The Spanishwoman's Kitchen

❧ PEPITA ARIS ❧

The Spanishwoman's Kitchen

Photography by David George

SEVEN DIALS

First published in the United Kingdom in 1992 by
Cassell

This paperback edition first published in 1999 by
Seven Dials, Illustrated Division
The Orion Publishing Group
Wellington House, 125 Strand
London, WC2R 0BB

Text copyright © Pepita Aris, 1992
Volume copyright © Cassell, 1992

Distributed in the United States of America by
Sterling Publishing Co., Inc.
387 Park Avenue South,
New York, NY 10016-8810

A CIP catalogue record for this book is available
from the British Library
ISBN 1 84188 016 7

Designed byu Yvonne Dedman
Map by Jonathan Wolstenholme
Typeset by August Filmsetting, Haydock, St Helens
Printed in Hong Kong

Half-title: Arab tiling is part of Spain's heritage
Frontispiece: An old mill kitchen in Durcal
Title page: Wild asparagus and eggs for a revuelta

❧ Acknowledgements ❧

My grateful thanks go firstly to Nan del Pozo, without whose enthusiasm this book would never have been written, and to Sue Macworth-Praed, who has shown such interest. So many people have helped, chief among them Manuel Carillo Díaz, Juan Díaz, Denyse Casuso, Beléta Child, Pilar Gernika, the family of Julián el Carnicero at Torrejas, Sarah and Alvaro Lozano Olivares, Jaime Manso Zubeldia, Janet Mendel Searl, Ampara Moreno, Vicente Muriel, Andres Núñez de Prado, Kristina and José Manuel Paredes Asencio, María-Angeles Pertierra, Angelina Portillo Giron, Alicía Rios-Ivars, Lola Ruiz de Javaloyes, Consuelo de Soto, Paloma-María Tomé Beamonte, Christina Venito and last, though very far from least, Gill Watling Ceballos.

My thanks are also due for support from Matilda Gladstone and Carmen Brieva at the Spanish Institute, Mercedes Reeves at Canning House and María José Sevilla and Janine Gilson at Foods from Spain in London.

I am also deeply grateful to the innumerable Spanish women who have answered my questions and my pointing finger, explained bits of recipes and family folklore to me, and guided me on my way.

Contents

ATLANTIC

SANTANDER

BILBAO

SAN SEBASTIAN

SANTIAGO DE
COMPOSTELLA

OVIEDO

ASTURIAS

CANTABRIA

BASQUE
COUNTRY

GALICIA

PONTEVEDRA

LEON

RIOJA

LOGRANO

NAVARRE

ARAGON

Duero

OLD CASTILE

Ebro

TARRAGO

SALAMANCA

AVILA

MADRID

Tajo

TOLEDO

NEW CASTILE

LEVANTE

EXTREMADURA
CACERES

LA MANCHA

VALENCIA

Guadiano

ALICANTE

CORDOBA

Guadalquivir

MURCIA

ANDALUSIA

SEVILLE

GRANADA

MALAGA

CADIZ

MEDITERRANEAN

IBIZA

IBI

Introduction

Spain, its women and cooking are the three themes I have explored in this book, for a cuisine grows out of the local culture.

The Spanishwoman's Kitchen reflects my journeys round the twelve very different regions of Spain and the conversations I had along the way. What interested me was the relationship between a particular place, its people and their food.

In Spain, geography and history have combined to create a cuisine that is unique in Europe. But Spanish food is also intensely regional in character. Politically, the people of Spain have resisted centralism and the same is true of their food. No one style dominates: the only dish found everywhere is *paella*.

The geographical reasons for this are clear. Spain is huge and varied, divided by towering mountain ranges. It embraces a wider range of climate and countryside than any other European country. In the north, verdant countryside with a mild Atlantic climate; in the interior, continental extremes of heat and cold. In contrast, the Alicante and Marbella coasts have the most covetable climate of the Mediterranean.

It is not surprising, then, that each place should have its own distinctive recipes. The mountains of Asturias contribute a rich bean pot, the rolling hills of Extremadura a hunter's hare stew and the Arab patios of the south chilled *gazpacho* soups.

There is a feeling among Spaniards that Spain is an especially privileged country when it comes to food, and that raw materials are better here than elsewhere. The ingredients are also more varied and interesting than in any other European country. For instance, common Mediterranean foods like *bacalao* (salt cod), garlic or tomatoes are found in more varieties, or are handled more subtly, in Spain than in Italy.

Spain's history is also quite different from the rest of Europe. It has a unique heritage, with cookery methods and ideas not found elsewhere. Nearly a thousand years of Arab occupation left it with ideas about frying (which were quickly copied), a distinctive sauce tradition and a spice palate that uses cumin and cinnamon with meat. A large and well-integrated Jewish population also contributed its dishes and food styles. And from Spain's empire in the Americas came a range of beans and peppers that are better exploited here than in neighbouring countries.

I travelled at different seasons, catching as I did so the traditional *fiestas* of the year which play such a part in all Spanish life. Food is still very seasonal, though it is all too easy to forget the bitter winters (and hearty game recipes) of the interior while enjoying the sun on a Mediterranean beach. Asking questions about ingredients, dishes, cooking methods and family traditions, I tried to fathom the Why? as well as the What? and How? of Spain's regional food.

I talked to grannies everywhere about the traditional dishes that took a day to prepare, and about the old patterns of life that went with them, so there is a portrait here of Spain's classic cuisine. I also asked younger women what dishes they admire and like to cook now. It is barely 20 years since Franco's death and the country is still coming to terms with the modern world, but changes – in food as in everything else – are proceeding rapidly.

This unusual collection of rural recipes easily stands comparison with those of France or Italy. There may never be so good a moment again to review the traditional domestic cookery of Spain.

Pepita Aris

7

CHAPTER 1

Andalusia

Every image that is Spain comes from Andalusia. Flamenco and bulls. The brown bare hills of the *sierras*, often topped with the silhouette of the bull that so splendidly advertises Veterano brandy. And the constant play of sun and shade – *sol y sombre* – repeated across innumerable white courtyards.

We were standing at the mouth of the Guadalquiver. Across the river the sand banks and pines of the Coto Doñana, Europe's major bird sanctuary, are silhouetted against a landscape of water. Beyond is Africa, a few short miles away and often visible across the Mediterranean.

This is the way the Moors came in 711, up Spain's most navigable river. At Seville the valley is flat and fertile as far as the eye can see – until it reaches the rim of the Sierra Morena to the north.

Andalusia is the huge underbelly of Spain. Wrapped by the Mediterranean, it stretches from Huelva on the Atlantic to Almería on the east coast. It is a land of tawny peaks and switchback roads, for the mountains within Andalusia are higher than those that define it. Three-quarters of Spain's grey-green olive trees grow here, and prosper where nothing else will.

In midsummer the sierras are bare and lifeless. The *pueblos blancos*, white villages, slip down their sides like a helping of cream. Approach one and the whiteness dazzles. By day they are silent, shuttered. No dogs bark. Streets are empty outside the social hours of evening. In the *semana dura*, the hottest (hardest) week of summer, it can be 30°C/90°F at midnight. No wonder the day is broken by a *siesta*, and tasks are put off until *mañana*.

Despite the dust and heat, this is a land of water. It plashes from village fountains by day, and at night from house jugs on to pots of scarlet geraniums. And luxuriant orange and lemon trees crowd the valley bottoms and surround every small dwelling.

The Moors built the great cities which became Europe's cultural centres: Seville with its high Giralda; Cordoba with its courtyard of bitter oranges, and a mosque like a marble forest, with glades between the columns; and Granada, with the wonder of the Alhambra! Here, in patios smelling of myrtles, or under fretted arcades, to the noise of fountains, the Moors ate ices made with the snows of the Sierra Nevada.

The Moors planted the citrus fruit and the gentle almond. They cultivated sugar cane and rice and brought aubergines, mint and spinach. Their influence is still present in the architecture: enclosed patios and horseshoe arches; heavy grilles on windows; and street doors studded with the great nails called the *media naranja* (half orange).

Africa is still an influence in the kitchen. Many food words start with the Moorish *al-*, beginning with *almuerzo*, lunch. The Moors brought barbecued and skewered meat, like the charcoal-scented *churrascos* of Cordoba or the popular little kebabs, *pinchitos morunos*, flavoured with Arab cumin.

Left: A dining room in Coín   9   *Above:* An Alhambra fountain

They brought the pestle and mortar whose cheerful clang is the prelude to an Andalusian meal. And with it came exquisite recipes, still in use, like *gazpacho* (see page 13) and recipes with pounded nuts, like the chicken *pepitoria de gallina* or the almond sweetmeat *alfajores*. The Arabs loved saffron and cinnamon as flavourings for fish and meat. Now the presence of these spices marks the dishes as Spanish. They introduced pickled fish: delicate, vinegared *escabeches* (see page 22). And they started the habit of frying in olive oil.

'Is it true Andalusia is the zone of frying?' I asked, repeating a popular phrase. 'Yes, at home we eat three fried dishes a week, four stews. These things are never done in restaurants.' I conveyed the Madrid idea that the locals were crude cooks. An explosion resulted! 'How dare they say we cannot cook! We have the best climate, we have the best vegetables! Spain taught Europe the meaning of civilized cooking. In the time of the Moors we led the way!' I gently took note.

With water, the land is highly productive. Almería, once stark, has now disappeared under plastic tunnels and, from the hills, these gleam like marshes. The modern miracle of the *invernadores* gives three, even four, crops a year of green beans and tomatoes. Vegetables go away boxed to the whole of Europe.

In these villages the pumpkin and the pepper are staple fare, with the tomato. They go in the *olla* (stewpot) and give Andalusia its characteristic sauce. Chick peas – the potatoes of Spain – are stewed with the red *chorizo* sausage, or are eaten (as are potato crisps) as a fried snack with the evening drink.

Capers from the hillside, wild asparagus and fennel: everything is used. For this is gipsy country, refuge for the legendary Carmen, and a land of simple inventions. In *huevos a la flamenca*, for instance, eggs are swirled with coloured vegetables, prawns, sausages: any and everything that comes to hand! Another gipsy invention is *tortilla Sacremonte*, a creamy omelette that now has brains in it. The most famous dish from the bullring is *rabo de toro*, (ox)tail cooked in sherry.

Tapas suits this society, morsels partnering drinks in a bar to stave off hunger. Once they were free: a few oval Jordan almonds or a saucer of olives. Now one must pay for a chunk of Manchego cheese on bread, or slivers of raw, scarlet *serrano*. Two of Spain's greatest hams are produced locally, at Jabugo and Trevélez. But lesser copies hang over every *tapas* bar, tipped (against drips) with a little upside-down paper umbrella.

First choice is still the magnificent olives, marinated *aceitunas aliñadas*. There are conventional green *sevillanas* (many grown within sight of the city), the purple-blotched heart-shaped Gordals, and the delicate small *manzanillas*. In a bar, however, the Spanish male can eat his favourite nursery dishes, something with gravy to dip the bread in: meat balls in tomato sauce, or *riñones al jerez*, kidneys with sherry.

The southern coast is famed for its fish. Boiled *gambas* (prawns) or *langostinos a la plancha*, big prawns cooked on the griddle. Fried battered rings of *calamares* (squid) are sold in every *tasca* (beach bar). But one must go to Cadiz harbour to eat the best *pescaito frito*, fried mixed fish. From this superb enclosed water the fleets set sail for America, and Drake rode in, to burn the gathering Armada.

The wine to partner fish is a *copita* of *fino* from the sherry cathedrals of Jerez de la Frontera. Made in a *solera* system, huge tiers of barrels, where one year is filled from another, it is one of the world's finest white wines – and not just an aperitif locally.

But it is oranges and sun that are the enduring image of the south, and the prospect of unwinding to a slower lifestyle. A continuing *siesta* symbolized by the sweating jug of iced *sangría*, soothing wine with chunks of orange and lemon gently bobbing.

Cooling red *gazpacho*, the perfect soup for a hot summer's day

❧ Gazpacho: the Famous Chilled Soup ❧

Spain's most famous soup, icy in the summer heat. What is real *gazpacho*? I asked. There was general agreement that it was made from puréed bread and the raw vegetables of summer. A peasant lunch served, in the old days, in olive-wood bowls.

And how do you make it so cold – here in the south? Ice is the modern answer, but '*gazpacho* should never be a pink liquid, tinkling in a glass. Nor should it be served with ice cubes in it. It is an old recipe, with the chill of cold, cold stones, standing all night on the cellar floor,' *en la bodega* – a familiar word as it also means a wine store. Or it might be diluted with clear, cold water from a deep well.

Where did it come from? Perhaps from the Arabs, perhaps from Roman times. It may simply be a way of using stale bread (from *caspa*, meaning bits in Latin). Cucumber might be an old partner, for it has grown round the Mediterranean for centuries, but the essentials are garlic to give it interest, and vinegar which makes it refreshing. With them go salt and oil.

A strong counter-argument ran that it is Arab, because it is dependent – at least until the invention of blenders – on the smooth pounding of the pestle in the mortar. Olive oil, beaten until creamy, accounts for its slip-down texture.

And what should go in it? Agreement broke down. 'It depends who is making it. Your *gazpacho* is like your accent; it says where you come from.' In far-away Madrid (and many restaurants) it even contains mayonnaise. One woman included cumin – an Arab spice, I noted.

I remember reading of an 18th-century traveller, named Richard Twiss, who admired a refreshing soup of bread, garlic, vinegar and oil, beaten till creamy with cold water. And this is probably the essence of it. Tomatoes, peppers, onions, cucumber, which are now so popular, are but pleasant extras.

Then the recipes. What a surprising diversity! The much-served *gazpacho rojo de Sevilla*, containing four or five puréed vegetables, and a bright scarlet version that was new to me. This, I found, was thought most typical by the Sección Femenina (see page 48), collecting classical recipes in the 1940s.

In the blistering heat of an Andalusian summer, herbs are rarer; occasionally there is parsley, and the Arab mint may go in. But the west of Spain shares the Portuguese fondness for fresh coriander. Another version, one of several called *porra*, has pounded fresh green garlic, the leek-like *ajos porros*.

Salmorejos have a slightly different consistency – and are unquestionably Arab. My favourite is an addictive garlic-scented cream, with a garnish of chopped egg and raw ham. It's so thick and creamy that I first thought cream must be an ingredient – but this is *gazpacho* without water. The liquid comes from tomatoes, though the original recipe (still sometimes served) has a longer history in Spain than does the tomato.

White *gazpachos* are older than the red ones. The region of Malaga is famed for its pounded almond version, with the grapes that make the local dessert wine. Nowadays there are even avocado versions. Much older is a recipe I found using dried broad beans, also called *porra*, a wonderfully receptive paste for displaying flavours like garlic.

My friends prompted that in winter *gazpacho* is a hot soup. Even in summer, in poorer times, land workers ate it as a thick, hot soup at midday, then watered it down for a cold soup at night.

Was this *gazpachuelo*, which I knew to be hot? No, was the answer. *Gazpachuelo* (see page 16) is not much like it, because it has no garlic – and the only vegetable is potato. But it's really a warm stock (sometimes fishy) made creamy with mayonnaise. The name probably comes because vinegar is the flavouring of both of them.

Zoque

RED GAZPACHO

The reddest of red *gazpachos* is much eaten in Spanish homes, though hardly known abroad.

1 garlic clove, finely chopped
½ teaspoon salt
5 slices of stale white bread, crusts removed
2 tablespoons red wine vinegar or sherry vinegar
4 tablespoons good olive oil
2 ripe red tomatoes, skinned and seeded
2 large red peppers, seeded and chopped
750 ml/1¼ pt iced water

SERVES 6

Everyone now uses a blender, but the recipe has been shaped by pounding with a pestle in a mortar. This is still the best way to crush the garlic to a paste with salt. Soak the bread in water, then squeeze it out and add morsels to the blender with the garlic, salt and vinegar. Purée until smooth.

Add the oil – a little at a time like mayonnaise. Add the tomato flesh and purée again. Add the chopped red pepper and reduce to a pulp. Chill well.

Stir in the icy water. Taste and season with more salt and vinegar if needed and serve very cold.

Right: Quail's eye view from a birdcage

Ajo blanco con uvas de Málaga

—— WHITE ALMOND AND GARLIC SOUP ——

WITH MUSCAT GRAPES

A soup so old that it is based on garlic and fruit, this is famed as white *gazpacho*. It was originally made by pounding almonds with icy well water – very soothing in the summer heat. The sultana taste of muscats is essential.

100 g/4 oz freshly blanched almonds
8 slices of stale white bread, crusts removed
2 garlic cloves, finely chopped
pinch of salt
3 tablespoons olive oil
2 tablespoons sherry vinegar
600 ml/1pt iced water
250 g/8 oz ripe muscat grapes, seeded

—————— SERVES 4 ——————

Soak the bread in water, then squeeze it gently. Grind the almonds in a blender until smooth, adding a little of the bread to stop them turning oily. Add the garlic, salt and olive oil and blend to make a smooth cream.

Add the remaining bread in pieces with the vinegar and enough water to blend smoothly. Chill for at least 2 hours, then dilute with iced water. Float the grapes on top before serving.

Gazpacho de primavera

—— GREEN GAZPACHO FOR SPRING ——

An unusual *gazpacho* because it is made early in the year, before tomatoes are red, and also because it contains fresh coriander. It comes from Huelva.

2 slices of stale white bread, crusts removed
2 garlic cloves, roughly chopped
½ teaspoon salt
2 large green peppers, seeded and roughly chopped
2 less-than-ripe tomatoes, skinned and seeded
1 lettuce, or the outer leaves of 2 (about 350 g/12 oz)

½ bunch of fresh coriander leaves and soft stalks
1 slice of onion
5 tablespoons olive oil
5 tablespoons sherry vinegar
pinch of hot paprika or a little cayenne
500 ml/18 fl oz iced water

—————— SERVES 6 ——————

Soak the bread then squeeze it out lightly. Purée it with the garlic and salt in a blender. Add the peppers and crush to as smooth a purée as possible. Add the tomato flesh and juice (they will need about 1 minute each in boiling water to skin them) and purée again. Add the lettuce leaves with the blender running. If you stop for any reason, cover the blender well before restarting. Add the coriander and onion.

Blend in the oil and season with vinegar and paprika. Chill the soup base well. Add iced water to serve, checking if more salt or vinegar is needed.

Salmorejo cordobés

—— CHILLED CORDOBA TOMATO CREAM ——

Not a soup (for it has no water), but an addictive, chilly cream, delicately flavoured with garlic and tomato. The tomatoes must have been added after the discovery of America, for the recipe 'goes back to Arab times'.

2 ripe red tomatoes, skinned and seeded
6 slices of stale white bread, crusts removed
2 garlic cloves, roughly chopped
½ teaspoon salt
6 tablespoons good olive oil
3 tablespoons vinegar
1 hard-boiled egg
about 40 g/1½ oz *serrano* or other raw ham,
such as prosciutto

—————— SERVES 4 ——————

Soak the bread in water, then squeeze out lightly. Purée about a quarter in the blender with the garlic, salt and oil until smooth. Add the remaining bread in pieces with the vinegar. Add the tomato flesh and juice. Purée again until very smooth, then beat hard for 2 minutes, to lighten it. The cream should be thick, but not stiff. Season and chill overnight.

Ladle into small shallow bowls and garnish with shreds of hard-boiled egg and raw ham.

Romería: the Village Pilgrimage

I saw the Virgin off in a taxi on May Day morning – along with half the village. She is about three inches high, crowned in gold like the child she holds, and enclosed for safety in a glass egg. Two bands with drums and bugles and a choir of women singing 'Hail Marys' escorted her to the edge of the village. The float she rode on was of shimmering silver, her halo standing high over the sheaves of pink and white carnations. Carved and gilded, the float was new, and had cost the village 5,000,000 pesetas. Andalusia is devoted to its Virgins.

Forty sweating lads carried her from the church, with many rests and a few beers, to the village border. She was off, for a month, to her summer hermitage at the Fuensanta. The hermitage is tiny, with a bell in a high white gable and two date palms which always fruit in summer. It used to be small and peaceful. Now the pilgrimage gets bigger every year and a space has been cleared for a vast all-night

picnic. A perfect opportunity for talking to village people about village food!

In the first week of June, the *romería* goes to fetch her home with all the splendour our village can muster. This year the procession took three hours to pass and travel the three miles to the Fuensanta.

All the neighbourhood horses are on show: normally they are working. But the Spanish love an elegant turn out and ride the high saddle that the US adopted for its cowboys. The girls ride pillion, with flamenco skirts billowing over the horse's hind quarters. There are also cropped jackets and riding skirts with a huge sweep behind that hangs on a button for walking.

A *burro* (donkey) in a hat and back and front numberplates leads out the procession. Forty carts follow, the products of nights of decoration. Lorries have awnings, with family and celebrators in the back, in the local costume. The one judged the prettiest has the honour of carrying home the Virgin. Most are financed by the *cofradías* (working-people's associations). The men march in front, wearing the group's ribbon and medal. I wave to my plumber, the man who sells me bread, the bank teller, and hand out drinks as the procession passes.

Finest are the old gipsy wagons with canvas on a bowed frame, as once they all were. These are each pulled by a couple of placid oxen (which still plough the steeper hillsides). The animals are decorated, with swinging tassels over the eyes that make me think of Cleopatra. There has been untimely rain and I notice the paper fans outside are now streaking on to the canvas.

On the mountain every *cofradías* has its stand, a one-night hospitality house for 50–100 people: big enough to take members' families, guests – and the kitchen. There is a sit-down supper for everyone, invariably *paella*. Then some space is cleared for dancing. How beautiful the girls look in the frilled flamenco skirts and spare fringed shawls, elegant hair-dos with high blossom! It suits even the fuller figure. With swishing skirts and arched backs they danced, a repeated rhythm with an elegant wrist that plucks the unseen apple from the air, puts it to the mouth, then behind the back discards it.

These are country dances, not flamenco with its stamping heels and insidious rhythms. August is the

Horsemen display their riding skill at the village fair

time for this, and the village *ferias*. In one village after another the lights go up and there are two or three days of music and drinking. I well remember my first flamenco, in the tiny village of Monda. There was the old dance floor then, on a promontory, to catch the slightest breath of air from the valley. The guitars started at midnight under a moon like a vast Manchego. We left at three, with the haunting guttural voice of the *canto jondo* echoing behind us down the valley.

Now the hermitage is packed, with a smell of lilies and tall wax candles. A procession of people passes in front of the Virgin, solemn, almost silent. A flamenco Mass follows on Sunday morning. Then the great procession returns again, the gold cups of the *cofradías* riding up in front of her. The Virgin is brought home to Coín, with infinitely more ceremony.

Gazpachuelo

WARM POTATO SOUP
WITH EGGS AND VINEGAR

A surprising soup: both that it should be so good, with such simple ingredients, and that it should be so creamy. 'Nowadays', I was told 'the egg whites don't often go into the broth, because the mayonnaise is made in a blender and that needs whole eggs.' A good example of how traditional recipes are reworked!

750 g/1½ lb new-season potatoes, diced
750 ml/1¼ pt water
½ teaspoon salt
2 small eggs, separated
about 4 tablespoons vinegar
250 ml/8 fl oz best olive oil

--- SERVES 4–6 ---

Cook the potatoes in the salted water. When tender, remove the potatoes, saving the liquid. Beat the egg whites into the liquid; they will set like a Chinese egg-drop soup.

Let the stock cool a little while you make the mayonnaise (see page 168) with the yolks, 2 tablespoons vinegar and the oil. Thin the mayonnaise to soup consistency by stirring in the stock and pour this over the warm potatoes in a serving bowl. Serve the soup warm, stirring in another 2 tablespoons vinegar. Or pass a jug of vinegar so the acid content can be judged at table.

Conejo en ajillo pastor

--- RABBIT WITH AROMATICS AND SAFFRON ---

Ampara Moreno in Coín gave me this recipe, which she learned from her mother. When I asked if it was written down, there was a smiling 'no': she cannot read.

2 wild rabbits, with kidneys and liver,
or 1.1 kg/2½ lb farmed rabbit
2 large mild Spanish onions, chopped
7 tablespoons olive oil
1 garlic clove, finely chopped
0.25 g saffron (50 strands)
4 tablespopons hot water
salt and freshly ground black pepper
4 tablespoons Spanish brandy or cognac
250 ml/8 fl oz white wine
15 black peppercorns, lightly crushed
6 sprigs of fresh thyme or
½ teaspoon dried thyme
1 bay leaf
about 125 ml/4 fl oz cold water

--- SERVES 4–5 ---

Fry the onions slowly in 2 tablespoons oil in a wide, deep pan until soft, then add the garlic. Meanwhile, wash the cleaned rabbit to remove any blood inside. Pat dry and split the front legs from the ribs. Cut free the flaps from the saddle. Cut the meaty back legs in half through the joint and halve the saddle with a heavy knife. Cut the thin pieces so they are flat.

Crumble the saffron stamens in your fingers and put to soak in the hot water for 5 minutes.

Remove the onion from the pan and add about 4 tablespoons more oil (there should be enough to coat the bottom and just float the rabbit). Salt and pepper the rabbit and fry the meaty portions – back legs and saddles – for 10 minutes. Tuck in the remaining rib pieces and flaps (and the liver and kidneys later, if present) and fry for about another 10 minutes until everything is golden. Spoon off all the oil.

Add the brandy and wine and stir to deglaze the pan. Pack in the rabbit pieces neatly and return the onion. Add the saffron liquid and peppercorns, and tuck in the thyme and crumbled bay leaf. Add the cold water, almost to cover the meat. Put on the lid and simmer very gently for about 1 hour, until the rabbit is tender, making sure it does not get dry. Check the seasonings and serve from the pan.

Yellow roses round a
window at the Alhambra
in Granada

Puchero de hinojos

FENNEL STEW WITH BEANS AND PORK

A dish from the *sierras* below Granada, this contains wild
fennel instead of the more usual onion. Simple but handsome with its white beans, green rings of fennel stalks and
maroon *morcilla* sausage.

250 g/8 oz white haricot beans, soaked overnight
1 piece of ham bone, or 1 small hock bone
(about 175 g/6 oz) with a little meat attached
2 pork ribs, cut through the belly
200 g/7 oz fresh streaky pork belly, cubed
500 g/1 lb bulb fennel, sliced
1 lt/1¾ pt water
250 g/8 oz new season's potatoes, sliced
200 g/7 oz *morcilla*, black pudding
or other mild smoked sausage, sliced
salt and freshly ground black pepper

SERVES 4

Put the beans in a large pot and fit in the ham bone,
pork ribs (rubbed with a little salt) and pork belly.
Add the water and bring slowly to the boil. Skim off
the scum. Simmer for 1 hour, or until the beans are
tender.

Add the potatoes, fennel and *morcilla* or sausage.
Cook for 20 minutes. Remove the bones, returning
their shredded meat to the pot. Season the dish and
serve garnished with the chopped fennel fronds.

Note: the local *morcilla* is mild, tasting largely of
onion, and can be replaced by any other mild sausage: I
use smoked kabanos outside Spain and a small gammon
hock bone for the meat in this dish.

⚜ A Day Buying Olive Oil ⚜

Close your eyes and try to imagine two million olive
trees: the world's largest grove at Sierra de Segura.
You can't see the extent of it, in a countryside broken
by cliffs and gullies. Baena, near Cordoba, is more
typical. The pattern stays on the retina: a grid of
grey-green trees against red soil.

Andres Núñez de Prado is the elder of two brothers who have 'an oil mill, not a factory'. In this
D.O. (quality-controlled) area, they produce some of
the finest virgin oil, sold in the square *frasca* bottle.
The family moved here more than two centuries ago,
though a tenth of the olive trees are older than this. 'But
these are being replaced with smaller ones, because now
olives for oil are handpicked.' In late November the

olives turn black and become sweet and full of oil.
Green olives are younger, and these are intensely bitter
when they are pickled for the table.

Lagrima is the finest grade of olive oil. The name
means 'tears', and the oil has only 20 minutes to drip
from the crushed olives. It is cloudy (unfiltered) and
greenish and has the freshness of young fruit, almost
appley. We eat it greedily on bread. 'The taste of oil is
accentuated by light warming,' I was told. I will try this
later at home.

The olives themselves are crushed by four rolling
stones, great cones that leave them like crushed mul-
berries. This purple paste is moved to a woven mat and
pressed. The flow of oil from it then separates in tanks

by natural density: a cold-pressed oil. The equipment was modern, but for the second grade oils they still used 200-year-old *tinajas*. These Ali Baba jars were buried up to their waists, so they would not dwarf the workers.

We sampled the local oils beside those of Catalonia, Spain's other quality oil area. The rivals were a lighter yellow – 'with a whiff of banana, rather than apple'. Most of these go to Italy 'and then onward, so it is said, as Italian oil'. The best virgin oils from Baena are sold locally, though it is difficult to buy them. There is no shortage of oil, though, for three-quarters of Spain's olive oil comes from Andalusia. Cheaper olive oils are lower grade products, produced by chemical refining.

Southern dishes, in the old days, included a lot of olive oil for nutrition, for it contains all the vital amino acids. Now olive oil is in fashion once more, but for the healthy heart, for it is mono-unsaturated and cholesterol-lowering!

I was amused to find it may also be an aphrodisiac for women, for it is high in oestrogen, the female hormone. Laughter here! Spanish girls, I notice, have a characteristic giggle, quite high up the register: '¡*he-he-he-he!*' And I always thought the effect of the south came from sunshine!

Olive oil is crucial for Spanish cooking: it is the perfect dressing, because it improves both the taste and texture of food. It makes sauces creamy (but is not as fattening as cream), for it remains in suspension when beaten with a liquid. It doesn't even separate when heated.

But Spain's supreme culinary talent is for deep-frying. How do they manage food that is so pure and greaseless? The reason is that olive oil forms a thin, dense crust round the food, so it absorbs less fat than it would fried in other oils: 'you can test this yourself!' Olive oil is the superior oil for frying, and it doesn't go rancid at high temperatures, so you can deep-fry in it 20 times. Other oils should be thrown away before this.

I took away some useful tips, such as that smoking, too-hot oil can be tamed by adding a piece of potato. To clean oil for the next frying, put in a strip of lemon zest. And parsley chucked in at the end of frying will reduce the house smell!

Remojón

SALT COD AND ORANGE SALAD

A popular Lenten salad, this recipe comes from Antequerra, an ancient town in the north of Andalusia. It's the classic recipe, using fish which is toasted before soaking – stronger-tasting and firmer, with a finely-judged exotic flavour. I am told this was once made with Seville oranges in season, but I found these too bitter for modern taste. Hard-boiled eggs are sometimes included.

250 g/8 oz thin outside piece or tail end of salt cod (or 200 g/7 oz canned tuna as a short cut)
8 oranges
75 g/3 oz marinated black olives, stoned
6 spring onions, chopped
½ small garlic clove, finely chopped
tiny pinch of salt
1 teaspoon sweet paprika
1 teaspoon vinegar (if not using Seville oranges)
5 tablespoons good olive oil

SERVES 4

Toast the salt cod in the oven at 200°C/400°F/gas 6 for 20 minutes. Break up the fish roughly and put it in a dish. Cover with water and leave to soak for 4 hours (the name of the dish just means 'soaked'). Taste the fish – it should be edible, but exquisitely salty.

Drain the fish, discard the skin and bones and shred the flesh finely with two forks so that it looks like pieces of wool.

Slice the oranges on a plate into rounds, quarter them and put in a serving bowl. Add the fish shreds, olives, and chopped white and green of the onion and mix gently. Make a paste with the garlic and salt, crushing it with the flat of a knife. In a bowl, mix with the juices on the plate, the paprika and vinegar and beat in the olive oil. Dress the salad 30 minutes ahead of eating.

Spring in the green olive groves – a sight the tourist rarely sees

Ensalada de alcauciles
y pimientos rojos

—— ARTICHOKE AND RED PEPPER SALAD ——

Alcauciles is the local Andaluz word for artichokes, called
alcachofas in the rest of Spain. Add a little tarragon (a Seville
herb) to the dressing if you grow it.

8 soft spring globe artichokes
1 large red pepper, seeded
6 tablespoons best olive oil
2 garlic cloves, finely chopped
2 large red tomatoes, skinned and seeded
salt and freshly ground black pepper
2 tablespoons vinegar
12 black olives

—— SERVES 4 ——

Prepare the artichokes, cutting off the stalk and tops
of the buds, then paring round to remove most of the
outside leaves. Cook in salted water for 20 minutes.

Meanwhile cut the pepper into thin strips. Heat 2
tablespoons oil in a frying pan and fry the pepper,
adding the garlic towards the end. Slice the tomato
flesh, add to the pan and cook for 5 minutes, then
season with salt and pepper.

Drain the artichokes. If they are very soft the
whole can be eaten. If not, push out the hairy choke
with a teaspoon and thumb and strip any harsh leaf
stubs from round the sides. Quarter them, add to the
pan and turn in the oil.

Make a vinaigrette by beating the vinegar with 4
tablespoons oil and seasoning. Turn the hot vegetables into a salad bowl, dress them, add the olives
and leave to cool before serving.

A Beach Party:
Little and Great Fish

It was Corpus Christi, the beginning of May, and a
tearing Atlantic wind blew fine sand sidewards along
the Malaga beaches. I went to grill sardines, on the
first fire of the year, with an expert: curly-headed
Juan Diáz, one of two fishermen brothers. Our fire
was a plank and pieces of driftwood, all laid in one
direction. Nothing like the wigwam fires of my
scouting youth. But the wind roared through it,
making it crackle and turning it swiftly to charcoal.

The sardines came from the market in the usual
polystyrene box, the cheapest of fish. Blue and green,
they were irridescent in the sunlight. When fresh, the
bodies have sequin jackets. Later the scales matted to
an overall aluminium glisten. He didn't bother to
clean them.

The skewers were home-made from bamboo, with
pointed tips. At the handle end the cane was intact,
but half of the rest was missing. The sardines were
efficiently stitched on, four or five to a prong, which
then stood parallel to the fire: simple and efficient.

Malaga is famous for miniscule *chanquetes*. They
are like crisp-fried seaweed, so small and transparent
only the eyes are visible. Now fished almost out of exist-
ence, they are protected, and tiny anchovies or sardines
are battered and fried in their place. Small fry under
$2\,cm/\frac{3}{4}$ in are used, and it struck me how meticulously
fish are sorted by size, as an aid to perfect cooking.

Anchovies, *boquerones*, are celebrated on this coast:
one of the best fish for frying. In Malaga they are often
made into 'fans' first, by sticking several tails together.
Their backs are green when newly caught, an inky black
a few hours later.

To learn about big fish, I had to go to the Atlantic
coast, to Cadiz. The real surprise were dog fish (with
mouths like rottweilers) and shark: *cailón* (porbeagle),
pez martillo (hammerhead) and *cazon*, known by the
harmless name of tope, and very white when cooked.
Cailón is a favourite here; the medium-lean meat (for
who would think of it as fish?) takes up a marinade and
high spicing of vinegar and paprika in the local *adobado*.
Cailón en amarillo is brilliant yellow with saffron.
Rosada (pink) covers other nameless predators.
Defeated and stripped of their rough skins, they look
like great meat bones on the market slab.

Sardines grilling on
bamboo skewers beside
a beach fire

Left: Peppers and
artichokes ready for a
summer salad

Fritura malagueña

MALAGA MIXED FRIED FISH

Always good, it is exceptional when one fish is pickled.

**4 small red mullet, about 175 g/6 oz each,
fresh or pickled** *(see* escabeche, *page 22)*
**8–12 small squid, about 7.5 cm/3 in long
oil for deep frying
2 small fillets of white fish, hake, sole etc,
about 400 g/14 oz together
lemon wedges, to serve**

BATTER
**125 g/4½ oz plain flour
1 teaspoon salt
large pinch of paprika
1 large egg
125 ml/4 fl oz tepid water**

SERVES 4

Don't bother to clean fresh mullet (their insides are neatly avoided on the plate). Just scrape them from tail to head to remove the scales, then rinse. Tiny squid don't need cleaning either. In spring and early summer they are full of soft milky roe, which keeps them moist when fried. (The stiffener in them is like soft plastic and easy to discard.)

Make the batter: season the flour, adding paprika, and beat in the egg, then the water. If possible, leave to stand for 1 hour.

Heat plenty of oil for deep frying (top heat on an electric fryer). Dip fresh mullet into the batter and fry them, 2 at a time, for 4 minutes. Drain on kitchen paper and keep warm.

Let the oil reheat, then dip the squid in the batter and fry in 2 batches – also for about 4 minutes, as there are more of them. Fry pickled mullet (if using), then the fish in pieces. Arrange on a plate with lemon wedges and serve.

Salmonetes en escabeche

RED MULLET SALAD

An old Arab way of preserving fish in lightly spiced jelly for a summer lunch, I ate this accompanied by avocado in the shade of a bignonia-covered terrace. The colours were perfect. Fennel, which is wild round here, is another green salad choice.

4 red mullet, about 200 g/7 oz each, cleaned
2 tablespoons olive oil
1 small onion, finely chopped
1 large garlic clove, finely chopped
175 ml/6 fl oz dry white wine
175 ml/6 fl oz wine vinegar
2 sprigs of fresh thyme or 1 bay leaf
salt and freshly ground black pepper

SERVES 4

Scale the fish by scraping from the tail towards the head. (Scales pop off easily, but look like dropped contact lenses.) Cut off the fins with kitchen scissors.

Heat the oil in a pan that will just hold all the fish and fry the onion gently until soft, adding the garlic at the end. Put in the fish, then the wine and vinegar. Add just enough water to cover them and tuck in the thyme or bay leaf and season. Bring to the boil, then cover and simmer for 10 minutes.

Move the fish carefully on a fish slice to a shallow dish. They can be served whole, or the fillets can be removed – easy when cooked and cold – and served without the bones. Strain the cooking juices over them and refrigerate until needed. Provided the juices completely cover the fish, the dish keeps 2–3 days.

A chilled *rosado* wine, like a Navarra Gran Feudo, perfectly matches the colour of the fish.

Urta a la roteña

FISH WITH ONIONS AND BRANDY

Urta is often baked, but this recipe, which was given to me by Doña Pepa, a gipsy in Cadiz, was made in a deep *paella* pan. The secret, she said, was to cook the onions very slowly till they turn quite sweet. With the brandy and wine they make a wonderful sauce. Rota faces Cadiz across the bay and this bream feeds on the shellfish, which flavour its flesh.

1 kg/2 lb *urta* in fillets, or monkfish on the bone
2 large mild Spanish onions, sliced very thinly
5–6 tablespoons olive oil
3 garlic cloves, finely chopped
1 large green pepper, seeded and chopped
3 large ripe tomatoes, skinned and seeded
1 bay leaf
salt and freshly ground pepper
freshly grated nutmeg
4 tablespoons Spanish brandy or cognac
4 tablespoons white wine

SERVES 4

Fry the onions very slowly in 2 tablespoons oil in a casserole until they melt. Add the garlic near the end. Turn up the heat slightly and cook until the onions caramelize and colour, stirring occasionally so the onions do not catch. Add the green pepper and fry for 5 minutes. Add the chopped tomatoes, bay leaf, salt, pepper and nutmeg and leave to reduce.

Meanwhile, if using monkfish, take the flesh off the bone and cut it into fingers. Season them. Heat 3–4 tablespoons oil in a wide pan and colour the fish on both sides. Spoon off visible oil. Warm the brandy in a ladle, then flame it and pour over the fish. Add the wine and stir to deglaze the pan. Stir in the tomato sauce and simmer for a further 5 minutes.

Mountain Hams

I went to Trevélez because I had heard their hams were cured in snow. Up the switchback road on the south side of Granada, climbing through the poor Alpujurras, whose Berber style of flat-roofed houses came from North Africa more than a millennium ago. Pass a tiny hamlet; an hour later pass it again, now 1500 feet above it.

In the highest village of Andalusia the hams are made in a rather ordinary-looking commercial factory. The glory of the place is rather the Mulhacén, 11,410 feet high, which commands the head of the valley: 'the ice lump in the heart of Andalusia.' So close to the Mediterranean it is unbelievable, a peak of snow-edged facets, cut white like a diamond.

The mountain site is important to the cure – hence the popular name for the ham, *serrano*, which means 'from the *sierra*'. For these hams are breeze-dried, not freeze-dried, in the clean icy air after a cure that for most hams is dry, though others are brined. In Jabugo, the most famous hams of all are buried in salt for four to ten days, then are hung in airy, shuttered rooms upstairs for up to six months. When the weather turns warm the hams begin to sweat salt, which is permitted for a week. They are then moved to cool cellars and hang there for the six warm months, sometimes longer.

The finest raw hams come from Trevélez and Jabugo, here in Andalusia, and from Montánchez further west. Most of them go to restaurants or as executive Christmas presents, long lean things, quilted in fat, and scarlet to a deep raw red when carved. Unusually they are carved along the bone, lengthways with the grain of the meat. The pieces are dry, flavourful, somewhat chewy, and in the very best hams the lean is flecked with a fat that moisturizes it. Other parts of the pig are cured too: the *caña*, which is the loin, and the cheaper *paletilla* (front shoulder), which was my purchase from Trevélez.

On the high mountain there were no pigs. But motoring through the national park of Grazalema, further west, I saw them under the dark holm oak that supplies their favourite food. They scuffled in the undergrowth and ran beside the car, lean, long pigs with black hair, unlike the fat domestic porker. I was told that, sadly, now only five percent of hams come from the native pigs, compared to a third 30 years ago.

Quality is graded by what the pigs eat. The best ham is *bellota* – fed on wild acorns. Alas, excise restrictions forbid the import into other countries of any meat whose diet is so uncontrolled. Only the *pienso*, a wild animal corralled and on a controlled diet for the last period of its life, is accepted abroad.

For Spain, rather than Germany or even France, is Europe's ham-maker. Spaniards consume a whole ham a year per person; that is, 9–10 kg/16 lb for every man, woman and child.

When it comes to cooking, I find my neighbours highly practical. Hams on the bone are for *tapas*, factory hams from the white pig, in vacuum packs, are used for cooking. These go further and are cheaper too, for a little chopped ham seems to go into almost every dish in Spain. Ham bones, ready sawn in rings, are also much used for cooking – the Spanish stock cube?

Andalusia is rightly proud of its raw ham, *serrano*, and devoted to its Virgins

Do you bury the hams in snow? I asked. 'Of course not; they would be frozen, wouldn't they? They say they feed the pigs on vipers in the Sierra de Viboras' (in Extremadura). Did I believe that too? I demurred.

In the many ham shops of the village the raw hams hang, the lesser-ranking ones from the white domestic pig, and the monarchs from the wild Iberian pig. The black trotters mark these *patas negras* and they hang on racks in a neat line, all the feet in one direction. Irreverently, they reminded me of leggy chorus girls. We bought our ham, carved with a knife in generous quantity, not paper-thin like *prosciutto*. It was not the black hoof (unobtainable sliced) but white pig, and we ate it in an Alpine-style picnic. It was soft and sweet.

The sale of little cakes augments the convent income

❧ The Nun's Story: Spain's Sweetmakers ❧

Her name was Sister Sorena-María and she stood, a pleasant smiling face, behind a grille of iron. At table level a small open wicket gate allowed her to pass us the bags of pastries for which we had come. It was a closed convent in the Barrio de San Francisco below the town at Ronda.

'Go through the green gate, cross the patio to the door in the corner, then ring,' I was told, when looking for the nunnery. There – the only feature of an empty hall – was the *tornador*, a heavy revolving wooden door. This one had shelves upon it, for it was

the means of communicating with the inside, sending letters and small presents. It was also the original means by which the nuns passed out sweets and pastries. For this is one of Andalusia's many orders where nuns live in *la clausura*. They never see an outside face. Nowadays, though, discipline is relaxed enough to allow a sister to speak to us through the grille.

Why should nuns be associated with baking? I asked. Egg yolks in Andalusia are a by-product of the sherry industry, where whites were used for clarifying the wine, and these were given to the convents for charity, sometimes in perpetuity. These yolks were then made into sweets and pastries for sale. In the 19th century, when many convents were stripped of their land, this often became their only source of income.

Less than 50 convents in Andalusia still make and sell pastries, some in houses reduced to half a dozen women. They are sold particularly at festivals like Easter and Christmas and some, like the *yemas* of San Leandro (round golden 'yolks'), made in Seville to a 400-year-old recipe, are famous all over Spain. Now 'fewer girls are called' and nunneries are closing. Ten years ago there were two convents in Ronda.

We discussed our small purchases: they were even called *dulces caseros* – home-baked goods. 'All made with love and no additives,' she joked, to traditional recipes. The nunnery sale list advertised *ganotes* (sweet potato cakes) and *mostachones*, S-shaped almond biscuits that pair to make a 'moustache'. But now they only cook things for which demand is steady: *roscones de vino* (small rings of a wine dough), *mantecados* (lardy cakes) and *polvorones*, little almond crumble cakes, rolled up in paper, for this is what they do too easily. Some titbits still have Arab names, like *alfajores* (almond saddlebags) and *pestinos* (see recipe), little fritters drunk with honey, that date back to Arab frying pans. These nuns might not like the idea, I thought, but they are the direct successors of the Arabs as bakers.

Soplillos de Granada

GRANADA ALMOND MERINGUES

A home-made version of *turrón*, their name suggests a gust of wind will blow them away. It is the just-perceptible amount of lemon that makes them such a success.

150 g/5 oz blanched almonds
2 large egg whites
grated zest of ½ lemon
200 g/7 oz vanilla caster sugar
2 teaspoons lemon juice

MAKES ABOUT 30

Toast the almonds in the oven at 150°C/300°F/gas 2 until biscuit-coloured and smelling pleasantly – about 30 minutes. Chop one-third of the nuts coarsely and grind the rest (in a food processor).

Whisk the egg whites in a large bowl until stiff, then fold in the lemon zest with two-thirds of the sugar, shaking in a spoonful or so at a time. Add the lemon juice and whisk until stiff and shiny. Mix together the remaining sugar and ground nuts and fold into the meringue. Fold in the chopped nuts.

Spoon the meringue into tall heaps on greased foil on two baking trays, spacing them out well. Put into the oven and immediately turn it down to 125°C/225°F/gas low. Leave to puff and dry for 1–1½ hours.

Pestinos

FRITTERS IN HONEY SYRUP

100 g/4 oz thick orange-flower honey
2 tablespoons sunflower oil
thinly pared zest of 1 lemon
½ teaspoon aniseeds, crushed,
25 g/1 oz butter
75 ml/3 fl oz white wine like Diamante (not too dry), moscatel or *amontillado* sherry
175 g/6 oz plain flour, plus extra for rolling
¼ teaspoon salt
4 tablespoons water
sunflower oil for deep frying
sugar for sprinkling

MAKES ABOUT 18

Flavour the sunflower oil by heating it in a small pan with the strip of zest until the latter browns. Discard the zest then, off the heat, add the aniseeds to toast them followed by the butter and wine.

Immediately add the flour and salt and beat them in to make a smooth dough. Turn on to a floured surface and knead briefly. Rest the dough briefly.

Make the syrup by melting the honey with the water. Heat clean oil for frying in a deep pan, enough oil to float the fritters.

Roll out the dough as thinly as you can on a floured surface and cut into squares about 7.5 cm/3 in. Fold two corners across diagonally, moistening and pinching to seal.

Lift the pastries on a wooden-spoon handle and slide them into the hot oil, 4 or 5 at a time. They will bob to the surface as they start to expand. Spin them over with a slotted spoon and fry until golden. Drain on kitchen paper while you fry the next batch.

Dip the fritters in honey syrup, then drain on a wire rack. Serve the same day, sprinkled with sugar.

CHAPTER 2

Extremadura

Pigs and sheep outnumber people here. It was probably always so, in the country that takes its name from 'extreme' and 'hard'. On the Portuguese border, in the most rural part of Spain, this is the land of the *conquistadores*, the men who left to make fortunes in South America.

The prickly pears are scarlet in November. They top the cactuses like a row of rifle targets, on all the rocky outcrops on the hill above Trujillo. Like the houses of the returning conquerors down below, they are conspicuous newcomers from America.

For this creamy-toned town, wrapped round a square like an arena, is the cradle of the *conquistadores*. Pizarro and Cortés, who conquered Mexico and Peru, Balboa, the first European to see the Pacific, Orellana, explorer of the Amazon, and Valdivia, founder of Santiago in Chile, all came from here. And there are palaces to prove it, chief among them that of Pizarro's brother on the main square. '*¡He hecho!* I made it!' boast the buildings.

How could they bear to leave a land so beautiful? Sparse plain gives way to the open *charro*. The undulating hillside, whose name appears on local dishes, is dotted with little populations of holm oak and cork. In April and May it is knee-deep in flowers, pink, yellow, purple, but now the turf was close-cropped and the long acorns were falling, to feed turkeys as well as pigs.

Montánchez is pigsville. This slight hill is famous for one of the three best raw *serrano* hams in Spain. It seems every street has a 'home sale', and they make *chorizos* besides. It is an unusual equation that so poor a region should be such a consumer of meat, but the pigs

and sheep provide for themselves. There is not the soil to grow vegetables.

Extremeñan hospitality is famous throughout Spain. Plates are so generously heaped, you are advised to share them between three or four people. The dishes urged on me were of the humblest: 'Don't do without the fry-up of eggs, ham, sausage and pork. *Migas* here are made with a magic touch' – breadcrumbs fried with streaky belly and dried peppers. And wonderful tomatoes appear in soups and salads with oregano, or stewed with peppers in the local chicken *pollo a lo Padre Pero*. A careful kitchen: figs here are cultivated, elsewhere wild.

In the north of Extremadura the lee of the Sierra de Gredos is famous for capturing sunshine. I drove past the slatted tobacco-drying barns, up the long valley of la Vera to Jarandilla. Here they make the best paprika in Spain. The new season's crop was just in (such a brilliant red!), heaped in sacks, and in three grades, sweet, piquant and *agridulce* – sweet and sour. It has, I learn, an exceptional amount of vitamin C. Perhaps this is why the population doesn't get scurvy on a pig diet?

Even fried eggs are served with paprika – and vinegar over the top. And paprika goes into the pork and the similar lamb *frite*. The flavours pair well with the cloudy *cañamero* wine, which has the appearance of beer but tastes of sherry.

Wild things are very conspicuous. Not just the storks, although half Spain's population breeds here and their great nests top the towers of Trujillo and Cáceres. Wild food is constantly on the menu. Frogs were abundant in November, their legs eaten crumbed and fried. Tench, barbel, trout and pike from the streams are eaten as *mojil de pesce*, with wild mint and green garlic, or cold and vinegered as *escarapuche* (see page 30). And in summer they eat lizards in Plasencia – caught with a loop of string and the help of a terrier. I also met a new way of barbecuing rabbit – *conejo a la teja*, on a roof tile. 'It retains the heat so well,' I was told. The method was also good for sardines and pork belly, for terracotta absorbs some fat.

A restless place – loved by many who cannot stay – the country is marked by invisible routes. The Romans carried their silver bullion through, going north. And a vast migration of sheep passed twice-yearly, following the *cañadas*, to and from the summer pastures round Soria and the north. Sheep still winter here – but take the train north.

There are famous lamb dishes – and in spring a celebrated ewes' milk cheese, too, called *torta de Casar*. *Caldereta* (see page 30) is made from young lamb, and named after its cooking pot. Mutton is still cooked in old ways – *carnero verde*, long simmered, then sauced with a green purée of parsley, mint and coriander. The latter is an unusual herb for Spain, only liked here in the west, though common in Portugal. I also met a sage sauce for partridges – and for sardines!

Orange and lemon trees, and dishes with Mediterranean names, make visible the connection with the south. But southern recipes are subtly changed. Extremeñan *gazpacho* is bulky with chopped onion, and its variants like *cojondongo* contain eggs, and even pig's lights in winter.

Pilgrims are other travellers, journeying to the great monasteries like Yuste and Guadalupe. The black Virgin of Guadalupe, with her exquisite pearly wardrobe, was a spiritual landmark for the *conquistadores*, and the monastery at one time fed 1000 pilgrims a day, with enormous basic stews of chick peas or *bacalao*, salt cod.

Equally famous, the monastery of Alcántara was sacked by a Napoleonic army, whose commander's wife sent their recipes to Escoffier. He made *faisán al modo de Alcántara* – awash with port and truffles – the most desirable pheasant dish in Europe.

Sopa de tomate con higos

TOMATO SOUP WITH FRESH FIGS

A peasant soup using two fruit – so simple it must be made slowly and correctly.

1 generous kg/2½ lb ripe tomatoes, chopped
8–12 ripe black figs
1 Spanish onion, chopped
3 tablespoons olive oil
2 fat garlic cloves, finely chopped
1 big bay leaf, crumbled
1 strip of orange zest (optional)
1 teaspoon sugar (if tomatoes aren't ripe)
salt and freshly ground black pepper
paprika
2 tablespoons virgin oil
4 slices of stale country bread

SERVES 4

Fry the onion in the olive oil very slowly until soft, then add the garlic. Add the tomatoes (these must be skinned and seeded first if you intend to blend them). Cook, with the bay leaf and orange zest, very gently down to a sauce – 30 minutes or so. (Ripe tomatoes don't need sugar, but supermarket ones might.) Season with salt, pepper and paprika.

Sieve or blend. Return to the pan and reheat. Add the virgin oil to give a creamy emulsion – don't boil from this point.

Lightly toast the bread, put it in 4 soup plates and pour the tomato cream over. Arrange the split figs on top of the bread, or pass separately.

A kitchen in Trujillo, where wild asparagus is being prepared

El matambre

CRISPY BREAD BALLS IN TOMATO SAUCE

Shepherds used to eat this filling dish, which I find makes an excellent accompaniment and sauce for a roast chicken – rather like boiled potatoes with parsley and garlic right through them. There is also a sweet version called *repápolos*, with sugar and warm milk.

250 g/8 oz stale country bread, crusts removed
about 250 ml/8 fl oz milk
4 tablespoons olive oil
2 fat garlic cloves, finely chopped
2 large eggs
8 tablespoons chopped parsley
salt and freshly ground black pepper
¼–½ teaspoon freshly grated nutmeg
plain flour for coating
1 hard-boiled egg, to garnish

TOMATO SAUCE
100 g/4 oz large spring onion bulbs
or shallots, chopped
2 tablespoons olive oil
1 kg/2 lb ripe tomatoes, skinned and seeded,
or 800 g/1 lb 14 oz canned tomatoes
½ teaspoon paprika

SERVES 4–6

Soak the bread in the milk. Put 2 tablespoons of oil into a saucepan and fry the garlic quickly; reserve to flavour the balls.

Make the sauce: fry the spring onions or shallots (quicker than onions) in the oil until soft, then add the chopped tomatoes. Season with paprika, salt and pepper and cook to a sauce.

Meanwhile squeeze excess milk from the bread, and beat in the eggs. Add the cooked garlic, crushed in a mortar, 6 tablespoons of the parsley, ¾ teaspoon salt, pepper and the nutmeg. Form into 18 balls. Sprinkle a tray with flour, add the balls and shake vigorously to and fro to coat the balls. Fry the balls in the remaining oil, rolling constantly until they are crisp and golden on all sides.

Press the tomato sauce through a sieve (or blend). Reheat briefly, pour over the balls and garnish with the chopped hard-boiled egg and remaining parsley.

Escarapuche

— COLD TROUT IN VINEGAR WITH CHOPPED SALAD —

When I was in Cáceres, tench were on sale everywhere, but this recipe makes a lovely summer dish for small trout. The name means pickled, though there is not enough vinegar to keep them. I was told small fish (carp, barbel etc) could be grilled uncleaned: not true of trout!

2 trout or tench, cleaned
salt and freshly ground black pepper
3–4 tablespoons olive oil
4 tablespoons finely chopped Spanish onion
6 tablespoons chopped tomato flesh
2 tablespoons chopped fresh coriander leaves
2 tablespoons red wine vinegar
2 tablespoons lemon juice

— SERVES 2 —

Salt and pepper the fish, then brush with oil. Barbecue or grill them for 4–5 minutes on each side.

Remove the skin, fins, heads and bones, on a foil-covered tray to catch the fish juices. If the fish were grilled on foil, some grilling oil may also be there. Put the fish and their juices in a flat dish in which they just fit.

Put the chopped onion, tomato and coriander in a bowl and add 2–4 tablespoons oil, the vinegar, lemon juice and seasoning. Spoon the dressing over the fish, spooning it back over them several times. (The gelatine in the juices is part of their dressing.) Chill and serve cold.

Caldereta extremeña

— STEWED LAMB FROM EXTREMADURA —

A rich dish, so quantities are quite small, this is often made with kid. Watercress grows abundantly in all the local streams and makes a good salad accompaniment. The *matambre* bread balls also go well (without the sauce).

700 g/1½ lb boneless young lamb, in large cubes
200 g/7 oz lamb's liver, in 2 slices
2–3 tablespoons olive oil
6 garlic cloves, unpeeled but smashed
2 tablespoons lard (or more oil)
salt and freshly ground black pepper
1 onion, finely sliced
1 dried *guindilla*, seeded and chopped
or a big pinch of cayenne pepper
1 bay leaf
2 sprigs of fresh thyme
1 tablespoon paprika, best from la Vera
200 ml/7 fl oz *pitarra* wine or Beaujolais Villages
175 ml/6 fl oz meat stock, warmed
6 black peppercorns
1 big red pepper, grilled and skinned
(see page 52) **or canned pimiento**
1 tablespoon vinegar

— SERVES 4 —

Heat the oil in a small flameproof casserole and fry the whole garlic cloves, then reserve them. Fry the liver quickly until stiffened, then reserve it.

Add the lard and the lamb, seasoned with salt and pepper, the onion, *guindilla* or cayenne, bay leaf, thyme and paprika. Fry until the lamb is golden all over, stirring every now and then. Add the wine and, as soon as it reaches boiling, a little warm stock. As this reduces add more stock, in 2–3 stages, letting it boil down to a sauce – about an hour.

Meanwhile slip the skins off the garlic cloves and pound them with the black peppercorns (or use a blender), working in the chopped liver and red pepper. When reduced to a paste, thin it with the vinegar. Add this to the lamb and simmer for 10 minutes. Remove the thyme and bay leaf and serve.

Moorish-style tiles in a
bar in Extremadura

Migas fried with pork fat are among the good things that come from the pig

❧ Matanza, and the Pig that Didn't Die ❧

Rain stayed execution: too wet to make sausages. They need dry air to cure them, so my pig need not die. *An auténtico rito*, I was assured, one of the great rituals of Spain. Indeed, for centuries the death and eating of a pig was a Christian rite, a demonstration that the participants were neither Arab nor Jewish.

Fewer families do it, in these factory days. Once it was done between St Martin (after All Saints) and the end of March. Now it is just during the coldest weather: *por Santa Catolina mata su cochino* – kill your pig on St Catherine's day – 25th November.

I was in Cacéres for the slaughter – and it was postponed. My farmer-contact fed me beers and the red *chorizo* sausage, his round black eyes concerned on my behalf. But the wait meant days as a noviciate in the rituals of the wild *ibérico*.

The black pig has skin the colour of an elephant, and it dies on the table when its throat is slit. The blood spurts into the *gran cuenco*, a brown basin with a small base and wide rim. The light hair is the next to go, the body down into a straw fire, and then a scrub and wash.

I was shown the equipment, the table with its splayed legs used for slaughter and dismemberment and the *atrevesa*, a trough to hold the chopped meat or the pieces for salting. Like a crib or manger, it was a hollowed half-log with sloping ends. Bigger troughs are used, filled with rough salt, to cure the *matanza* hams.

31

His moustache moved apologetically. 'Sorry. No death in this drizzle.' I eat *prueba de cerdo* (see recipe), delicious hot pork in paprika. It is the dish to test the quality of the newly killed pig. We arrange to telephone again.

Another day: he is still jacketless, and in short shirt sleeves, despite the drizzle. We discuss *chorizos*. The hams can be salted and the loin eaten fresh, or everything can be made into *chorizos*, which are then graded by their meat of origin. Ears and tails are invariably salted. Muzzles etc go into stews. Ribs can be eaten fresh or are chopped (to my surprise) and are then preserved in the major gut. *Cachelada*, a soup with the lungs etc and cumin, is made on the first day; very good it was too. I learn sausages are usually made on the second day. More *cañas* (beer), and *morcilla*. The black pudding is magnificent here, cinnamon-flavoured, with blobs of fat like clotted cream.

Another day, and we contemplate the rain from shelter. His fingers appear from the left-hand pocket (where they had been so glued, I wondered if he were disabled). They flutter... 'Maybe, *quizás*.' I go to telephone Julian, *el carnicero* (butcher) in another town. After a three-day diet of pig (relieved only by bread and alcohol) I began to wonder about this pig thing. Pig palls.

In the end three pigs died. I have gutted an animal once, and it is best not described, except to observe how very near death is to birth. Its legs splayed, the pig delivers its membraned packages, all of them useful. You can, as they say, eat everything from a pig but its squeak.

The pigs hung in the garage, heads into margarine pots lest they drip, bellies splayed with a stick to get plenty of air. Their insides were like an 18th-century cabinet – neat, well-designed fittings. The caul and belly flaps (with teats) hung on washing lines to air. The latter goes to make pumpkin sausages further north. I helped the owners wash out the stomach and intestines into the ditch with a hose.

They make three sorts of sausages in Spain: dried *chorizo* with the red pepper that gives them their name, black pudding or *morcilla*, with either onion or rice, and fresh *embutidos* or *longanizas*, so called because they have no links. The women were reluctant, I found, to make *morcillas*. 'Blood is a messy job – for us, and to be sure to be clean. Oh yes, we like to eat them,' in answer to my question.

There was snow in the air, and in the crevices of the black sierra, on the day we finally made sausages, in a small kitchen warmed by a stove with a pipe through the ceiling. There was a faint, sweet, oppressive smell of meat. The pig died yesterday and weighed 80 kg/176 lb, so we hoped to get 25 kg/55 lb good *chorizos*. The meat was hand-chopped first. Barely five per cent fat, each kilo was flavoured with 3 garlic cloves, 27 g/1 oz salt and 28 g/1 oz paprika (half *piquante*, half sweet) and made into balls, ready for the mincer.

Three women is the natural team for sausage-making, and I joined Julian's wife, her mother and daughter. The youngest wound a massive mincer. Mother fitted the casing on to its solid spout, and pricked the sausage as it formed, and granny tied them. The intestines lay in a bucket under water, 45–60 cm/18–24 in long. Loop and knot at the bottom, then fingerfold it on to the machine. The meat spurted into the skin which swelled, a gentle rhythm as the handle turns.

A good reef knot, granny tied, not a granny, starting in the middle, for this was solid meat which cannot be squeezed. A quick flip of a knife to remove the ends and a new string of six sausages went down into the bucket. The bigger intestine of the pig made fatter sausages: into a different bowl, for they have a different drying time.

We carried six huge bowls and trays into the back kitchen behind the cow byre, where the windows were open on to the mountains. Ceiling hooks were hung with extra strings and wooden poles posted through the loops. We draped our strings of sausages. As they dry the ends are tied in loops.

'Drying takes a week ,' I was told, 'if it doesn't rain.' They shrink and turn bright scarlet. 'If it rains we light the fire' – a wood oven in the wall. 'Sometimes we conserve them in oil.' We rested, and ate bread and *chorizo* from the previous batch, as night closed in.

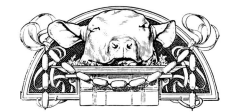

Above: Pass this way for a good meal

cayenne, thyme and bay leaf and fry, stirring every now and then as the onion softens.

Add half the water and 2 tablespoons vinegar. Cook until this is gone, then add more water and vinegar. When the liquid has reduced to a couple of spoonfuls of sauce, sprinkle with the parsley and serve.

Costillas con niscalos

PORK RIBS WITH WILD MUSHROOMS

The pig's ribs are often eaten the day it is killed, either baked with cinnamon, black pepper and salt or, as here, in sauce. Crude food, it is the kind enjoyed by men and boys. *Niscalos* (see page 145) are in season in late November, meaty orange slices. I think them overrated and that brown mushrooms have the better flavour.

1 kg/2 lb meaty pork belly ribs
350 g/12 oz *niscalos* or brown mushrooms,
cleaned and thickly sliced
salt and freshly ground black pepper
2 tablespoons olive oil
1 cinnamon stick
½ dried chilli pepper, seeded and chopped
150 ml/5 fl oz red wine
about 250 ml/8 fl oz water
1 onion, chopped
1 fat garlic clove, finely chopped
1 teaspoon paprika
1 tablespoon plain flour

SERVES 4

Rub the ribs well with salt and pepper. Heat the oil in a big frying pan and fry them until browned. Pack them into a flameproof casserole and add the cinnamon stick, chilli, wine and water to cover. Simmer gently for 20–30 minutes until tender.

In the oil remaining in the frying pan, fry the onion slowly until soft, adding the garlic towards the end. Sprinkle with the paprika and flour. Stir and then add the mushrooms. Cook gently.

When the ribs are tender, add a ladleful or so of their liquid to the frying pan and stir until thickened. Bed the ribs down into the frying pan, adding as much of their cooking liquid as needed to make a sauce. Cover the frying pan and simmer 5 minutes more: it will wait without harm. This is a messy finger-and-bread dish, so serviettes are needed.

Prueba de cerdo

FRIED PORK WITH PAPRIKA AND VINEGAR

The dish that 'tests' the newly killed pig. My guess is that the vinegar was once stale wine. A simple dish which can be an elegant one when made with 2 whole pork fillets or tenderloins, cut into rounds.

800 g/1¾ lb boneless pork, diced
2 teaspoons paprika, preferably from Jarandilla
salt and freshly ground black pepper
4 tablespoons olive oil
1 onion, chopped
3 garlic cloves, finely chopped
1–2 *guindilla*, seeded and chopped
or a pinch of cayenne pepper
4–5 sprigs of fresh thyme
1 bay leaf
175 ml/6 fl oz hot water
4 tablespoons red wine vinegar
2 tablespoons chopped parsley

SERVES 4

Season the pork with paprika, salt and black pepper. Heat the oil in a flameproof casserole on your hottest burner. Put in the pork in handfuls, turning it and keeping it moving with a wooden spoon, adding more when it is sealed. Add the onion, garlic, *guindilla* or

❧ Game: a Passionate Hunter ❧

'We have to be careful not to let the children go out on Sunday into the rough grass' – I was admiring the parkland so close to the city – 'because of the guns.' Over three-quarters of Spain is hunting country, I discovered – the rest city! Even in the suburbs of Madrid you can hear the noise of gunshots.

Spain has some of the best hunting country in Europe. *Caza major*, big game, is plentiful in most mountains – red deer, boar and others; wolves and bears are protected. But it is *caza menor*, small game, that is the common sport. It needs countryside and Spain still has it. On the main bird-migration routes

south, birds come through in great numbers: 'I once saw a band of *paloma torcaz* (pigeon) passing over that stretched three miles wide. And it took three hours to pass!' Spain also combines the variety of Africa with that of Europe.

Dr Alvaro Lozano is out every weekend, Saturday or Sunday. He has been shooting partridges since he was eight years old, and learned it from his father: 'a living

The *charro*, the countryside of holm oaks and rolling turf, where pigs and sheep graze

thing' he wants to see passed on. 'There are very few bad things about hunting. You get to know a lot of people, like the shepherds. I walk 25 miles in a day with a dog. From dawn to 2–3 pm, perhaps six hours, with a *taco* (a little something) – a *bocadillo* and wine.'

He launched into a passionate defence. 'Hunters are preservers, not killers – *cazadores no matadores*. Ecologists understand this. But lots of people come who don't understand: they don't differentiate. *Caza* is an art, like a profession.' He will go out for something and select it. 'A piece is a trophy, a record of success. Others will take a bird on a partridge hunt, even if it is not a partridge. They get in a great wall and shoot everything that comes over, big and little.' He wiped a trembling moustache.

'In Spain there are 4 million partridges, 10 million quail, 7 million rabbits. Partridge is good in October, but wood pigeons, *palomas*, are there all the year. They're now cross-breeding with European pigeons. Turtle dove is just midsummer.

'Quail are summer birds. There is a short season for birds which breed here – 15–20 days, then they are on to Africa. But the wild bird is far superior to the farmed one. The Spanish red-leg partridge is not found elsewhere.' I demurred but he insisted that it is now cross-breeding. 'They fly in vast clouds, on the way to Africa.

'About a third of the birds that pass over Spain are killed: the rest are for reproduction. We kill about a million partridges, but not more. The *fincas*' – there are 27,000 private shooting clubs in Spain, as well as vast national parks – 'count the dead to keep control.

'Starlings used to be taken with a line decoy. You can shoot 400 a day with a bait like this. It's not a sport, but it's been done like this for centuries. Two or three men and a dog can get 140 without a trap.'

I asked about hanging. 'In November the temperature is still high at midday, and a pheasant can easily get tainted in five hours. But they might hang one–two days in winter. In summer it's in the 40s (over 100°F) and you can't even leave turtle doves a day. We carry them in canvas bags – there is the danger of flies. You must get them into the fridge, and into the freezer in two-three days.' Normally he sold the carcasses. But at home the man cleaned them, the maid cooked them.

What did he like best to eat? 'Thrushes in rice, but turtle dove is even more exquisite and wild quail also wonderful stewed. Woodcock – it's more from the north – stuffed with its own innards. Hare – you find it in La Mancha and Extremadura – is good with chocolate, and rabbit with either garlic or tomato: you should eat it with thyme, oregano and rosemary, the natural herbs, picked at same time. It's smaller and slightly darker than the tame ones – like boar is to pig, harder flesh and stronger.'

Aquatica, duck hunting, is a special branch. Out came the photographs, himself in hunting waders with braces, car bonnets covered with ducks – green-headed, red-headed, striped-winged – 20 years of successes recorded under plastic covers. A good shoot was when three or four people shot 70 ducks one day, 20 on another. He watches the temperatures across Europe, and so knows when the ducks will come. 'But others rely on barometers!

'Acquatics are very varied: there are ducks for winter and ducks for summer. There are mallards in all the lakes of Spain. We hunt them in October, standing in water up to the armpits, hidden in reeds. Wigeon come later, when it is cold in Europe. There are shovellers in winter too.

'Ducks are very serious sport, and few people specialize in it. You must distinguish them in flight. Once I was waiting when a flight of 100 descended – *cosa impresionante*, a marvel! We watched without shooting for an hour and a half – it would have been a massacre – and they wheeled and then left, little by little.' Portrait of a happy man!

Liebre guisado

HARE IN RED WINE, SPANISH STYLE

A rich dish, originally cooked with hot charcoal on top of a heavy iron lid. At the end of cooking the sauce was thickened with some of the hare's blood. When I explained blood was difficult to get back home, I was given the tip to replace this with a small glass of mixed brandy and sherry. Another suggestion was 15 g/½ oz dark chocolate.

1 hare, 1.5 kg/3½ lb after cleaning
100–200 g/4–7 oz streaky pork belly,
fresh or salt, such as Italian pancetta
4 tablespoons olive oil
6–8 tablespoons plain flour
1 onion, finely chopped
1 celery stalk, finely chopped
salt and freshly ground black pepper

MARINADE
75 cl bottle of red wine
6 parsley stalks, bruised
2 sprigs of fresh thyme
1 bay leaf
1 inner celery stalk with leaves
1 cinnamon stick
6 black peppercorns, roughly crushed
1 tablespoon olive oil

CONDIMENT
25 g/1 oz almonds, toasted *(see page 129)*
3 garlic cloves, smashed
¼ teaspoon salt
25 g/1 oz pine nuts, dry-fried *(see page 122)*
2 tablespoons Spanish brandy or cognac
2 tablespoons *fino* sherry

SERVES 6

Two or three days ahead, rinse and dry the hare well. Cut it into serving portions, severing the flaps and taking the ribs off the front legs. Put it in an earthenware casserole – of the kind that can be used for cooking. Make a bouquet garni with the herbs, celery and cinnamon and add this and the peppercorns (but no salt, because this would make the meat tough). Add 1 tablespoon oil and the pork belly and pour in wine to cover. Leave this 2–3 days, covered.

Take the hare and pork out, blotting them well with kitchen paper. Cube the pork. Heat the oil in a frying pan and, just before putting the meat in the pan, sprinkle with flour. Brown the meat on all sides and return to the empty casserole, packing it tightly.

Fry the onion and celery in the fat remaining in the pan and add to the casserole. Pour the marinade and bouquet garni over the hare pieces. Cover and bring to simmering (I started with the oven at 170°C/325°F/gas 3, turning it down after 30 minutes). Cook the hare at 140°C/275°F/gas 1, barely simmering, for about 2½ hours.

The condiment will also thicken the sauce. Purée the garlic with the salt in a mortar (or small blender) and add the toasted almonds and pine nuts. Reduce to a paste and dilute with the brandy and sherry. Check the amount of sauce (remove the hare and boil if necessary). Stir the paste into the sauce and simmer briefly to thicken. Check the seasoning, and serve from the casserole. Serve with boiled potatoes.

A glass of wine and a *hornazo*

Pato con aceitunas a la antigua

—— DUCK WITH OLIVES THE OLD-FASHIONED WAY ——

An older recipe than duck with orange, the olives serve the same function as the bitter Seville juice: to cut the fat.

1.9 kg/4 lb duck, with its liver,
or 3 chicken livers (75 g/3 oz)
24 green olives, stoned (200 g/7 oz jar)
50 g/2 oz pork fat (back or belly)
or bacon fat, cubed
1 tablespoon olive oil
1 slice of stale bread
salt and freshly ground black pepper
125 g/4 oz raw ham or gammon, cut into strips
freshly grated nutmeg
1 bay leaf, crumbled
150 ml/5 fl oz red Rueda or *fino* sherry
250 ml/8 fl oz stock, from the neck and giblets
1 tablespoon chopped parsley

—————— SERVES 4 ——————

Sweat the fat cubes in the oil in a flameproof casserole, then remove. Fry the bread and cook the liver lightly, then reserve.

Remove the wing tips from the duck. Cut off the excess neck skin by slashing it across at the end of the breast, then use a little knife to remove the wishbone. Cut off the parson's nose, then the pad of fat on either side of the tail. Rinse and pat dry with kitchen paper. Prick all fatty pads and season inside and out.

Put the duck, breast down, in the casserole, then turn it, propping it against the side, so that it colours on all sides – 15–20 minutes. On the last turn, add the ham strips.

When the duck is golden, remove it and drain all the fat from the casserole. Quarter the duck and cut the backbone free. Sprinkle the meaty sides well with nutmeg. Return the duck, backbone, pork cubes and ham to the casserole and add the olives, bay leaf, Rueda or sherry and enough stock almost to cover. Cook over a gentle heat, covered, for about 45 minutes or until tender.

Pound (or blend) the liver and the bread with the parsley. Remove the backbone from the casserole and stir the liver mixture into the sauce to thicken it, seasoning as necessary with salt, pepper and nutmeg. Use a slotted spoon to move duck and garnish to a serving plate and pass the sauce in a sauce boat.

CHAPTER 3

New Castile and La Mancha

South of Madrid, La Mancha forms the greater part of the Castilian plateau. The hottest and driest part of Spain, the region is so backward that when Cervantes wanted to bring a smile to the lips, he chose it for his good knight, Don Quixote de la Mancha.

I joined the train at Chamartín, Madrid's main station. It is like an airport. Distant places flash up on the indicators, with their gates, then roll away. All tickets bookable and every ticket guarantees a seat. Outside, the platforms are low-slung for Continental trains. Oh the glamour of those long-distance engines, with great headlights, and the carriages with flights of steps up into them! A period of frenzied activity followed, as old ladies with cardboard boxes (fortified with rubber ties) were shoehorned by half the family into their compartments.

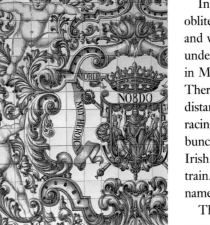

'Only 20 minutes late,' said my companions with approval, as the engine started to take the weight. In our compartment three jolly chaps settled down to play cards, then there's me and a granny, and a couple of mums with small children. Out came colouring books and new crayons. We knew we had ten hours to reach the south!

La Mancha means 'bone dry', from *manxa*, the Arabic for parched earth, for this elevated plain is not irrigated. Cereals, vines and olives grow here, fields of saffron and a vast production of sunflowers. The river Tajo lies south of Madrid, with Toledo and the summer palace of Aranjuez in the last green valley. Then the plains go on for ever. There are six or seven market towns, and fewer cities, at the plain's four corners.

In summer the sun's heat obliterates all thought but shade and water. La Mancha survives under a sky of molten metal. But in March rain hangs in the air. There is a sense of space and far distant horizons. Cyclists in racing colours, fast-moving in a bunch like racehorses on the Irish Curragh, sweep past the train. The *rapido* (unlike its name) proceeds at a stately pace.

The pruned vines look like rows of black stopcocks, close to the earth. This is the winelake of Spain, Europe's biggest and poorest vineyard. It produces rough yellow wine: as someone said of Madrid's river in summer, 'contributed by mules'. Hour after hour the train rattles across it. Every field has a small white building and water wheel, with an attendant almond tree. Spring is late here, icy like Britain's, and the trees are covered in pale pink blossom. There really are windmills in La Mancha, clustering on the slightest ridge.

Castile is a region of poor man's food. I can see why. Simple hearty garlic soups, beans with cardoon, lentils with rice, and meals with chick peas or potatoes plus items from the *tocinería* (pork shop). But it has some of Spain's best-known dishes: *garbanzos con chorizo*, chick peas with the spicy red sausage that so perfectly flavours them; *potaje* (chick peas with spinach and salt cod), eaten particularly in Lent; and *pisto* (see page 42). *Olla podrida* is an everyday pot with chick peas and humble things from a pig, rather than Madrid's meat-filled *cocido* (see page 56).

Tortilla was invented in New Castile, a dense egg cake, quite unlike a French omelette. And eggs go into everything. *Mojete* (which just means moist) is another tomato mixture, this time with fried potatoes and garlic, to which a poached egg is added 'for charity'.

They like strong flavours here, to combat the climate: raw tastes against winter cold and summer furnace. Cumin, from Arab times, is backed up by thyme in unheard-of quantities. Cumin goes into *sopa castellana* (see page 42), into the local *gazpacho* and on to tomato, or red pepper, salads. It is noticeable in the tomato-sauced beans, *judías a lo tío Lucas*. Another strong flavour is that of toast: toasted bread (which can dominate a dish), but often the taste of cinders or the grill. *Tiznao*, fish started in the ashes and then finished in pepper sauce, is the most elegant example.

Escabeches – also Arab – are foods cooked in wine and vinegar then marinated in the cooking juices. Most famous is the red-legged partridge, which breeds here (see recipe). And all the village *ferias* sell aubergines pickled with hot peppers from Almagro. This is partly cereal country, and there are ancient bread-thickened dishes like *gazpacho manchego*. The country recipe is nothing like the tourist dish. It starts with large flat pieces of unleavened dough, as thin as a coin, cooked between two heat sources. The result is like a Jewish matzo. On a good day, a stew of rabbit or pigeon was cooked separately, and broken pieces of wafer added to soak up gravy. It was then served on more wafer, to use as a spoon. Some days no game was caught.

Castile also has its famous products. Saffron is grown in both Castiles, and Toledo is celebrated for inventing marzipan some 800 years ago. Better wines are made at Valdepeñas. When driving you know you have reached it by the vast Ali Baba jars beside the road. These *tinajas* are still used for wine-making.

La Mancha also make the most famous cheese in the country. Much copied, Manchego is the Castilian cheddar, sold at all ages. It may be mild and soft or sharp and crumbly, sometimes in a gold rind, sometimes a black one, with braid marks on it. The taste of mature Manchego cheese is haunting and addictive, reminiscent of good Parmesan. It is more expensive, though, for Manchego is made from ewes' milk, Parmesan from cows'.

Out came the cheese and ham *bocadillos*, then our compartment settled down to sleep.

Crema de Aranjuez

ARANJUEZ CREAM-OF-ASPARAGUS SOUP

Aranjuez has Spain's Versailles – a purpose-built summer palace, where the fountains play on festival days. It is a place for summer outings, and so the so-called 'strawberry train' runs there from Madrid at weekends and on public holidays.

500 g/1 lb asparagus
50 g/2 oz butter
1 leek, white and pale green parts sliced
1 carrot, sliced
4 tablespoons rice
1 lt/1¾ pt light stock or water
2 tablespoons finely chopped parsley
200–250 ml/7–8 fl oz milk
2 egg yolks (optional)
salt and ground white pepper
tiny pinch of cayenne pepper
4 tablespoons whipping cream

SERVES 4

Reserve the asparagus tips, and peel and slice the stalks. Melt the butter in a pan and add the stalks with the leek and carrot. Sweat them for 20 minutes, covered, then add the rice. Cook the tips separately in the stock – about 8 minutes; drain and reserve tips and stock.

When the rice has absorbed the pan juices, add the stock and simmer for 30–40 minutes. Press through a sieve with the parsley (or blend together). Bring back to simmering and thin with milk to a creamy consistency, reheating the asparagus tips in the soup. Stir in the egg yolks, if wished, for extra richness. (They are traditional but not, I think, needed.) Season, including a discreet amount of cayenne, and serve hot with a dribble of cream.

This also makes an excellent chilled summer soup, diluted a little with good jellied chicken or meat stock. Purée the tips with the soup and garnish with a delicate herb and 1 chopped hard-boiled egg.

Perdices estofados

PARTRIDGES IN WINE AND VINEGAR

'Stewed partridges are a gift: fried ones are heavy on the stomach,' she told me. The wine-and-vinegar sauce sets off game beautifully, but can also be used to give character to a small chicken. Easy, successful – and also good cold.

3 partridges
salt and freshly ground black pepper
3 tablespoons olive oil
1 large mild Spanish onion, chopped
1 tender celery stalk, finely diced
3 garlic cloves, finely chopped
1 bay leaf
2 cloves
175 ml/6 fl oz dry white wine
4 tablespoons sherry vinegar or red wine vinegar
about 200 ml/7 fl oz chicken stock
boiled potatoes (to serve hot)

SERVES 6

Reach into the neck of each bird and run finger and thumb nails up the wishbone to the top and pull it out. Salt and pepper the birds inside and out. Choose a flameproof casserole into which they fit snugly. Heat the oil and fry the birds, turning them over and propping them against the sides of the pan, until they are coloured on all sides. Remove the birds and keep warm.

Fry the onion and celery in the same oil, adding the garlic when they soften. Return the birds. Add the bay leaf, cloves, wine, vinegar and sufficient stock to cover the legs. Simmer, covered, over low heat until cooked – about 30 minutes.

Remove the birds to a hot serving platter. Strain the stock, pressing the solids through back into the casserole. Alternatively blend the solids, discarding the bay leaf. Skim the stock and add about half to the blender. Purée, then reheat in the casserole. Check the seasoning. The Spanish like their potatoes soggy and often reheat them in the sauce.

Divide the birds in half, surround with potatoes and pass the sauce in a sauce boat.

Queso frito

FRIED CHEESE

Cut hard cheese, such as young Manchego, young Parmesan, mature cheddar or mature Double Gloucester into slices about 5 mm/$\frac{1}{5}$ in thick. Dust with flour, then coat with beaten egg and crumbs. Fry in enough olive oil to nearly float them for about 1 minute in all, turning once. Serve with bread and/or fruit – ripe figs, grapes or an apple.

Alajú

ARAB HONEY AND NUT SWEETMEAT

An old, old Arab sweetmeat, famous in Cuenca and clearly related to Siennese panforte. It is very more-ish, despite simple ingredients. The touch of orange lends it magic.

250 g/8 oz honey, warmed by standing in hot water
150 g/5 oz almonds, toasted *(see page 129)*,
or $\frac{2}{3}$ almonds, $\frac{1}{3}$ walnuts
grated zest of 1 orange
150 g/5 oz stale bread without crusts
$\frac{1}{2}$ teaspoon orange flower water
2 sheets of rice paper, each 24 cm/9 in square
(or 4 smaller sheets)

MAKES 18–24 PORTIONS

Put the honey in a saucepan with the orange zest, grated on a coarse cheese grater. Leave to simmer for a couple of minutes. Grate the bread into crumbs – grating on the same grater as the zest to pick up all the orange oil. Add the toasted almonds (plus walnuts – recommended!) to the honey, then the crumbs. Stir continuously for about 5 minutes; the mixture will stiffen and come away from the side of the pan. Off the heat add the orange flower water (it otherwise evaporates during cooking) and stir it in.

Turn on to the rice paper and pat into a disc, or make 2 smaller discs. Cover with another piece of rice paper and press down gently, to less than a finger thickness. Work round the edge with a table knife, to neaten it. When the sweetmeat is cold, trim the rice paper to fit. Keep in an airtight tin and slice off chunks then cut into pieces to serve.

In Search of Don Quixote

I saw what Cervantes saw, with a shock of recognition. Driving north across the plain, featureless in the dusk, towards Consuegro, the castle was silhouetted against the evening sky. And to its left, along the ridge, were six giant figures. The famous windmills of Don Quixote! But at this distance all scale was missing. They looked like giants with lances.

Windmills, I discovered, were introduced from Holland about 20 years before Cervantes began his epic book. No wonder his hero found them striking! Was Don Quixote, then, an early Luddite, battling against the machines? Now it would be the electricity pylons. Built like figures, a row marches across the plain north of Toledo. He would have fared worse.

Don Quixote opens with food: 'His habitual diet consisted of a stew, more beef than mutton, hash most nights, *duelos y quebrantos* (sorrow and suffering) on Saturdays, lentils on Fridays and a young pigeon as a Sunday treat. This took three-quarters of his income.' The puzzle is: what are *duelos y quebrantos*? 'Boiling bones' says the Penguin translation. This is not what is served now in La Mancha.

There are eggs for certain. I've been offered eggs-and-brains hashed. Eggs with *chorizo*, whose paprika is the wounds, says another. In the end I found an academic who had given it a corner of his mind. It's the same as 'scraping the barrel'. And finally to Calderón de la Barca (in the 1650s): *huevos y torreznos bastan que son duelos y quebrantos*. We are back to eggs and bacon!

Torreznos are very typical of Castile and essential fare at *la matanza* (see page 74): made of cured streaky pork belly (streaky bacon a finger thick) or what is called 'pancetta' in Italian delicatessens. The correct way to make them is to fry them, without fat, in a heavy pan over low heat until they give off fat, then raise the heat and fry until they are very crisp and light. Like an empty sponge (for the fat has gone) and full of flavour, they are better than English crackling. Now it is common in La Mancha to serve them with fried *chorizo*, as well as the Don's scrambled eggs.

Sopa de la abuela castellana

—————— GRANNY'S GARLIC AND BREAD SOUP ——————

4 garlic cloves, chopped
6 tablespoons olive oil
4 slices of stale bread
1 lt/1¾ pt light stock or water
100 g/4 oz raw ham or gammon, finely diced
salt
1 teaspoon paprika
½ teaspoon cumin seeds, very well crushed

———————— SERVES 4 ————————

Put a casserole over the heat and add the oil and garlic. Remove the garlic the moment it looks cooked, and keep it. Then fry the bread on both sides until golden. Add the stock or water and the ham and bring to simmering. Return the garlic and season with salt and paprika. Simmer for 5 minutes, stirring to break up the bread.

Check for salt (it probably won't need it because of the ham) and sprinkle the cumin over the top just before serving. This adds special flavour.

Pisto Semana Santa

—————— PEPPERS, TOMATOES AND ONIONS ——————
WITH CANNED TUNA

Pisto for Holy Week (for fasting), with the favourite *escabeche* (pickled fish), rather than the ham it so often includes. Good hot, better still cold.

3 large green peppers, seeded and chopped
5 big ripe tomatoes, skinned and seeded
(or 800 g/1 lb 10 oz canned tomatoes, with juice)
2 Spanish onions, thinly sliced
3–4 tablespoons olive oil
3 garlic cloves, finely chopped
3 big courgettes, thinly sliced
salt and freshly ground black pepper
4 tablespoons chopped parsley
200 g/7 oz canned tuna
2 hard-boiled eggs
2–3 tablespoons virgin olive oil (to serve cold)

———————— SERVES 4 ————————

Soften the onions in the oil in a flameproof casserole, over medium heat so they caramelize. Add the garlic

Peppers, aubergines, courgettes, onions: the ingredients for
pisto manchego

near the end. Add the chopped pepper, then the tomatoes and courgettes, as they are ready. Season with salt and pepper and cook gently for 20 minutes until the flavours blend.

Stir in the parsley and flaked tuna and check the seasonings. Garnish with the chopped eggs. Sprinkle a little virgin oil over the cold dish (or use more in cooking if planning it this way).

Torrijas

—— SUGARED WINE TOASTS ——

A children's breakfast or tea when made with hot milk, this little nothing is quite something when made with wine – crisp on the outside and resembling custard within. I was recommended to try it with Málaga, cream sherry or red port too, but red wine was delicious. I'm told it is eaten on Christmas Eve in the Basque country.

8 rounds of stale French bread,
a good finger thick
about 100 ml/3½ fl oz red wine
2 eggs, beaten
4 tablespoons sunflower oil
sugar for sprinkling
pinch of ground cinnamon, to serve

—— SERVES 3–4 ——

When ready to fry, dip the bread rounds into wine on each side and then into beaten egg. Fry in hot oil on both sides briefly, until crisp and golden, then drain on a platter covered with sugar until the rest are ready. Move to a serving plate, and sprinkle with sugar mixed with cinnamon. Eat hot.

Saffron: October Gold

Flying fingers pull the scarlet stamens from the centre of each crocus. It is like sewing with fine silk: meticulous repetition. I wonder they do not get cramp, from so intense and seasonal an occupation.

The purple *rosas* are tipped upon the kitchen table and three stamens and a pistil must be plucked from each one. When they are heated during cooking, they produce a heavy aromatic scent, an aromatic oil and a water-soluble colour. But at this stage a good day's work is 50–70 g/2–3 oz plucked and a week to get a pound! 160,000 blossoms are needed for a kilo.

Last of all comes *el tueste*, the toasting. Only older women are trusted to do it. To dry the stamens, they are put on a sieve over a pan of charcoal. Moments when weeks of labour are at risk. No wonder this is the world's most expensive spice!

Mancha *selecto* is the world's best saffron: deep-red, inch-long stamens, packed and date-stamped. Lesser types, like sierra saffron, have shorter stamens and a quantity of white and yellow flower parts. They also have a more bitter flavour.

The festival in Consuegro is the cheerful public side of muscle-aching labour. It starts on the Friday with a *chupinazo*, when sweets are scattered to the children in the Plaza de España, the town square which is commanded by the handsome wooden balcony and pantile roof of the museum. Here, too, there is dancing by the local girls in dark red skirts and black aprons. There are bull fights and the election of a beauty queen. In her gold-and-scarlet sash and 16th-century costume, she is called La Dulcinea after Don Quixote's enamorata. There are saffron-plucking races between the girls from different villages, and even a children's competition.

Saffron, by weight, costs more than gold, but little enough of the latter sticks to the hands of those who produce it. Landless labourers plant the bulbs on rented land, as an insurance policy. Anywhere suitable: round the grapes, or where winter wheat will grow later. Always the poorest, I was told, and always the same families. Some years they don't want to do it.

The flowers of *Crocus sativus* appear overnight, round Santa Teresa's day, 15th October. In a landscape burnt brown by the sun, they are more like purple rugs than carpets. They must be hand-picked the same day, so it is out at dawn, for perhaps 19 hours of stooping. Not surprisingly the crop has dropped by half since the 1930s!

The Arabs worked out the secret of saffron cultivation – and gave the spice the name yellow, *za'fran*. The Romans brought it to Spain. Now it grows in Aragon, Murcia and Old Castile, though the best quality is from Manchuela, from Cuenca south to Albacete.

It has been exported since the 1400s, when adulteration was also a problem. In Spain the substitutes are safflower, the yellow *cártama*, and packets of dye labelled *colorante*, which contain tartrazine.

A 0.125 gram pinch of stamens, about 20 strands – and about $\frac{1}{2}$ teaspoon by eye – will colour and flavour a dish for 4–8. Italian packets of powder (usually 0.1 g) serve about the same. In Spain stamens are crushed in a mortar – though crumbling with fingers is easier – and are often then soaked for five minutes.

I asked round Consuegro for local recipes. The ideas were simple – *patatas amarillas*, yellow potatoes (containing up to 4 packets of saffron), rice with saffron, and *cocido con garbanzos*, a pot of chick peas with a golden broth. Indeed saffron seemed to go into most things, regardless of its price. In with the eggs for meat balls, into the onion for a sauce for pork steaks, or for *pisto manchego* (a tomato dish like ratatouille). They also made a sweet saffron sponge cake.

Tortilla de patatas con azafrán

—— POTATO CAKE WITH EGGS AND SAFFRON ——

A dense moist cake of egg, really yellow because of the presence of saffron. Don't use too large a frying pan – the old-fashioned iron one with vertical sides, about 22 cm/9 in across, is ideal to produce a cake shape.

3 potatoes (rather larger than the eggs), diced
100 ml/3½ fl oz olive oil
1 onion, chopped
0.1 g saffron (20 strands)
3 tablespoons hot stock
6 large eggs
salt and freshly ground black pepper

SERVES 4 AS A STARTER,
—— 2 AS A SUPPER DISH ——

Heat a generous quantity of oil until very hot, add the potatoes and onion and stir to coat. Reduce the heat and cook until soft without letting them colour. Meanwhile crumble the saffron in your fingers, then soak in the stock for 5 minutes.

Move the potatoes and onion with a slotted spoon to a bowl with kitchen paper at the bottom. Drain the oil from the pan, leaving about 2 tablespoons oil. Beat the eggs with the saffron liquid and seasoning. Remove the paper and pour the eggs over the potatoes, so they are well coated.

Pour into the hot oil, spreading the potatoes evenly. Cook a minute at high heat, then turn down to low. Use a spatula to pull the egg off the sides of the pan, shaking it to and fro occasionally, to make sure the bottom isn't catching.

When the top has ceased to be liquid, cover with a serving plate and reverse the pan. Return the *tortilla* and cook for a further minute. Serve hot, or cold, cut in portions and speared with cocktail sticks.

Pollo con salsa de ajos

—— CHICKEN WITH SAFFRON AND GARLIC SAUCE ——

Old-fashioned fried chicken, the saffron sauce is thickened at the end with a typical *picada* – a mash of mild garlic and toast.

1.2–1.4 kg/2¾–3 lb free-range chicken,
cut into 8 pieces
salt
1–2 teaspoons paprika
4 tablespoons olive oil
1 slice of country bread, crusts removed
1 bulb of garlic, cloves smashed and peeled
0.25 g saffron (50 strands)
125 ml/4 fl oz white wine
125 ml/4 fl oz hot water
5 black peppercorns
1 tablespoon Spanish brandy or cognac

—— SERVES 4 ——

Rub salt and paprika into the chicken pieces with your fingers. Heat the oil in a wide shallow flame-proof casserole and fry the bread quickly on both sides, then reserve. Give the chicken pieces a turn in the hot oil with the whole garlic cloves. When the chicken starts to look golden, take out all the garlic and reserve with the bread, but continue frying the chicken (about 15 minutes in all).

Crumble the saffron with your fingers into the wine and add to the casserole with the water. Cover and reduce the heat to minimum. Simmer for 10 minutes.

Crush the black peppercorns in a mortar (or small blender). Add the garlic cloves with a pinch of salt and reduce to a paste. Add the fried bread in pieces and pulp it all. Stir this into the cooking liquid, spooning it over the chicken. When the chicken is cooked through, sprinkle with the brandy and serve.

Left: New meets old in a
Spanish kitchen: modern
plastics with a marble sink

CHAPTER 4

Madrid

At the high centre of the country, Madrid was the obvious capital when the country united 500 years ago. A city of broad avenues and epic plazas, it must be a pleasant place to live in, despite extremes of weather, for the Guadarrama mountains are visible from city offices.

Madrid in March. No leaves, yet, on the trees in the Paseo de Castellana, the avenue which bisects the city. But the Metro posters are all of beauties in wedding dresses. The sun has banished overcoats, and dark-stockinged legs are visible everywhere. It seems a pity I am not a fellow.

Fashionable eating, I soon discover, is in the *casas regionales*, many round the Plaza Santa Ana. Every region has an authentic restaurant here, and there are Michelin-starred ones too, as well as institutions like Lhardy's (a bar, restaurant and charcuterie all in one) and Botín's, oldest restaurant in the world.

I ask about Madrid food. *A la madrileña* used to mean short-order food, I discover – restaurant dishes, cooked to order – when all the old ones were all-day affairs. 'Oh yes, Madrid has its official dishes, *cocido*, *callos* (boiled meats and tripe), but they're drawn from the countryside. Grannies might cook them.' The implication was, they are not for us.

'A chicken has four legs in Spain' (meaning two are needed for a family meal), joked a mother. But big families are a thing of the past. Spain has the lowest birthrate in Europe. Women are well represented in the *Cortes* (parliament) and in the cabinet, as well as in top jobs such as head of RENFE (the state railways) and regional governorships. There are even women dustmen and miners! But over all, I find, only one-third of all women have a job.

I maintain also that it is slightly easier to get domestic help. 'Forty years ago there was one maid to cook, one to serve at table.' I notice the little dining-room bell (for ringing for the next course) still in many houses, even where the mistress cooks. Spanish maids (and men servants) get free accommodation and have time off for a good part of the day, and there is a lot of demand from South America. They work at night.

Madrid is a place where there is always a fresh food market near, always a little shop round the corner. There is fresh fish daily and wonderful takeaways. The population has trebled since the 1950s.

It is the hours that are so punishing. 'I have never had more than five hours sleep a night, and I have never had a siesta,' said one *madrileño*. Madrid has the most robust nightlife (and appalling hours) in Europe, with restaurants opening at 10, smart to arrive at 11. How can executives dance till three on a Friday night? – but they do. The rush hour often starts at 3 am. At home families eat late, nine is early. Even young children eat late (with a nap after tea). I wondered just how they managed.

The old pattern was to have meat at lunch, then fish at night, with a vegetable as the first plate. Now women who work all day only want to make a sandwich and salad at night. Both the men and the children eat two courses at lunch.

And the women like some social life. 'Work, home, shop, sleep is not a good enough life. Life is for having fun.' The men don't go home straight from work. And the women don't either. They have a *merienda* (tea-time snack), meet friends, go window shopping. The food shops are generally open till eight, chain stores much later. The pattern is to get home at nine and eat at 10. Back to the office at eight or nine next morning, as there is a long lunch hour.

A week in Madrid, and I got used to calling on women in their offices – going for a gossip and a *tapa*, asking how they cooked, how domestic life had changed with the coming of democracy. Christine was a secretary in her mid-50s. Her father had been a commandante of the Guardia Civil. And the first thing I learned about her mother was that she had beautiful handwriting. She was also intelligent, generous, independent. But in those days a good hand was a virtue in a woman, just as people praised a good dressmaker. 'Such skills are valued no more! Women prefer promotion to housework. The children go to a *guardía infantil*,' a child minder – which means very long hours in Spain. 'Marriage seems more solid in the provinces. In Madrid people have affairs and then split up.

'Of course life was different in Franco's time. There was the Servicios Social de la Mujer – compulsory service for the state.' Anyone who is over 35 now must have served under Franco. 'You did six months service at the age of 17. And you needed a certificate saying you had done it to get a job or a passport. It worked out as three months at school, learning politics for four hours each morning. Then in the afternoon there were cooking lessons, sewing etc. Everyone learned to make a *canastilla* (basket, i.e. layette) for a baby. Then there was three months office work or visiting old people.

'Initially a woman had to obtain a certificate from her husband granting permission for her to work. And women were kept separate at work. Channelled towards charity, culture, education, health, that sort of thing.'

The Sección Femenina was run by Pilar Prima de Rivera, the formidable daughter of dictator Miguel (and sister of José Antonio) – it was like a Women's Institute, but run by the Movimiento. 'It did some good things. It made people record the singing, dancing, cooking of their region in the 1940s. Pilar Primo de Rivera belonged to the left – the Falange,' (or purist wing of the party) 'traditionalists, wanting to maintain roots in the regions. To save the traditional values of Spain.'

They also published a classic cookery book. Just called *Manuel de Cocina*, it is on its 27th edition, still printed from the old type blocks. Many brides are given it. The other classic book, that many own, is Lourdes March's *La Paella y de los Arroces* (*paella* and rice).

'Female employment came on the big scale in the 1960s. Mainly to save labour costs. But it was short-term labour, perhaps five years. Recruitment slowed when employers discovered that women wanted to return after having babies.' Now legislation for women is highly protective – such as the right to return home to breast-feed a baby during office hours. It may not be an advantage. I met employers who said they now think seriously before employing a young woman.

A house in the Santa Ana area, a very traditional part of the city

Madrid Markets: a Day Shopping

You can cross Madrid in half an hour by Metro, yet everyone owns a car. And they use it: even to go to a bar five minutes' walk away. There are different words for parking while shopping, and parking more permanently. You can do neither in Madrid, despite the broad avenues. Complaints (and scrapes) are constant.

I was met by Jaime in a green buggy with no door-locks and a Palma de Mallorca number plate. 'The Madrid police process 25,000 infractions a year,' he explained. 'With these it will be a while till they get round to me.'

We start with a market that has no food, a fine 1930s building, near the Rastro, of soaring concrete in the Fascist style. Built for fish, it now houses antique booths. The fish moved to Mercamadrid. Fish shops are first on our list, to reach them early in the morning. The Casa Francisca, in the Calle Bailén, he

thought the best for cod, La Marquinesa best for fresh tuna, Pescaderías Coruñesas best for shellfish. The Carnecería Frances was the best meat shop.

The Pescadería Pardiñas on Calle de Alcalá 131 shone white, the tiles reflecting the morning light. The fish lay on marble desks, garnished with false bay leaves and mimosa. Here we hoped to find *gallo* (Madrid's answer to plaice) and the best sea bass. Fish is so fresh in the capital (despite an 8-hour drive from the sea) that one popular local dish is called *mata mulo* – the mule killer. The speed getting to Madrid did the animal in!

There are mussels and the beautiful, eccentric barnacles called *percebes* (see page 79) at 7900 pesetas per kg/£20 per lb. I study clams: *almendras* are rounder; *chirlas* have stripes gathered up at the middle. A minute pink shrimp is called *camerones*, bigger are *quisquillas* and orange-pink *langostinos*, which are deep-water

The freshest fish: a big buey crab and clams for sale

50

prawns. The small *necoras* – one of the top crabs to eat boiled – have hairy legs and red knee joints. The Basque *kokotxas* (see page 106) are obviously popular in Madrid too, for they fetch 6500 pesetas per kilo.

Fish include *reo*; the sea trout looks more like a carp, short, stubby, brown. There is *bonito* in a great joint like a lamb saddle, and swordfish, *pez espada*, grey-pink round a central bone. 'You can buy foreign produce like South American swordfish. It's cheap, like sardines. And big prawns from Thailand with red and pink rings, but I don't advise it.' Jaime was back from solving our parking problem. 'Canned anchovy comes from Chile and Peru, but the best comes from Gerona, from L'Escala. Ortiz makes the best canned *bonito* (tuna).' Out it flowed. Information like bullets: the best pickled aubergine (*berenjenas de Almagro en escabeche*); the amount of fish needed for *paella*. I know there was a kilo of rock fish for the stock and crabs to go on top. I was fascinated – but unable to take in so much advice.

Back to the buggy and we whirl through Madrid to the Mercado de la Paz in the Barrio Salamanca. Madrid buys splendid beef from Galicia and the Basque country. But most families eat veal instead. The famous producers are at Avila. Jaime didn't like it: 'Insipid!' Better pink veal (the popular taste) to milk-fed. The market sells veal haunches for roasting, labelled with their age: one year, two years. There is also beautiful *lomo cebon*, wing ribs in a perfect triangle, from veal fed on barley. Like the hams, the labels say what the animal ate, to indicate the quality.

Walking across the street, the Frutas Vazquez (Calle Ayala 11) was so pretty I would like to have it as a doll's house. The shop front folded back on either side, with shelves all the way up, to flank the space.

Dramatic crookneck squash, pumpkin, pineapples in baskets and asparagus 60 cm/2 feet high framed the door. And the shop apron was full of good things: fresh ginger in flat hands and new potatoes from Almeria. The very best from the regions: *cogollos* (lettuce hearts) from Tudela and spicy pointed peppers, *pimiento de piquillo* at 1500 pesetas per kilo. And any Frenchwoman would covet the fresh bouquet garnis, a dozen herbs tied up with string, at 100 pesetas each.

Spring fruit is quite different in Spain: *fresas del bosque* (wild strawberries) and raspberries from Segovia. *Escarola*, I note, is the Spanish name for frisé. And much like it were enchanting *cardillos*, tiny hearts of curling stalks, part of the artichoke family, purplish

on the outside. There were also spring chanterelles (*rossinols*), and I bought a small bag of white *criadillas*, summer truffles, from Cáceres. There were South American fruit too: *pasionaria de Brazil* (passion fruit) and fragrant yellow *pitahaya*, bigger than a prickly pear, with the spines taken off.

We stop for a beer at Cervecería Alemana in the Plaza Santa Ana, a favourite with Ernest Hemingway. Then work through the backstreets, past La Casa de la Abuela, famous for its *gambas* (prawns). I comment on the fish heads on the floor. 'They couldn't sweep it, or the place would seem unpopular', was the answer.

Up the Calle Victoria where the bullfighters drink, and along Echegaray. We pass the Villa Rosas, patterned tiles on the street, and look into Los Gabrieles, whose amazing wall tiles advertise wine or biscuits for Galletas Olibet. Another panel is a pastiche on Velásquez' *Los Borrachos*, the drunkards. Then into a dark brown cavern, with stacked sherry butts, to drink *fino* and eat *mojama*. This cured tuna is a speciality from the south and east coasts. It looks like dried beef and is made from tuna back, sundried and seawashed.

Several people had advised me to go to the Antiqua Posteria de Pozo, Calle del Pozo 8, as Madrid's best pastry shop. Puff pastry is their forte, in salmon pies and desserts with cream filling or the favourite squash jam, *cabello de angel*, and Roscon de Reyes at Christmas time.

Back to the Mercado de la Cebada, near where we started. There were problems (again) with the parking. Jaime disappeared for hours and I inspected the Galician charcuterie. It was more dreadful than I feared. Aged *unto*: dark sheets of fat wrapped round each other. *Unto* is also the word for the fat round a man's heart (this floats from my unconscious): this loaf has pagan uses. There are paprika-dusted pig's belly (*tocino*) and *cecina* (beef ham) from León. 'It fed the conquerors of America.' Jaime has reappeared – we were double-parked. I gather that the ship stores were garlic, onions, salted *tocino*, *cecina*, *mojama* and *membrillo* (sweet quince paste and full of vitamin C). Half Magellan's crew died of scurvy, but on this diet the officers kept healthy.

Even food, it seems, is subject to politics. The Franco era kept the shutters down for 30 years – nothing from outside. One woman told me, 'People were asking: What is a raspberry? Even by 1980 broccoli hardly existed.' Earlier in the week an old lady had given me two very ordinary broccoli recipes, with some pride at being modern.

Today the market is flooded with small, sweet Canary bananas. There are oranges (*tavernes*) and huge artichokes. But I am impressed by *ajetes*, green sprouting garlic, the bulb much the same size as spring onions, but with much more leafy top. Their mild flavour is a favourite, especially with eggs.

Back to my Metro station, we divide the shopping and I try to pay for mine. 'Don't give me money, especially here! Someone might see you!'

Chuletas de cordero con pimientos asados

LAMB CUTLETS WITH SOFT RED PEPPERS

Lamb is the festive choice in Spain. These cutlets have a simple garnish of sweet red pepper.

**12 best-end lamb cutlets, 50 g/2 oz each,
the bones cleaned of fat down to the eye of meat
4 red peppers
paprika
salt and freshly ground black pepper
2–4 teaspoons olive oil**

SERVES 4

Grill the peppers for about 20 minutes, giving them a quarter turn every 5 minutes, until they are charred on all sides. Put them in a plastic bag for 10 minutes, then strip off the charred skins and pull out the stalks and seeds. (Do this on a plate to catch all the sweet juices.) Open the peppers to remove the last seeds and cut them into strips. Save them in a saucepan with their juices.

Rub the cutlets with paprika, salt and black pepper. Brush lightly with oil and grill them for 3–4 minutes on each side. Arrange them with the bones overlapping in threes on a big serving plate. Reheat the pepper strips in their liquid, with a little oil if needed, and garnish the dish.

Mama's merluza

MAMA'S HAKE WITH TWO MAYONNAISES
AND A SOUP COURSE

An elegant and easy cook-ahead dinner for a hot day. Hake is perfect as the fillets roll off the backbone like the breasts of a chicken. It is cooked in a pressure cooker – a popular time-saver in Spain – and left unopened all day. The stock is then used for soup. Quicker to do than explain!

Cod, poached in the normal way, is also delicious with these mayonnaises: I like to serve one plain, one coloured, though there is a choice of green or saffron-flavoured.

**1 kg/2 lb middle piece of hake
salt and freshly ground black pepper**

STOCK
**100 g/4 oz small onions, halved
100 g/4 oz baby carrots, in sections
4 small new potatoes
1 strip of lemon zest
1 bay leaf
about 400 ml/14 fl oz water**

TWO MAYONNAISES
300 ml/½ pt thick home-made mayonnaise
(see page 168)
**0.1 g packet powdered saffron
1 tablespoon boiling water
pinch of paprika
1 sliver of garlic
¼ teaspoon salt
5 tablespoons finely chopped parsley
1 tablespoon capers
1 tablespoon lemon juice**

SOUP ADDITIONS
**1 hard-boiled egg (optional)
100 ml/3½ fl oz white wine or dry vermouth
100 g/4 oz cooked peeled prawns
2 tablespoons chopped parsley**

SERVES 4, IN TWO COURSES

Put the stock ingredients in the bottom of a pressure cooker. Put in the bottom plate with enough water to reach it. Salt and pepper the fish, put it in and close the pressure cooker. Bring up to high heat with the vent open. Close the vent, according to your model, turn down the heat and start timing for 9 minutes. When this is reached, remove from the heat and leave unopened, untouched, until cold.

Prudent Spaniards love cooking with a pressure cooker

Torta de gambas

— PRAWN-GLAZED SALAD LOAF —

Quick, modern and with the pizzaz and colour *madrileños* love. The stuffings are changeable – tomatoes plus basil are good. The layers must moisten the bread; sprinkle the bread with a little vinaigrette if in doubt.

500 g/1 lb big whole boiled prawns, peeled
1 small round white bread loaf,
about 18–20 cm/7–8 in across, 1 day old
100 ml/3½ fl oz fish stock or white wine
1 scant teaspoon powdered gelatine
(or fish aspic)
1 drop of cochineal (optional)
parsley sprigs, to garnish

STUFFING
250 ml/8 fl oz mayonnaise
100 g/4 oz smoked salmon
2 tablespoons lemon juice
2 ripe avocados
pinch of garlic salt
pinch of cayenne pepper
freshly ground black pepper

SERVES 8 AS A STARTER,
— 6 AS A SALAD LUNCH —

Open the pressure cooker and skin the fish, removing it from the bone on to a serving plate.

Make the mayonnaises: for saffron mayonnaise dissolve the spice in the boiling water and stir into half the thick mayonnaise. Dust paprika – from a height through a tiny strainer – over it.

For green mayonnaise, pound the garlic sliver with the salt, then reduce it with 4 tablespoons parsley and the capers to a green paste (easy in a small blender). Stir into half the master recipe for mayonnaise with the lemon juice. To serve, sprinkle with a little finely chopped parsley.

To make the bisque soup, remove the lemon zest and bay leaf and sieve (or blend) the stock base with the hard-boiled egg yolk (if using). Return to the pan, add the wine or vermouth and reheat. Add the prawns and season to taste. Garnish with the parsley and finely chopped egg white (if using).

Note: this is adjusted to the British standard of 15 lb per sq in. Continental models of pressure cooker (such as Tefal, Duromatic, Silvinox and Sitram) all cook at much lower pressure than this and require about double the time.

Make the glaze for the prawns (or use fish aspic): heat the stock or wine, sprinkle with the gelatine and leave 3–4 minutes, then dissolve over hot water. Add a drop of cochineal to a spoonful of cold water and add half to the jelly. Leave to cool until starting to set.

Slice the bread loaf horizontally into three layers, removing the domed top if there is one. Turn the loaf over, to give it a flat crust top.

Spread the bottom bread layer with two-thirds the mayonnaise. Cut the salmon into strips (*tiritas*) as long as the radius of the loaf and arrange over the top, pointing into the middle (easier to cut). Sprinkle with 1 tablespoon lemon juice. Cover with the next layer of bread and press down well. Purée the avocados in the blender and season with 1 tablespoon lemon juice, garlic salt, cayenne and black pepper to taste. Spread over the bread with the back of a spoon.

Cover with the bread lid (once the bottom). Spread lightly with mayonnaise and arrange the prawns in a wheel on top. Dribble with the just-setting glaze and decorate the centre with parsley sprigs. Leave to set for 6–24 hours. Slice like a cake.

The Marquesa's Cook Book

I was invited to *merienda*, a glass of lemonade and cake round teatime, by the Marquesa's daughter, an imperious figure in black with pearls. Titles pass in Spain to the eldest child, I learned, and her mother had been Marquesa in her own right.

Her cookery book was put into my hands, bound in flowered cotton. We have just such a book at home, which had belonged to the poet Robert Southey, and was bound by his wife with one of her petticoats. Its neat writing documented a past life. No crossing out, no hesitating. Obviously every recipe was written out then copied, and she planned every page to look handsome. Presentation – what the dish looked like – came first. 'Ingredients' and 'Preparation' were titles in a larger hand.

Started by a young bride, it opened on a note of economy with Sensible consommé. Higgledy-piggledy she entered things as she met and enjoyed them, growing in confidence: skewered kidneys, how to cook a tongue, a recipe for artichokes from Cadiz, with a note that the local word for them was *alcauciles*, and a recipe for sweet almond soup, that everyone eats at Christmas.

There were Spanish classics such as Basque salt cod, Catalan *zarzuela* (mixture of fish) and Asturian pie. Humbler items too, like fried breadcrumbs (*migas*) from La Mancha. And friends gave recipes, chicken breasts from a Doctor Villegas and a hot liver mould from María Palau (see recipe). A period piece, I asked for *Huevos Generalissimo Franco* (see recipe). I guess the maid who copied it for me approved of the General, for she underlined the title with the colours of the flag – red, yellow, red.

Ravioli a la milanesa and lobster *a la americaina* showed the Marquesa looked abroad. Spanish women, like women in Wiltshire or Maine, do not only cook their national dishes. It took me a little time, though, to work out exactly what *noquis* were. And I had never heard of *frivolodades moscovitas*. They seemed very Spanish to me: eggs coated with jellied mayonnaise with herbs and truffles; tomato cases stuffed with diced small vegetables in mayonnaise – *ensaladilla rusa* in Spain, which may explain it.

But the charm of the book was the record of a life. A holiday in Biarritz (barely over the French border), perhaps, had yielded fillets of sole *café de Paris de Biarritz*, sole garnished with mussels and prawns, then grilled with a thick hollandaise. It may have been a fashionable dinner party recipe in the 1930s, for it was mentioned again by other older women. Or perhaps the holiday in France was itself the fashion?

Pastel de higadillos de ave, María Palau

MARIA'S HOT POULTRY LIVER PÂTÉ

An elegant and delicious hot pâté

FOR A 15-CM/6-IN CHARLOTTE MOULD

OR DEEP CAKE TIN

12 chicken livers (350 g/12 oz) *(see note)*

300 g/11 oz boneless veal

200 g/7 oz boneless lean pork

a piece of bread the size of a small lemon, soaked in 2 tablespoons milk

1 small egg

salt and ground white pepper

2 tablespoons *amontillado* sherry

75 g/3 oz butter

6–7 slices of stale bread crusts removed, enough to fit the mould

100 g/4 oz tiny button mushrooms (caps only)

2 tablespoons olive oil

MEAT SAUCE

250 ml/8 fl oz hot meat juice

or concentrated meat stock

2 tablespoons *amontillado* sherry

2 teaspoons cornflour, mixed with 1 tablespoon cold water

SERVES 6–8 AS A STARTER

Note: the livers incorporated into the minced meat can be replaced by the same weight of foie gras.

Preparation: Wash the livers, cut them in half, put them into a pan and cover with cold water to whiten them for

15 minutes. Keep 12 liver halves and put the rest with the veal and pork through the mincer. Put this mass of minced meat through 3 or 4 times (or process thoroughly) and the last time include the bread soaked in milk. Add the egg, salt and white pepper and mix it well. Add the sherry and mix again.

Smear two-thirds of the butter round the mould. Cut a big bread round to fit the bottom and halve the remaining slices lengthways if they are roughly square. Toast them lightly and while still warm arrange in the mould to line it, overlapping them slightly.

Put the mushrooms into hot water with the oil, taking them out when boiling point is reached. Add a couple of spoonfuls of the liquid to the mince, to make a very wet mixture. Sauté the reserved livers and mushroom caps with the remaining butter.

Divide the mince into 3 parts and put one into the mould, pressing down well. In the middle put half the livers and mushrooms, then add another third of the minced meat. Put in the remaining liver mixture and top with the last of the mince. (Cover with foil.)

Stand the mould in a bain-marie, pour in boiling water to come halfway up the sides and put into a fairly hot oven (190°C/375°F/gas 5) to cook for 55–60 minutes, until done.

For the sauce, mix the hot meat juices and sherry with the cornflour mixture, then simmer briefly.

Presentation: once the pâté is cooked, turn it out on to a round serving plate. Cover the top with a little meat sauce and serve the remainder in a sauce boat.

Huevos Generalissimo Franco

POTATO NESTS

WITH EGGS AND MUSHROOMS

A little period piece with overtones of nursery food, as have so many dishes popular with Spanish men. The Marquesa's recipe was topped with summer truffles, coloured pink with cochineal and arranged as a rosette on each one. I have substituted brown mushrooms.

4 large eggs
1 teaspoon vinegar
250 g/8 oz summer truffles or brown mushrooms, sliced
50 g/2 oz butter
salt and white pepper
15 g/½ oz Parmesan or Manchego cheese, grated

DUCHESSE POTATO
750 g/1 lb 10 oz floury potatoes
50 g/2 oz butter
freshly grated nutmeg

BECHAMEL SAUCE WITH CHEESE
25 g/1 oz butter
1½ tablespoons plain flour
300 ml/½ pt milk, warm
15 g/½ oz Parmesan or Manchego cheese, grated
freshly grated nutmeg

———— SERVES 4 AS STARTER OR SUPPER ————

Preparation: to make duchesse potatoes, cook them in salted water until soft (but not breaking up). Pass through a vegetable mill and beat in the butter, nutmeg, salt and white pepper. Use a piping bag (with nozzle no 5, said the Marquesa) to make four nests (about 14 cm/5 in across with a shallow base, on a greased baking sheet).

Make the sauce: melt the butter in a saucepan and stir in the flour to a paste. Add the warm milk, stirring vigorously with a whisk (or wooden spoon) to make a smooth sauce, and simmer briefly. Incorporate the cheese and season with salt and nutmeg. Strain the sauce into the top of a bain-marie to keep warm.

Poach the eggs lightly in a pan of boiling water: add the vinegar, make a whirlpool with a slotted spoon, then tip in each egg, from a cup, using the spoon to wrap the white round the yolk and keep the shape. Cook for about 3 minutes, then drain and trim.

Fry the mushrooms in the butter, and season.

Presentation: in each nest put a tablespoon of sauce. Cover it with a poached egg, then add another tablespoon of sauce and sprinkle with grated cheese. Dribble each one with a teaspoon of melted butter and put in a hot oven (220°C/425°F/gas 7) briefly (3–4 minutes). When the top has coloured take it out and arrange a rose of truffles on each one – or cover with mushrooms.

Cocido: Capital Fare

'As a young bride I could not believe that people could eat so much,' said Denyse Casuso, when I asked about *cocido madrileño*. 'When it came out, I looked at all those platters, and thought: what can I eat? Then there was often a second course of *filetes con patatas fritas* (steak with chips). Then they would ask if anyone was hungry? Would any one like a fried egg? and some did!'

A world-famous dish, several courses come from the slow-simmering *cocido*, where many meats make a slow exchange of flavours. First course is the *caldo*, broth from the meat, often with rice or pasta in it.

'The chick peas were cooked with the meats, but they were put in a bag, so they could be served in a separate dish. My mother-in-law served green beans and tomato sauce too. Then there were the meats, all carved: beef, chicken, cooked *serrano*, black pudding, *chorizos*, pork belly – all together. The last dish was carrots, turnips, leek, potatoes – all the vegetables – but all the platters came out together.

'The *chorizo* and *morcilla* (black pudding) were cooked in the *caldo* to colour it pink, but they were only added at the end. *Morcillo* breaks up if cooked longer than five minutes. The whole thing must be cooked slowly, in the traditional way. Not in a pressure cooker.'

The *cocido* was cooked in two casseroles. A complementary pot held the vegetables: chard, drumhead cabbage, green beans or cardoons, to keep the taint of cabbage away from the pure broth of meats.

The joke is that Queen Isabella's Catholic Spain inherited its most famous dish from the Jews who were expelled in 1492. Spain's national *cocido* dates back to the pot left to simmer all the sabbath, the *adafina* (also on three plates), and based on chick peas.

True, pork and sausages went into it, at this point, to make it Christian. Black puddings from Extremadura and Asturias and *chorizos* from Cantimpalo in Segovia are now the ones sought after. And the *cocido's* almost pure meat content made it an aristocratic dish.

In wealthier Madrid households fried balls of the finest minced meat are added towards the end of cooking, another sign of an earlier tradition. For these *pilotas* are the symbolic traces of the hard-boiled eggs in the Sephardim *adafina*. In the humble south the balls are made with minced chicken livers and meat, sour-sweet with bread, egg and pine nuts.

Cocido is at its most famous in Madrid, but it is made in every region of Spain, with local changes. Its vegetable content increases away from the capital, and it was this that led to its slide down the social scale in the 18th century, to become a popular dish.

The Basques use red beans instead of chick peas, the Gallegans include their favourite turnip leaves, and in the contrary Maragatería (León) everything goes on the table backwards, ending up with soup! Onion, carrot, pumpkin or squash, sweet potato – even pears and quince – make the *pucheros* of the south much sweeter. And in Catalonia *caldo* becomes an *escudella* with noodles and the *carn d'olla* (meats of the pot) are veal, black pudding and one huge dumpling of minced pork seasoned with garlic – plus the usual fresh and dried vegetables.

Though it was never cooked on Sundays, the *cocido* of Madrid had, before the 1940s, the same ritual place of the Sunday roast beef in Dickens' time. It went on to make the hash of Monday. The most famous derivative is *ropa vieja* (old clothes) where leftover meat and chick peas are reheated in a newly made tomato sauce.

Redondo de ternera mechada

—— POT-ROAST BEEF LARDED WITH HAM ——

Watching the layer of fat being carved from the outside of an exquisite Jabugo *serrano* ham, I commented on the enormous cost of something that was to be discarded. 'Oh we keep it all, to lard Mama's pot-roast beef,' was the response. Now I save the fat from Christmas hams – brown-sugared and clove-scented – for this, and own a larding needle. But I give the recipe by the hand method as I first tried it. It sounds tricky but was fun to do. It is a very Spanish thing to cook beef with a liquid. Only young animals are roasted.

1.1 kg/2½ lb beef rump in a long shape, tied
100 g/4 oz ham fat or pork back fat
4 garlic cloves, cut in slivers
200 g/7 oz jar or can pimiento-stuffed olives
salt and freshly ground black pepper
4 tablespoons olive oil
400 g/14 oz green beans, in short lengths, to serve

Madrileños love good meat

MARINADE
good olive oil
2 onions, chopped
2 garlic cloves, finely chopped
125 ml/4 fl oz dry white wine
125 ml/4 fl oz Spanish brandy or cognac

BRAISE
2 big ripe tomatoes, skinned, seeded and chopped
freshly grated nutmeg
1 bay leaf
125 ml/4 fl oz good meat stock

——— SERVES 6 ———

A day ahead, cut the fat into thin strips, each about 4 cm/1½ in long. Lay them in a metal tray and freeze until stiff. Working on one cut end, jab a thin knife blade into the beef, a finger's width from the meat edge (and parallel to it). Go halfway through. Then jam in the handle of a wooden spoon.

Push in a sliver of garlic, then a stiff strip of fat, then another garlic sliver. Work round the outside – I got the hang of it by the fourth or fifth time. Then repeat the holes nearer the middle, pushing in olives. Then more fat in the centre. Repeat at the other end of the beef. Allow time, as this is fiddly.

Rub the beef all over with plenty of black pepper and olive oil. Put it in a small deep bowl with the marinade ingredients and leave for 24 hours, turning.

Heat the oven to 150°C/300°F/gas 2. Dry the beef with kitchen paper and salt lightly. Heat the oil in a small flameproof casserole and turn the meat until browned on all sides. Add the drained onions from the marinade and fry until softened. Add the chopped tomatoes, a good sprinkling of nutmeg, bay leaf, half the marinade juices and the stock. Cover and cook in the oven until tender, about 2½ hours. Check occasionally that the liquid is just barely simmering and turn the beef over halfway through.

Remove the beef from the casserole and leave to rest for 10–20 minutes. Meanwhile, discard the bay leaf and purée the remaining solids. Skim the pan juices, add half to the purée and season the sauce.

Cook, drain and season the green beans. Carve the beef and arrange overlapping slices on a hot platter. Garnish with the beans and pour a little sauce over the meat. Heat the remaining marinade juices and add to the rest of the sauce; pass in a sauce boat.

Surtido de verduras rellenas

STUFFED VEGETABLE SELECTION

Two grannies gave me almost identical recipes for this dish of concentric rings of stuffed vegetables – much appreciated by their families, for it needs time to make (and cook) and also requires careful shopping. Buy a selection of vegetables that match (or can be cut to) a 50 g/2 oz tomato – about 36 in all. Potatoes can be used as cups, though one granny recommended a ring of tiny new potatoes between the stuffed vegetables.

FOR A 30-CM/12-IN DIAMETER
EARTHENWARE CASSEROLE

8 smallish tomatoes

8 small onions

4 oversize courgettes

8 small peppers

6 tiny aubergines

1 garlic clove

1–2 lemons, sliced in rounds

3 bay leaves

MEAT BALLS

500 g/1 lb minced veal

500 g/1 lb minced pork

150 g/5 oz raw ham or raw smoked gammon, finely diced

4 garlic cloves, finely chopped

salt and freshly ground black pepper

6 tablespoons finely chopped parsley

2 slices of stale bread, crusts removed, soaked in milk then squeezed dry

2 teaspoons ground cinnamon

1 teaspoon ground cloves

1 teaspoon freshly grated nutmeg

2 teaspoons paprika

SAUCE

200 g/7 oz onion, including inside of onions

3–4 tablespoons olive oil

4 garlic cloves, finely chopped

6 tablespoons finely chopped parsley

2 tablespoons tomato concentrate

200–300 ml/7–10 fl oz dry white wine

SERVES 12 AS A STARTER, 8 AS A MAIN COURSE

Rub a garlic clove round the inside of the casserole and rub with little oil.

Prepare the vegetables by cutting off and keeping the tops and scooping out the insides to make cups.

(Even onions respond to a firm revolving spoon.) Cut lengths of courgettes, and cut the peppers and aubergines short to fit the scale of the other vegetables. Arrange them all in rings in the casserole. Keep the scooped-out onion, tomato and aubergine for the sauce; discard the courgette seeds.

Combine all the ingredients for the meat balls, first reducing the garlic to a purée with 1 teaspoon salt in a mortar. Traditionally the parsley and the bread are puréed there too, before being worked into the meats. Make walnut-sized balls and use to stuff all the vegetables, then put back the vegetable tops as hats. Anything that has no hat can have a lemon slice. Use the remaining meat balls to make another ring inside the outermost vegetables, to stuff the spaces. Push the bay leaves in round the edge.

Make the scooped-out onion insides up to 200 g/7 oz, chop well and fry slowly in oil in a saucepan until soft. Add the garlic and the other chopped vegetable insides and cook until soft, then add the parsley and rub through a sieve (or blend). Return to the pan, add the tomato concentrate and some of the wine and season well.

Reheat the sauce and pour round the vegetables, adding more wine as needed. Bake the vegetables at 200°C/400°F/gas 6 for 1 hour, then turn down the oven to 180°C/350°F/gas 4. The dish needs a good $2\frac{1}{2}$ hours to cook: cover with foil if the tops are burning. It reheats well, so is best made ahead.

Pineapples on sale for Christmas

Above: Fine tiles on the outside walls of the Villa Rosas

Christmas in Madrid

The lights were stretched over the Calle Serrano, the fashion-shop part of town, and Velasquez, which runs parallel to it. Patterns of twinkling bulbs, like London's Regent Street or Fifth Avenue in New York, festive for the Advent shopping season.

Christmas is coming in the food shops, too. Behind the glass, next to the door, appear bottles of Vega Sicilia, Spain's most expensive and difficult-to-buy red wine. Just two or three of them, in a place where you cannot miss them. There are big baskets of glacé fruit in the corner of Lhardy's window, near the Puente del Sol, and El Riojana, in the Calle Mayor, has *tarta de Mondoñedo* (Spain's answer to treacle tart) covered with candied fruit. And every *ultramarinos* (specialist grocer) has Roscon de Reyes,

low ring cakes of yeast dough, decorated with the odd almond. It is traditionally the Twelfth Night cake. 'All wrong,' moaned one granny. 'People eat it right through January now, instead of just on the 6th.'

Christmas is coming because there is *cardo* (cardoon) in the market, vast heads like celery but three times the size. White ribbed stalks with a grey frizzle down the side where the leaves were stripped, this is a relative of the globe artichoke. With white sauce and ham, it is a Christmas Eve dish for many.

Turkeys are on order with a choice of stuffings: Roquefort, York ham and wild mushrooms, raw *serrano* with mushrooms and the like. And the hams! The Cortes Ingles and the Museo del Jamon have a wonderful display. King of the mountain, the lean black-footed

Jabugo *serrano* commands 4900 pesetas per kilo (Sanchez Romero – the home brand – more expensive at 6500), down to the Extremeño rounded golden *blanco* at 1299 pesetas and even cheaper *blanco* (white pig) from Murcia. At 6–7 kg/13–15 lb each these are no cheap purchase. Many end up as executive Christmas presents.

You can see the snow on the Guadarrama from the suburbs of the city. The Puerto de Somosierra, which commands the road to the cities of the north, had its first blizzard in early December, fir trees bending under the snow's weight. A more traditional Christmas season here than in the cities near the English Channel! At weekends the Madrid commuter stations are peopled with skiers going a few stops north.

The famous quote about Madrid is: '*Nueves meses invierno, tres infierno*' (nine months winter, three months hell). Chill grips the city, the beggars look hopeless, and blind guide-dogs have a mat to sit on when the owner stops.

Pay packets hold two months' pay at Christmas (salaries are divided into 13 – bad luck to miss December). And there is always the hope of winning the Christmas National Lottery, *¡Hay lotería de Navidad!* Bars, cafés, even cloth shops, display the coloured tickets. Dark green, yellow or to local choice, printed with the location where they were sold (and the bank that guarantees the issue). For a month they take over from ONCE, whose kiosks dot the city. The prize is not vast – 2,500,000 pesetas (£16,000) – but the draw on 22nd December will guarantee some family a happy Christmas.

The English word 'Christmas' is used in Spain for the exchange of cards and gifts: *recibíamos Christmas*. Wondrous nativity scenes of painted pottery figures appear in shops such as Heyca, behind the Plaza Mayor. Not just the three kings, angels and a crib, but a castle of Herod and figures from the Spanish countryside: windmills, shepherds and sheep, people washing, frying eggs on camp fires, log-cutting. At home, on the side table, each day the three kings are moved one step nearer to the manger.

La Nocebuena (good night) supper on Christmas Eve is the family celebration before midnight Mass, *la Misa de Gallo* (at cock's crow). Seafood and roast lamb are favourites. But by tradition it is red cabbage, later a stuffed bird (turkey or capon), and above all the pink-fleshed bream (see page 62) baked in oil and lemon.

Sopa de almendras, a sweet milk from soaked almonds, is the approved dessert. 'Put a cloth on the table,' I was told, 'the nuts in the centre and another above it. With a wooden hammer give them little sharp blows till you have a paste.' Every granny advised against machine grinding!

'Put a casserole with 2 litres milk and a stick of cinnamon, and when it begins to boil add $\frac{1}{2}$ litre ground nuts and remove the cinnamon. Stir with a wooden spoon. Add 4 spoons (more) of sugar and simmer some more. When the milk is used, add more. At the end of $1\frac{1}{2}$ hours, sieve it and put it in cups and powder with cinnamon.' But there is no longer any need to make it. Many pâtisseries sell it ready-made. *Turrón* (see page 157) from Valencia and marzipan *figuritas* (see page 63) end the meal.

Aceitunas a la importancia

— PARTY OLIVES —

WITH ANCHOVIES AND PEPPERS

A decorative plate of olives to go with drinks before dinner: big 'queens' or the purply heart-shaped Gordals are used. Cross the top with a small thin strip of canned pimiento and another of split, canned anchovy fillet, halved. Jab in a cocktail stick to hold them. To vary the taste, mix in short lengths of pickled cucumber treated the same way.

Oranges waiting in the kitchen
for the Christmas table

Tigres

STUFFED CRUMBED MUSSELS

One of Madrid's most popular *tapa*, this is not normally served at home, except as a first course. The addition of chopped pepper and tomato comes from a friend. The traditional way to make these is to egg and crumb them, then fry them in two-fingers depth of oil, flipping it over the top. It must date to before the days of overhead grills, which are much easier.

1.5 kg/3 lb mussels, cleaned *(see page 91)*
4 tablespoons dry white wine
1 garlic clove, finely chopped
175 g/6 oz butter
6 tablespoons plain flour
500 ml/18 fl oz milk, hot
2 tablespoons finely diced red pepper
2 tablespoons finely diced green pepper
1 teaspoon tomato concentrate
salt and freshly ground black pepper
freshly grated nutmeg
pinch of cayenne pepper
about 20 tablespoons stale white breadcrumbs
4–5 tablespoons olive oil

SERVES 18 AS A TAPA,
8 AS A BIG STARTER

Heat the wine with the garlic in a large saucepan. Add half the mussels, clap on the lid and cook over high heat for a couple of minutes until the mussels are all open. Remove with a slotted spoon and add the rest, meanwhile removing the bodies from the shells. Save half of the biggest shells and the cooking liquid.

Melt half the butter, stir in the flour and cook for 1 minute. Off the heat work in the hot milk, stirring until smooth and thick. Simmer for 2–3 minutes. Strain in the liquid from the mussels, through muslin inside a sieve, and stir again. Add the diced peppers and tomato concentrate and season, adding nutmeg and cayenne.

Chop the mussel bodies into 2–3 pieces and stir into the sauce. Use a spoon to fill the mussel shells, laying them out on a cake rack. Fry the crumbs in the remaining butter with the oil and sprinkle over the tops. Refrigerate until needed on 2 baking trays.

Put under a hot grill for 2–3 minutes before serving and pass serviettes to hold them. Remember dishes for the empty shells!

Besugo al horno

BAKED WHOLE FISH
WITH LEMON AND POTATOES

A classic dish, and an ideal recipe for any whole fish, though red bream, with a black spot on its shoulder, is the favourite – and the perfect shape. It is cooked with lemon and wine in many Spanish homes on Christmas Eve – either with parsley and breadcrumbs or with potatoes. 'It is important to the dish', said the retired diplomat's wife who gave it to me 'that the potatoes are crisped round the edge and brown. They catch this from the lemon and oil.' She admonished me to 'be sure that the potatoes are pre-cooked, otherwise they will not be ready with the fish.'

1.1–1.2 kg/2½–3 lb whole red bream,
sea bass or salmon, cleaned
3 lemons
100 ml/3½ fl oz olive oil
2 bay leaves
350–700 g/12 oz–1½ lb potatoes *(see note)*, sliced
1 onion, preferably purple, sliced in rings
salt and freshly ground black pepper
1 garlic clove, cut in slivers
a little dried *guindilla*, seeded and chopped
or a pinch of cayenne pepper
100 ml/3½ fl oz dry white wine
1 tablespoon chopped parsley

SERVES 6 AS A LIGHT MAIN COURSE

Cut off the fins and rinse and dry the fish inside. Squeeze 1 lemon and sprinkle the juice and 4 table-spoons oil inside. Leave to marinate for 2 hours.

Reserve the marinade juices. With the point of a kitchen knife make slashes on the sides of the fish. Slice the second lemon, halve the slices and fit into the gashes, pointing backwards like fins. Oil an oven-proof oval dish and put in the fish with the bay leaves under it.

Cook the potatoes in salted water until just tender. Arrange round the fish, scattering with the rings pushed from the onion. Season lightly with salt and pepper and cover with thin slices of the third lemon.

Heat the remaining oil in a small pan with the garlic slivers and the *guindilla* (if using), discarding them when they brown. Add the marinade juices, wine and cayenne (if using) and pour over the fish and pota-toes. Cover with foil and put into a fairly hot oven (200°C/400°F/gas 6). Cook for 35–45 minutes (according to fish size).

Remove the foil and cook for a further 15 minutes to colour the potato edges. Sprinkle with a little parsley.

Note: an excellent recipe for a big hot salmon, though longer, slimmer fish shapes mean baking in a large roasting tin. If you do this, fill the space with a few extra potato slices.

Figuritas de marzapan

MARZIPAN PIECES

Figuritas – about the size of a thumb – are fun to make. These shapes are collected from three people.

My bread shapes are a French loaf, slashed in a few places, an oval bun loaf (also slashed), an *ensaimada* (well-known as a breakfast roll) – simply a fat spiral – and a pretzel (a slim sausage with the ends curled back and crossed over in the centre).

Successful musical instruments are a violin, a French horn (with a wide horn end and the tube curled round)

Home-made *figuritas*, marzipan to end the Christmas feast

and a drum, with V-marking round the sides and crossed sticks on top.

Animals include a serpent, with a diamond head and the tail coiled on to its back, a mouse with blob ears and tail, and a turkey with tiny head, puffed breast and spread tail (marked with a fork). Everyone makes rabbits, though they are the most tricky: two rolls of marzipan are doubled to give the dominant crouching back legs, the head is a U, with tapering ears (to cover the front) and a blob tail. I was pleased with mine.

To make marzipan, blend 250 g/8 oz ground almonds, 200 g/7 oz caster sugar, 1 small egg and 1 teaspoon lemon juice in the food processor. Paint the tops of the *figuritas* with beaten egg yolk and glaze briefly under the grill. Bought marzipan models beautifully, but cannot be glazed: it melts!

Intxaursalsa

CHRISTMAS EVE WALNUT CREAM

Rather than a hot almond milk, this delicate chilled walnut cream is preferred in the Basque country – especially for dessert on Christmas Eve.

125 g/4½ oz shelled walnuts
500 ml/18 fl oz milk
125 g/4½ oz sugar
strip of lemon zest
½ cinnamon stick
1 slice of stale bread, crusts removed,
lightly toasted
100 ml/3½ fl oz single cream
ground cinnamon, to finish

SERVES 4

Bring the milk to the boil with the sugar, lemon zest and cinnamon stick. Meanwhile grind the nuts to powder. Be careful, if using a food processor, that they don't become oily. Add the nuts to the milk and simmer for 30 minutes.

Crumble the bread and add it. Simmer briefly, then remove the zest and cinnamon. Beat to a creamy texture with a wooden spoon (or process). Enrich with the cream.

Pour into individual bowls and cool, then chill. Serve very cold, lightly powdered with cinnamon – through a strainer from a height.

CHAPTER 5

Old Castile and Rioja

The high centre of Spain. The language (which is called Castilian) and the strength to battle back against the invading Moors were both forged in Castile. A line of castles, extending across what is now wheatland, marks each surge towards the south.

I entered Castile by the back door, driving up the Valle de Jerte. It's the south-western corner of the province, coming round the Sierra de Gredos, the mountain rim west of Madrid. The road weaves and climbs to the Castilian plateau, through mile on mile of cherry trees. The leaves were golden in October. On to the Puerto de Tornavacas and over the top, to meet the first castle.

El Barco de Avila is a small town, with a tiny, shabby square. It is famed across Spain for its round white kidney beans. In the autumn sun, the cartridge belts hung up along the high street, and the sausage skins, dried *tripas*, fluttered brown like massed condoms. I bought the *judías* (beans) and the local paprika, a deep, deep red. What prodigality, to see a whole sack of such a spice!

Despite the presence of historic cities – Avila, Segovia, Salamanca – this is a poor region. Beans and peas, not meat, are daily fare. Marisa, a schoolteacher in Segovia, feeds her children *guiso* – lentils on Monday, chick peas on Tuesday and beans on Wednesday – typical Castilian fare. They are 'a rosary of riches,' I was told, '*muy distinto* – very distinctive.'

Lentils were eaten with chicken giblets and fried *chorizo* or pig's ear. Beans were cooked with *chorizo* and *tocino*, pork belly, 'but less now everyone is down on pork, for health reasons. Bay and parsley are added:

some use cumin or spring garlic. If possible, let them get cold, then reheat.' Garlic is the flavouring, par excellence, as it is in New Castile, away to the south-east. 'And 14th December, the feast of St John of the Cross, is the day to eat *garbanzos*. In Arévalo, huge cauldrons are set up in the markeplace.'

There is, however, no lack of meat, just of money. The wide valley of Amblés rears the best veal in Spain. I was more conscious of the sausage factories and the smell of piggeries.

Light snow was in the air as I stood by the walls of Avila: 88 perfect turrets, and part of the second line of fortifications, which included Segovia and Salamanca. Fur tippets were in fashion, I noticed, and pony coats, in the highest city in Spain. Santa Teresa is an ever-present figure, for from Avila she reorganized the convents which once held one in ten of Spain's women.

The heartbeat of history pulses near the surface here, as successive lines of castles mark the fight against the Moors. It is impossible to ignore them, or get away from the fighting presence of Queen Isabella *la Católica*. Born in one castle, at Madrigal de las Altas Torres, died in another, at La Mota, fighting a battle here, giving birth there (wherever she happened to be stationed), she had her way just as effectively as Santa Teresa. Spain may not be a feminist country, but it certainly has a tradition of strong women!

North of here, in León, the Tierra de Campos is the granary of Spain, round Carrion de los Condes, with its red brick villages, and south towards Zamora. The wind blows through the seas of frozen wheat in winter and the sun crushes it in summer. They grow the best wheat in the country here and still make the *hogaza*, the large loaf – the *pan de padrenuestro* ('our daily bread').

Ancha es Castilla goes the saying – Castile is wide: there is room for people to be themselves. Driving westwards at sunset across its open, undulating vastness, space and time blend and it seems that, by driving fast enough, one could catch the night and stay permanently suspended in that blood-red light.

The great plain is framed in the north by the Cantabrian mountains and, to the south, by the Sierra de Gredos and the Guadarrama, that hides Madrid. The east, too, is high, so the plain tips west. The *tierra del vino* has four major wine areas; three lie along the Duero. Spain's single most expensive wine, Vega de Sicilia, is produced at La Ribera del Duero, as are good whites. Rioja lies well to the west, immediately south of the Basque country and, in the higher, cooler Rioja Alta, produces wines with the possibility of great maturation.

South of Rioja is the Meseta, where fortunes were made from sheep and are recorded in stone, in cities such as Burgos and Soria. Sheep, which wintered in the south, walked north in summer, to graze the higher plateaus, a massive shift of animals, twice a year. Not surprising, then, that *lechazo* (roast milk-fed lamb) is the culinary glory here, a dish unchallenged anywhere in the world. Lamb also stars in the September wine fairs, *chuletas de cordero*, diminutive lamb cutlets (four, even five, to a portion), grilled over vine-prunings, *al sarmiento*.

The plateau is so cold in winter that goat and pig as well as lamb are cooked in the round beehive ovens. There are also good lamb stews, and in the little *tascas* (bars) they serve *conejo al ajillo*, rabbit with garlic. Other simple stew pots (see recipe page 74) are made in the Béjar region, to the west.

Cold winters mean good sausages, like *chorizos* with oregano, the Burgos *morcillas* with blood and rice, and the ugly but delicious *botillo* from the Bierzo. Salamanca also has a *farinato*, a bread sausage with paprika – they consider it a mid-morning snack – and *hornazo*, a pie with a mass of meats inside: *chorizos* and ham, pork belly and birds, topped with criss-cross pastry.

Piles of *hogaza:* the flat wheat loaf of Castile

Tucked into the northern rim of mountains to the west is the ancient kingdom of León. With the mountains of El Bierzo behind it, game such as roe deer – *ciervo* – is abundant. There are also hundreds of miles of trout streams, and the fish end up cooked in the local red wine. Frogs' legs are eaten battered in La Bañeza, and with garlic in Zamora, and Herrera del Pisuerga is famous for its crayfish festival. Game birds pass south over much of Castile, to winter away from Europe. 'It rains *codornices* (quail) in season.' The stewed partridges (see recipe page 41) are wonderful, and typically Castilian.

Old Castile on its western side also has a longstanding tradition of little cakes, like the golden, sugar-rich, round *yemas* (the size of a bantam's yolk) in Avila, *mantecados* (small square sponges) in Astorga, and one in León called *polverones ¡Jésus que me ahogo!* – 'crumble-cakes – may I choke on them!'

Menestra de pollo

CAULIFLOWER, ARTICHOKE AND
CHICKEN HOTPOT

'*Menestras?* Oh they can be a fiddle, but when they are good they are very good. They are no good in Madrid!' – my interlocutor was an arrogant Basque. 'The best ones come from Palencia.' Often vegetables stew with fresh beans or peas with a backbone of ham: she thought this one unusual. Big fried artichoke bases give it a more interesting texture, but small ones, boiled whole, are quicker.

½ small free-range chicken (about 500 g/1 lb),
in serving pieces
the bases of 4–6 large globe artichokes
(*see note*)
300 ml/½ pt light meat or good chicken stock
175 ml/6 fl oz dry white wine
1 small cauliflower, in florets
2 tablespoons diced ham fat or olive oil
175 g/6 oz raw ham or gammon, in thin scallops
salt and freshly ground black pepper
6 tablespoons stale white breadcrumbs
4 tablespoons chopped parsley
1 hard-boiled egg, chopped (optional)

CONDIMENT
2 tablespoons olive oil
2 onions, chopped
6 garlic cloves, finely chopped
6 tablespoons chopped parsley
2 teaspoons paprika

SERVES 6

Cook the chicken in a small pan in the stock and wine for 30 minutes (originally it just came from the *cocido*, with some stock). Prepare the artichoke bases.

Next make the condiment: heat the oil in a frying pan and soften the onions, adding the garlic towards the end. Remove the onion to a mortar (or blender) and purée with the parsley and paprika.

Cook the cauliflower in boiling salted water in a flameproof casserole for about 5 minutes, then drain. Fry the quartered artichoke bases for 5 minutes or so in the frying pan, with any ham fat, adding more oil as needed. Fry the ham briefly.

Turn the chicken and stock into the casserole (removing unsightly bones) and stir in the condiment purée. Check the sauce seasoning. Gently mix in the cauliflower, ham and artichokes. Fry the crumbs in the

frying pan, mix with the parsley and sprinkle on top, adding chopped egg if you wish. Eat with spoons and forks.

Note: to prepare artichoke bases snap off the stalks (if these are stringy, the artichokes are tough and will need an extra 5 minutes' cooking). Trim the bottom flat and cut through the top leaves just above the choke, leaving a base about 3 cm/1¼ in deep. Trim away the side leaves with a small knife until the white base shows. Cook in boiling salted water for 10 minutes, then drain upside down until cool enough to handle.

Flip off any soft leaf stumps with your thumb, revealing the hairy choke. Remove it with spoon-and-thumb, leaving a smooth cup base. This needs about 5 minutes' more cooking (braised or fried etc) depending upon toughness.

Judías del Barco de Avila

WHITE BEAN POT

Subtle – and a change from beans in tomato sauce. It is also an excellent dish combined with roast game birds – try a roast mallard. Meat shreds and pan juices go into the beans: the carved bird is served on top.

400 g/14 oz *judías del Barco* or white haricot beans,
soaked for 12 hours
150 g/5 oz salt pork belly, Italian pancetta
or boiling bacon (*see note*)
½ leek
½ onion
2 cloves to stick in the onion
4 garlic cloves
1 fresh bouquet garni of a sprig of rosemary,
3 sprigs of thyme and 1 bay leaf
600 ml/1 pt water
3 tablespoons olive oil
1 big green pepper, seeded and finely chopped
4 tablespoons sieved tomato (passata)
or tomato sauce
½ teaspoon paprika
salt and freshly ground black pepper
½ teaspoon vinegar

SERVES 4

Drain the beans, put them in a pot with the pork and add the leeek, ½ of the onion (stuck with 2 cloves) and the garlic, all unsliced, plus the bouquet garni. Just

Sacks of dried beans at El Barco de Avila, with the celebrated local paprika

cover with the water and put over low heat. When it starts to simmer, add 1 tablespoon of oil. Leave to simmer (with no bubbles), covered, until the beans are tender – about 1 hour. Keep an eye on it, adding a little water if needed.

Heat the remaining 2 tablespoons oil in a saucepan with the remaining onion quarter, finely chopped, and the green pepper over low heat. After a few minutes raise the heat to medium and cook, stirring occasionally, until they start to colour. Then add the sieved tomato and paprika and cook a minute longer.

Fish the leek, onion quarter and garlic cloves out of the beans. Discard the bouquet garni and cloves and purée the vegetables (peeling the garlic cloves first) with a little of the bean stock. Return this, plus the green pepper sauce, to the pot. Shred the pork and return it. Taste for seasoning: it may not need salt, if the pork gives it. Add pepper and a little vinegar to add piquancy. Cook gently for another 10 minutes.

Note: a little fried, crumbled bacon (cooked with the vegetable sauce) can replace the pork.

Menestra de ternera

— VEAL WITH NEW VEGETABLES —

'It's not modern,' Lola said 'it comes from the time of my grandmother. Very good and plain.' I agree with the first, not the second. Use fresh peas if you can, or fewer frozen ones if you can't. The potatoes are discretional, as they also make a good accompaniment.

1.3 kg/3 lb boneless pink veal, cubed
4–6 tablespoons plain flour
salt and freshly ground black pepper
4–6 tablespoons olive oil
2 onions, chopped
2 garlic cloves, finely chopped
1 teaspoon paprika
175 ml/6 fl oz white wine
300 ml/½ pt meat stock (or more)
500 g/1 lb chard
(or 250 g/8 oz spinach or lettuce)
250 g/8 oz tiny new potatoes
300 g/10 oz fresh shelled peas (150 g/5 oz frozen)
250 g/8 oz fresh broad beans (or frozen)
2 large carrots, sliced
4 small globe artichokes, halved
or 2 artichoke bases *(see page 67)*
1 leek, sliced
2 tablespoons chopped parsley
½ lemon

— SERVES 6 —

Coat the meat with seasoned flour. Heat the oil in a frying pan and fry the meat in batches, then remove to a large earthenware casserole. Fry the chopped onions in the frying pan, adding the garlic near the end. Sprinkle in 2 tablespoons flour and cook, stirring, until darkened. Add the paprika, a little salt and pepper and, stirring slowly, the white wine and stock. Pour over the meat in the casserole and cook, covered, in a medium-low oven (170°C/325°F/gas 3) for 1 hour. (It can also be casseroled on the top of the stove.)

Meanwhile prepare and cook the vegetables. Remove the stalks from the chard and cut them into lengths (like celery). Tear up the leaves. Bring a large pot of water to the boil and add the potatoes, fresh peas and beans, carrots, halved artichokes and chard stalks. Small potatoes and summer peas can take up to 15 minutes, though 10 minutes is average, so judge

the cooking sequence by size. In a second pan of boiling water cook the leek and chard leaves for 5 minutes. If using spinach or lettuce, simply pour boiling water over it, then drain.

Drain all the vegetables and add to the meat with the parsley and a couple of ladlefuls of vegetable water (or stock) as needed. Check the seasoning and give the dish 10 more minutes' cooking.

To lift the flavour, grate a good pinchful of lemon zest on your smallest grater and stir it in with the juice of the lemon half. Do not boil after this, to keep the savour of fresh lemon oil.

Carne con chocolate

— BEEF STEWED WITH CHOCOLATE —

'This is my mother's recipe,' said Consuelo. 'Very good. It's really a recipe for quail, but she changed it to beef, (*ternera fuerte*).'

1 kg/2 lb braising beef, cut into short fingers
about 6 tablespoons olive oil
2 onions, chopped
3 garlic cloves, finely chopped
2–3 tablespoons plain flour
1 teaspoon paprika
salt and freshly ground black pepper
2 big carrots, cut into short sticks
1 bay leaf
175 ml/6 fl oz red wine
150–175 ml/5–6 fl oz meat stock
25 g/1 oz dark chocolate, in pieces
1–3 teaspoons vinegar

— SERVES 4 —

Heat 2 tablespoons oil in a casserole and fry the onions until soft, adding the garlic towards the end. Season the flour with paprika, salt and pepper and lightly coat the beef. (Putting it in a plastic bag and shaking, in 2 batches, is the easiest way. This controls the amount of flour in the sauce.)

For speed heat more oil in a frying pan and fry the beef, in 2 batches, until well coloured. Transfer to the casserole. Add the carrots and bay leaf and pour in the wine and enough stock to cover. Put on the lid and simmer for 40 minutes. The sauce should just clothe the meat. If there seems to be too much, remove some, boil to reduce it and then return to the casserole. Add the chocolate and stir until melted. Add the vinegar to taste (stirring it in well): the amount will depend on the wine used and the brand of chocolate. Check the seasoning. Boiled potatoes are the best accompaniment.

A good stew of beef with chocolate – and plenty of it!

70

Roast Lamb, Sucking Pig and Arab Ovens

Sepúlveda is stretched along the ridge, a small town north-east of Segovia. Easy to see, difficult to reach, as this means snaking round the valleys. The site is so narrow the town can barely manage a main square, houses stacked on stepped streets or squeezed out along the promontories. It is famous for its *asadores*, the lamb ovens. My children were at baby ages (round five) when they ate their first roast *lechazo*. They still speak of it with wonder 15 years later.

The ovens are on Arab models. I have just such a one in my orchard, further south. Built for a private house, it is bigger than a wheelbarrow inside – rings of brick rising to a low domed ceiling with a small door for putting in wood and baking. It needs time, and much wood, to heat it.

Sucking lamb, from the surrounding hills where they sup on thyme and rosemary, is the speciality in Sepúlveda. A leg to a single portion, it has an unmatched flavour. Aranda de Duero and Burgos are other great places to visit.

The west of Castile is equally famous for its ovens, but here they roast sucking pig instead of lamb. Where

was the line? Arévalo and Segovia were piglet country. On, then, to Arévalo to eat the rival *tostón*, hoping for a recipe. 'We get them from the baker. We ring up and tell him what time we want to eat and he delivers them hot.' Some takeaway!

I went to visit my lunch cooking. The smell of roast meat wafted down the street, as we walked into a wood shed. The baker opened a small iron door and there, on a revolving turntable, were 30 little piglets. Golden skin, fatless, they are cooked split-and-flat, each in an earthenware dish. Head and tail up, legs splayed, they meet their apotheosis in cheerful abandon as though they were sky-diving.

The cooking process is slow, with nothing in the way of secret herbs or spices. What was the recipe, I asked? The wood, the baker said. 'Holm oak, the mothers from which they come, the age at which they are killed' – 15–20 days old. 'And four generations of experience!' Such things are wedding fare here. The golden skin is ceremonially carved with sharp blows from the side of a plate. I have the shoulder-blade of that piglet still; it matches my car key.

Tostón

ROAST SUCKING PIG

In Spain these piglets are 2–3 weeks old, and are roasted very slowly. Elsewhere they may be older – but 6.5 kg/15 lb uncleaned (for 20) really is the limit of a domestic oven. A smaller one for 12 people is a more comfortable size. To get this going in a small oven – and make that famous crisped skin – it needs high heat.

4.5 kg/10 lb sucking pig, cleaned
about 100 ml/3½ fl oz olive oil
salt and freshly ground black pepper
bunch of fresh thyme sprigs
¾ × 75 cl bottle *fino* sherry or dry white wine
juice of 2 lemons

SERVES 12

Continue the belly cut up to the neck and then press hard with both hands on the shoulders of the piglet, so that it opens completely flat like a fish. Put the piglet, skin up, in the sink and scald all over with boiling water. Make sure ears and trotters etc are

Right: A roast lamb shoulder from a domestic oven

clean, then drain and dry with a cloth. Hang it up in a cool place for the skin to dry completely for a couple of hours.

Heat the oven to top heat (240°C/475°F/gas 9). Brush the piglet inside and out with olive oil, seasoning it well inside. Put the thyme sprigs under it in a large earthenware dish or roasting tin and pour in a couple of glasses of sherry, wine or water to stop the juices burning. Splay the legs out sideways (or diagonally, if the oven is small).

Roast for 40 minutes, until the skin starts to look golden. Then remove from the oven, turning this down to 180°C/350°F/gas 4. Baste the pig well with a mixture of oil and lemon juice. Add more wine to the pan juices as needed; make sure these don't burn. Wrap the snout, ears (which puff up), tail and trotters in foil, to prevent them burning. Roast for about another $1\frac{1}{2}$ hours, basting again with the wine from the pan and keeping an eye on the skin colour. You can check that the piglet is cooked by a skewer in the shoulder – the juices should not run pink. Then leave it to rest in the turned off oven for 10 minutes before carving.

I was advised to prick any bubbles that start to form on the skin at the high heat stage, but this didn't happen for me. Skim the pan juices and serve a couple of tablespoons with each portion.

To carve, cut across the base of the head – take a slice from either side of the neck. Take the shoulder plus front leg as a portion, and again a whole leg when you reach the hams, cutting them through the natural joint – male portions, these. Carve the loin at right angles to the backbone, then cut down either side of the backbone to release them. Finally the pig is left looking like a child's hobby horse – a golden head connected by the backbone to its crisp curly tail.

❧ Rioja Red Peppers ❧

La Guardia, on the hill, looks out over Rioja, a balcony to view the vineyards. Scrubby, ground-hugging vines, sprawling on small hills, have an uncared-for air to those accustomed to the neat vineyards of France or Germany.

Our journey up here took us past walls bearing famous names. Viña Ardanza going through Haro, Marqués de Cáceres in Cenicero and Marqués de Riscal (and a fine group of conker trees) in El Ciego. I was reminded of my grandfather's story of a French general who made his troops present arms to the vineyard of his favourite burgundy.

La Guardia also has the most colourful medieval portal in Europe. Its saints seem freshly painted, for the citizens built a porch with a door, which saved it from the weather. But in late September the colour was in the streets: bright with peppers. Scarlet, long and pointed, they were festooned from every balcony. Against the walls were also silver necklaces of foil balls. 'Those are prunes, drying for Christmas,' I was told.

Surprisingly *a la riojana* means a dish with peppers, rather than one with wine. Potatoes with peppers, for instance, or with *chorizo* sausage, which is flavoured by them. The nation is pepper-proud, and the subtle use of peppers – and tomatoes – distinguishes Spanish cooking. Tomato plays the cello role in sauces: not dominant and scarlet, as it is in Italy. Here it just conveys the pepper, sweetness balancing the heat, with an occasional addition of vinegar to make a sauce more spicy.

Columbus went to the Americas to discover a cheaper source of pepper, and chilli peppers were the most immediate gain. Spain has three main dried ones. The heart-shaped *choriceros* go into old dishes like *chilindrón* (see page 122) and *bacalao a la vizcaína*. The red hue of these dishes was once soaked, pulped pepper (up to two per person), not tomato as it is now. But *choriceros* are most associated with the sausages to which they lend colour and piquancy. Oregano is a frequent partner in *chorizo* sausages across the country.

Noras, small squat balls, are favoured for rice in Alicante and Murcia. Their Catalan name is *romesco* and in Catalonia they make their greatest sauces (see page 140) in association with the local hot *bitxo* chillies. *Guindilla* is the one national hot chilli, small and pointed. Spain also has three paprikas (to Hungary's five), sweet, sharp and *agri-dulce*. The best comes from Jarandilla in the Sierra de Gredos. Paprika is now Spain's basic pepper.

Right: The fist-shaped peppers that go to make salads and stews in Spain

Fresh peppers are notable too. The knobbly *morrones* are baked, if they are red, to develop their sweet juice, then used like a tomato for some distinguished salads (see page 20 and 149), or puréed for a sauce. *Pimientos de Padrón* (see page 79) are tiny – a thumb's length – while the *pimiento de piquillo* is one of Spain's star ingredients. It is long (the name means 'beak'), thin-skinned, wonderfully spicy – and famous stuffed. And, like a wine, the pepper has D. O. (Denominación de Origen) status.

Pimientos rellonos de merluza

—— RED PEPPERS STUFFED WITH HAKE OR COD ——

The great stuffed red pepper dish? It balances the flavours of two types of pepper, one whole, one dried, with a white fish filling. The sauce tastes of cream and tomato, but has neither. All Spain makes this dish with bottled *piquillo* peppers, which are smaller and spicier than our knobbly peppers. However, I have made Palomita's recipe with common red peppers, and adjusted the seasonings.

8 smallish red peppers
400 g/14 oz tail fillets of hake, cod
or other white fish, without bones (or canned crab)
3 tablespoons water
about 5 tablespoons olive oil
1 onion, finely chopped
2 garlic cloves, finely chopped
4 tablespoons chopped parsley
salt and ground white pepper
plain flour for dusting

BECHAMEL AND PEPPER SAUCE
2 tablespoons plain flour
25 g/1 oz butter
200 ml/7 fl oz milk, warm
4 dried *choricero* peppers, soaked for 2 hours,
or 1 tablespoon paprika
1–2 teaspoons lemon juice

SERVES 4 AS A STARTER,
—— 2–3 AS A SUPPER DISH ——

Grill the red peppers until charred on all sides, giving them a quarter turn every 5 minutes. Leave to cool in a bag, then peel off the skins on a plate, to catch the juices. Remove the stalk and most of the seeds through the stalk hole with a teaspoon.

Arrange the fish, in fat fingers (skin down), in an oiled baking dish in which they fit exactly. Sprinkle with the water and 2 tablespoons oil. Bake in a fairly hot oven (200°C/400°F/gas 6) for 10 minutes.

Meanwhile fry the onion in 2 tablespoons oil until soft, adding the garlic towards the end. When the fish is ready, flake the flesh into the onion and add the parsley and seasoning.

Make the sauce: cook the flour in the hot butter for a couple of minutes, then stir in the warm milk and simmer for a couple more minutes. Add 4–5 tablespoons sauce to the fish mixture, then divide this into 8 and stuff the peppers. Lay these in an oiled baking dish (or individual casseroles), brush with oil and sift flour lightly over them.

Add the reserved pepper juices to the remaining sauce, together with the *choricero* flesh or paprika and bring back to simmering. Taste and balance the sauce with a little lemon juice and seasoning. Pour round the peppers. Reheat in a low oven (150°C/300°F/gas 2) for about 10 minutes – or 25–30 if prepared ahead and cold.

Note: one of the great ways to cook fish to be eaten cold, or as part of another dish.

Calderillo bejarano

— POTATO, GREEN PEPPER AND RIB STEW —

A filling potato pot from the snow-covered Sierra de Béjar in the west, the recipe was made with veal ribs (unobtainable elsewhere) in a copper pot, and is normally eaten hot. It also makes one of the nicer potato salads, in front of barbecued sardines.

6 pork ribs, cut through the belly

2 kg/4 lb potatoes

500 g/1 lb green peppers, seeded and chopped

4 tablespoons olive oil

2 Spanish onions, chopped

salt and freshly ground black pepper

½ tablespoon paprika

4 garlic cloves, peeled

6 tablespoons chopped parsley

2 tablespoons white wine

pinch of cayenne pepper

2 bay leaves

800 ml/1 pt 7 fl oz water

6 tablespoons (or to taste) virgin olive oil,
if eating cold

— SERVES 8 OR MORE —

Heat 2 tablespoons oil in a wide flameproof casserole and fry the onions over low heat. When they begin to soften, push them to the sides and add 2 more tablespoons oil. Put in the ribs, well seasoned with salt, pepper and paprika. Turn up the heat a little and fry them, stirring occasionally to make sure the onion doesn't catch. Add the chopped peppers as the ribs are browned.

Pound the garlic with the parsley (or blend), adding the wine. Add this paste, plus any remaining paprika and a little cayenne, to the casserole with the bay leaves and water. Let this simmer while you peel and dice the potatoes.

Add the potatoes and bay leaves to the casserole with a little extra water if absolutely necessary to cover. Simmer for 30 minutes, or until the potatoes are ready. (If there seems to be too much liquid, ladle out, boil to reduce and return.) Season with salt, turn the stew over gently and serve hot with the ribs on top.

To serve cold, shred the meat, discarding the bones. Check the seasonings again and dress with a little virgin oil.

❧ The Pig Feast ❧

The squealing had stopped when I arrived, for pigs die at dawn. We were there to celebrate, not to witness the sacrifice, in a vast hall in Burgo de Osma. The bibs round every neck said Virrey Palafox, *la catedral de buen comer* – the cathedral of good eating.

We started with a toast to the president – ancient and extremely short, in a new striped smock and black ribbon – and the Virgen de Pilar. I envy the Spanish capacity to be merry before the drinking even started. The band in fringed velvet breeches processed, and the trail of music started big hips swinging and a little burst of dancing. We praise *la fiesta de San Firmín* with one long-held note, and 20 people down one side of the table swing together. Two lines of chorus and it melted away 30 seconds later.

A scurry of waitresses and the arrival of the first course: cured meat from 'last year's pig', then a rest, with scrambled eggs and green garlic (see page 46). Enter the first hot pork, and into serious business. A trio of red *chorizo*, *morcilla de arroz* (black pudding made from rice and cumin) with *torreznos de alma*. These pork belly strips cooked almost to crackling are admirably Chinese: succulent, not greasy. Brain pudding followed, with gravy. It was the last dish I finished: I was growing wiser.

Next a salad of chicory, a few strawberries on top and boiled pig's ear. I was so glad that I tried it: membrane with a delicate texture. More bottles of *rosado* and ties were loosened. Expansive, pink and sweaty, we were starting to resemble Walt Disney's pigs in clothing.

A squealing like bursting bagpipes announced the arrival, at our table, of the band. Dressed in black velvet, there were two oboes and big and little drums. They played old tunes, with many repetitions, so everyone knew when to sing '*Olé*' at the right moment. Then bravura blowing from the oboe. All on one breath, phrase after phrase, cymbals banged and clicking drumsticks marked off the moments, lungs bursting and crowd clapping.

The hot starters, next, were more ambitious cooking: pig's tongue in white wine with peppercorns, brains with oyster mushrooms (more Chinese overtones), and pig's tail with carrots. Stewed trotters in the slight red juice from *choricero* were cooked to a succulent jelly; Spain values a range of textures. My attention must have wandered at this point, for I missed the grilled

Café chairs waiting for the evening *paseo* or a fiesta

spare ribs entirely. It was because my neighbours had a side order of meatballs and grilled salmon.

A *jota de ragón* started down the table and the clatter lessened. A large (blonde) lady singing, in quarter-tones and with Arab sorrow, of past loves. Just discernible, her young child sang with her, a high echo of the mother's *basso*, matching the line exactly.

It called itself a pause – but was a course without meat. New dishes of stewed beans, of potatoes with saffron and ribs and an excellent soup. Feeling a trifle full, there was a people-movement, flapping bibs and general calling for *sorbete*. It came: short glasses of iced *cava* (champagne-style wine). 'Drink this, to clean the system.' Indigestion pills came out of handbags. Down the table were shouts of '*Mandales la botella*' – 'pass the

bottle'. Tara-tan-tara: a hunting horn came from someone's pocket.

The start of the main course meant serious pig-eating, a roast loin that had been marinated for a week, a roast leg with raisins (see page 46) and – high point – the roast sucking pig, *cochinillo asado*. So small, so succulent and wonderful! A gold skin like a net of grilled sugar enveloped meat without fat, tender and creamy. What could follow? Pork fillet, roast wrapped in raw ham, and served with tiny vegetables.

More wine, more drinks, puddings, an orange sorbet in the fruit shell and little cakes. Counting up, in four hours we had eaten 30 dishes. Dancing – and drinking – started in earnest. Before next year I must, must, must learn to dance a good *paso doble*!

Orange peel drying,
ready to flavour sauces
or a bouquet garni

Revuelto de ajetes o puerros

COLD SCRAMBLED EGG WITH LEEKS

AND MAYONNAISE

An unusual starter, or something to join the summer salad plate, this combines the smooth, smooth texture of a baked custard with subtle flavouring contributed by the onion family. In Spain, where everybody owns *paella* pans in several sizes, it is cooked in a bain-marie, one pan inside the other. Quantities can be larger. Put 2–3 dried beans between the pans, so the top one is not sitting directly on the bottom one and on the heat source.

4 large eggs
25 g/1 oz butter
4 green garlic shoots, or 2 small leeks, or 2 bunches
of spring onions, white and palest green, chopped
2 tablespoons whipping cream
salt and freshly ground black pepper
mayonnaise, to serve

SERVES 2–3 AS A STARTER

Heat the butter in a saucepan until frothing. Add the garlic, leeks or onions and soften for 2–3 minutes. Beat together the eggs, cream and seasoning (I strain this, wanting a perfect texture.) Pour on to the garlic or leeks.

Move the pan, to stand it in a small roasting tin of simmering water. Scramble the eggs, stirring regularly with a wooden spoon and removing from the heat while still just liquid. Turn on to a dish and leave until cold, then slice. Serve with 1–2 tablespoons mayonnaise each.

Jamón asado con pasas

ROAST PORK WITH

RED WINE AND RAISIN SAUCE

A *jamón* is a hind leg, but a loin is more convenient outside Spain – and also a typically Spanish cut. The sauce has rich Christmas flavours.

900 g/1 lb 14 oz eye of pork loin
(6–7 chop loin, boned, skinned and flaps removed)
salt and freshly ground black pepper
2 garlic cloves, smashed and peeled
1 bay leaf, crumbled
100 ml/3½ fl oz red or white wine

RED WINE AND RAISIN SAUCE

75 g/3 oz muscatel raisins, preferably from Malaga
8–10 prunes
250 ml/8 fl oz red wine
2 tablespoons sugar
zest of 1 orange, pared in a spiral, plus juice
pinch of freshly grated nutmeg
pinch of ground cloves
1½ tablespoons chopped candied orange peel
2 teaspoons cornflour
1 tablespoon lemon juice

SERVES 6

A day ahead, rub salt and pepper into the pork and marinate it with the garlic, bay leaf and wine (a plastic bag is easiest). Turn once.

Heat the oven to 200°C/400°F/gas 6. Stand the joint on a rack in a small roasting tin. Add the garlic and bay leaf from the marinade to the tin and pour in a glass of water. Roast for 1½ hours, keeping an eye on the juices so they don't burn. Add the marinade after 1 hour and baste twice. Leave the joint to rest for 10 minutes.

Meanwhile, make the sauce. Cook the raisins (seeded if you wish) and prunes with the red wine, sugar, orange zest, nutmeg and cloves until they are well plumped – 20–30 minutes. The wine should reduce well at this point.

Turn into the roasting tin and stir to deglaze. Discard the garlic and zest and add the candied orange peel and orange juice. Mix the cornflour with the lemon juice and a little of the hot sauce, and stir back into the sauce to cook this. Taste and add salt and pepper (and more lemon) if needed. The trick is to balance the sweet and sour, with salt and pepper – but don't overdo any of them.

Carve the joint thinly and pass the wine and raisin sauce separately in a jug.

❧ Awful Offal: Salamanca ☙

The Plaza Mayor in Salamanca is one of the grandest in the country, a rhythm of balconied windows on three storeys. Its arcades were packed at the evening *paseo* hour – and deserted again next morning. This spacious honey-coloured city has had a university since the 13th century, one of the oldest in Europe. The chiselled double entrance to the school came later, now one of the best examples of Spanish plateresque. Like Oxford, Salamanca has the reputation of swimming against the tide. I found my own lost cause – innards – downstairs in Salamanca central market.

The first thing to catch the eye was the row of baby piglets. They were so very tiny! Hanging in a line on hooks, their white eyelashes closed in death, they could easily have been in church, not a market. Each bore a small slit in the breast, through which it had been bled. It reminded me of the bleeding heart of Jesus, in so many church pictures.

One thinks of innards as scarlet, but these were pure white. Like a Chinese laundry, the *casquería* had the white of much blanching. And for once it was not dominated by the pig, for it sold lamb and veal innards too. White muzzles under glass, rows of nostrils that had breathed their last. There was tripe, too, like blankets of mohair, smooth or curling honeycomb sections. And ox feet – not veal, for they were enormous.

I watched a woman peeling off the horn hooves. They came away in four neat sections, receptacles that would have been made into an inkwell or a button box in the 19th century. It left four pink raw toes, below a massive ankle. This was then split for slow-stewing with pulses.

But it was the tiny lambs' feet that really gripped me. I had refused a recipe for these, knowing I would never cook them. Now I regretted it. They were so exquisite, with their porcelain toes, smaller than a pair of fingers, and so delicate they reminded me of Nicolette in the French fairy story about Prince Aucassin: the whiteness of her feet shamed the daisies as she passed.

I ate these later – 12 feet at one sitting – in a mild sauce that had something of tomato. They were as smooth as custard (one with a bay leaf flavour). The toes left on the plate were like molar teeth. Later, too, I ate lamb's intestines, *zarajos*, the entire thing wrapped round two sticks, like a ball for knitting. It was grilled until crisp outside but remained succulent within. These inside things are delicious! As the traveller Richard Ford said of cat-stewed-for-rabbit: 'It is only knowing that hurts.'

Right: Veal muzzles waiting for a rich stew or bean pot

CHAPTER 6

Galicia

Europe's western corner, the stormy Atlantic sweeps Galicia on two sides. America next stop! Green, wet and misty, the northern coast is the Celtic fringe of Spain. It has more in common with Wales or Scotland than the sunny Mediterranean beaches.

Rocking in the wind, like upturned green skirts, the cabbages identify the place as Galicia. Hundreds of them, waist high, in every cottage patch and village field. And every homestead has its *horreo* outside. They look like coffin-houses. Grey and stone-roofed, with a cross at one end and slatted sides, they are lichened by wet weather. These long store-cupboards are used for storing vegetables, maize for the poultry (secure from rats) and the local soft cheeses.

I was driving south from Santiago out of the wind in the valley behind the coast: down the E1, Europe's first highway. It crosses broad, calm rivers which emerge on the unseen coast as deep fiords. There are trout, salmon and lamprey (to which salmon is host) in those brown waters. It was December and I passed stands of brown maize, still in the husk, and bright orange osier branches, from which two-handled baskets are made. Vines here grow on overhead trellises to catch the sun. (Elsewhere in Spain they are earthbound.) The wine they make is reminiscent of hock.

I was on the way to Padrón, famous for a tiny pepper. *Pimientos de Padrón* are so small that 20 form a portion. Deep-fried and served with coarse salt, they are a lottery as in every plateful two or three will be hot ones!

In honey-coloured Pontevedra the camellias in the main square were flowering for Christmas. With its old streets and good pilgrim museum, the port is at the head of a river. It was the perfect place to stop for lunch and sample shellfish.

Plain-boiled, there are plenty to choose from. Huge deep-water prawns (*langostinos*), pink-clawed scampi (*cigales*), wonderful small shore crabs called *necoras*, and St James's own lobster with a flat head (*santaguiños*). There is also a curious (and very expensive) barnacle called *percebes*, which stands from the rock like a miniature bear's claw: black and white fingernails. We snap, break, squeeze, peer and poke into the shells, smashing with crackers, picking with forks, sucking at heads and legs, trying to extract every last succulent white piece from piles of shellfish, from the best fishing waters in the world.

Half Spain's fish is caught off this ragged, rocky coast: Vigo is the main fishing port of Europe. Oysters are exported by the barrels: 'their flavour is spiritual,' I was told. Locally, fish goes into *caldeiradas*, different fish layered upon each other (often six types at a time), with onions, potatoes and vinegar. Turbot are now farmed here (on the island of La Toja), as demand is so great for them. *Rodaballo gallego* is cooked with potatoes, peas and paprika, with a garnish of baked pepper.

Galicia is divided from the rest of Spain by more than mountains. For a thousand years it was occupied

Left: The Galicia coast to the west   79   *Above:* Scallops of St James

A favourite cheese, the soft-textured *tetilla* of Galicia

by the Celts, never the Arabs. They left a different culture, the shadow of an ancient paganism. The cuisine stems from them and is based on pork fat. You can see it in Santiago market: great yellow rolls of *unto*, marked with string. *Lacón*, the salt-cured pig's foreleg, is another speciality and the tripe is excellent.

Galicia is a place with its own language and legends. The Romans came – and brought the bagpipes. The worship of nature and natural things is an enduring strand that ran for centuries beside the Christian one. It survives now in herbal medicine from the village healer and local cures, given on the radio. Bread still has rituals attached to it. Great rye loaves, wrapped in leaves, are sold by the chunk and there are also breads with cornmeal. Vast tub-moulded rounds were on sale with *pasas* (raisins) in them for Christmas.

Galicia claims to have invented the double-crust pie: flat affairs with bread dough (see page 86) or wheat or cornmeal pastry. These are festive fare – and also work pies: stuffed with *xouba* (a skinny sardine) or lamprey, *raxo* (the local name for pork loin), and *zorza* (paprika mince, ready for sausages).

One can still see a sight here that has almost died out in Europe: women carrying shopping on their heads. It used to be commonplace. In Santiago market they used baskets of interwoven chestnut, broad thin wood strips, with a square bottom and round opening.

With rain and a rich black earth, northern Galicia raises vegetables for the whole of the country. The potatoes are famous, eaten as *cachelada* with *chorizo* sausage. The turnip trinity reigns: three parts are eaten. The roots now go mainly to animals (though duck with turnips is claimed as a local invention). The leaves (*grelos*) and young flower buds (*navizas*) are the favourites. These are eaten with prawns or ham and go into a *tortilla* (omelette). Galician beef is better than most,

and there are cows, and milk puddings, like those of Asturias. Cider is made and quince paste, called *marmelo* here, which gave us the English word marmalade.

It may be a medieval society, but Galicians are innovative farmers. They claim to have introduced watercress as a salad. The kiwi fruit is farmed here, and even the horned melon is grown.

Villalba market squeezes into the streets below the tower of Los Condes de Vallalba. Octagonal and crenellated, this now houses the main room of the Parador. I had come for the Christmas market, for the town is famous for capons, which used to be king of the Christmas table. Sunday is market day and there were lemons and fresh walnuts, garlic bulbs and great heads of domed *repollo*, the local cabbage. Black-waxed Manchego as well as the local smoked St Simon cheese, like a shiny brown pear, and a breast-shaped one, appropriately called titty (*tetilla*) were being unloaded from a van. A man selling Christmas *turrón* candy was talking-in the clients, through a microphone.

In the smaller squares the sellers were all local: eggs on sale from shopping baskets, or two or three rabbits gently pulsating in cardboard boxes. The hens were magnificent: red-crested, russet and ginger. I watched a man feel their breasts with a gesture that looked sexual. Capons are vast, I discovered – 5 kg/11 lb like a small turkey. They are fattened on maize, down a tube, in the same way as foie-gras geese.

Further south in Galicia are hills – too many of them – with pines, oak and chestnut. Like Britain's Celtic uplands, many people have departed. These are called the 'goodbye' lands and every family has its *defuntiños* – missing people.

Aguardiente (eau-de-vie) is the local distillate, a drink to keep out winter weather. A headache-maker called *orujo* is poured from unlabelled bottles in the bars, and made (like French marc) from grape pips and skins.

For me, Galicia is a land of stones and magic, and the *meigo* (male witch), in his triple cape and hood-of-straw, chanting to San Telma. This is the ritual of *queimada* – which is no mere punch. Into the three-legged pot goes, in proportion, 2 lt/3½ pt clear *orujo*, strips of lemon and 1½ glasses red wine for colour; 250 g/8 oz of sugar (it must be cubed) will also be included. The *meigo* sets fire to a ladle of liquid, with islands of sugar, lowering it to ignite the rest of the liquid. Blue flames leap up! They are used for divination: foretelling someone's death or marriage.

Gallina a la gallega

— BUTTERED GALICIAN CHICKEN WITH NOODLES —

A good use for a boiling hen, I was told, especially with a few yolks inside (added with the saffron) to give colour and richness to the sauce.

1 boiling hen or 1.3 kg/3 lb free-range chicken
salt and freshly ground black pepper
100 g/4 oz good butter
250 ml/8 fl oz dry white wine or strong cider
1 fresh bouquet garni of 2 sprigs each of
thyme and parsley, plus bay leaf
1 onion, very finely chopped,
100 g/4 oz raw ham or gammon, in small strips
1 tablespoon tomato concentrate
about 700 ml/1¼ pt vegetable water or light stock
pinch of sugar
0.25 g saffron (50 strands)
freshly grated nutmeg
175–200 g/6–7 oz *fideos*, small elbow macaroni,
or spaghetti broken into short lengths
2 tablespoons chopped parsley, to garnish

CONDIMENT
2 garlic cloves, finely chopped
3 tablespoons chopped parsley

— SERVES 4 —

Cut the hen into 16 pieces (halving the backbone, breasts and thighs), removing or shredding any thick chicken skin, and season. Melt three-quarters of the butter in a large frying pan (with any lumps of chicken fat). Add the chicken pieces and fry them over the highest heat until well-coloured.

Move to a flameproof casserole with all the butter and add the wine and bouquet garni (include the bony extras from a boiling hen). Cook over medium heat, basting regularly with the juices, until most of the wine has evaporated.

Melt the remaining butter in the frying pan and cook the onion till softened, frying the ham at the same time. Stir in the tomato concentrate and half the water or stock. Add a pinch of sugar and balance it with salt. Crumble in the saffron with your fingers. Bring to simmering, then pour over the chicken. A boiling hen is simmered until tender at this point.

Check the seasonings, adding nutmeg to taste, then more water or stock, judging enough to cook the noodles. Add these to the casserole.

Mash the garlic with $\frac{1}{4}$ teaspoon salt and pulverize with the parsley (or use the blender); add the paste to the pan. Cook until the noodles are ready (about 15 minutes) and the chicken falling off the bones. Remove the backbone and bouquet garni (plus bony extras from a boiling hen), and garnish with more parsley. Good with Brussels sprouts and plenty of cider to drink.

Sardinas rellenas asadas

BAKED SARDINES
WITH OREGANO STUFFING

Sardines are at their best in August. A rich dish as it includes the juices from the head and the fish are uncleaned. Ideally it is accompanied by the deep-fried miniature *pimientos de Padrón*.

1 kg/2 lb very fresh sardines
salt and freshly ground black pepper
6 garlic cloves, finely chopped
2–3 shallots or the whites of a bunch of spring onions, finely chopped
6 tablespoons chopped parsley
1 tablespoon fresh oregano leaves
8 tablespoons dry white breadcrumbs
$\frac{1}{4}$ teaspoon finely grated lemon zest
4 teaspoons lemon juice
1 tablespoon paprika
about 1 teaspoon olive oil

SERVES 4–6

Scale the sardines by rubbing tail-to-head and rinse them. Slit them open from the back, cutting down one side of the backbone. (The guts are nothing much in small fish.) Open the pocket with 2 fingers and salt and pepper them inside.

Mash the garlic with $\frac{1}{2}$ teaspoon salt in a mortar (or a small blender), then purée with the shallots or onions, parsley and oregano. Add the breadcrumbs, lemon zest, 1 teaspoon lemon juice and the paprika and reduce everything to a paste. Taste and season.

Stuff the sardines and lay them in a lightly oiled earthenware dish. Mix 1 tablespoon lemon juice with the oil and brush or dribble over them. Bake in a fairly hot oven (190°C/375°F/gas 5) for 25 minutes. Serve immediately, with crusty bread.

Callos con garbanzos y costillas

TRIPE WITH CHICK PEAS
AND PORK RIBS

An intelligent update of *callos a la gallega*, which is a popular Sunday treat in the local taverns. Nutty chick peas contrast perfectly with the meat and the smooth, creamy texture of tripe. The tripe almost disappears – an angel passing. In this version pork ribs replace the traditional calf's foot. Buy meaty ones, cut through the belly, not spare ribs.

500–700 g/1–1½ lb tripe, par-cooked *(see note)*
400 g/14 oz chick peas, soaked overnight
3 pork belly ribs, with meat, chopped by the butcher into squares
150 g/5 oz raw ham or smoked gammon, cubed
175 ml/6 fl oz white wine
100 g/4 oz *chorizo*, or any smoked paprika sausage such as kabanos, sliced
1 tablespoon lard or oil
1 teaspoon paprika
pinch of freshly grated nutmeg
pinch of ground cloves
salt and freshly ground black pepper

CONDIMENT
3 small onions, peeled (250 g/8 oz)
2 bulbs of garlic
12 cumin seeds
1–2 dried *guindilla*, seeded and chopped or a good pinch of cayenne pepper
2 tablespoons chopped parsley
1 slice of stale bread, crusts removed, toasted

SERVES 4

Put the drained chick peas in a pot with the ribs and ham and just cover with cold water. Bring to simmering, then skim off the scum. Add the whole onions and bulbs of garlic. As soon as these are cooked – about 20 minutes – remove and reserve them.

Add the tripe and continue to cook over very low heat, or in a low oven (150°C/300°F/gas 2), until the meat falls from the rib bones and the chick peas are tender, 2–2½ hours longer. Check occasionally that the chick peas are not drying out and add the wine about three-quarters of the way through, when you can judge liquid levels – the final dish should not be too sloppy.

For the condiment, crush the cumin and *guindilla* in a mortar. Peel the cooked garlic and mash in the mortar (or blend everything), adding the onions in pieces. Reduce to a paste with the parsley and toasted bread, adding liquid from the pot as needed.

Fry the sausage in lard or oil. Add the sausage with its juices and the condiment to the pot. Taste and season, adding the paprika, cayenne (if using), nutmeg, cloves, salt and pepper; the spicing should be quite discreet or it will distract attention from the texture. Cook it all together for 30 minutes before sending it to the table. The dish reheats well, and we ate it from individual casseroles, heated in the oven from a big family stewing pot.

Note: the recipe as given to me started: first wash the tripe well, both in cold water and in warm water. Rub it with lemon juice and vinegar. Cut it into bite-sized pieces and put in a pot with cold water. When it boils, throw away the water and start again, simmering (usually with calf's foot) until tender. However, because tripe is more often sold par-cooked, I have started at a suitable point. Check cooking times when you buy it.

The Pilgrims' Way and Scallops

Santiago de Compostella – the name has the reverberation of great bells tolling. It holds the shrine where St James the Apostle is reputed to lie. In the Middle Ages it was the most visited place in Europe. His saint's day, 25th July, is now Spain's National Day, and we made the pilgrimage through France to celebrate it.

The pilgrims once walked across Spain to get here, wearing a scallop shell, the badge of Santiago. Modern pilgrims may still wear them, on a string round the neck, and some carried a staff with the traditional gourdshell for water.

We travelled the pilgrim highway south of the mountains, the *camino francés*. Each night was spent in old pilgrim resting places, like San Marcos in León. Outside, its Renaissance frontage is more suited to an opera house; inside it is a monastery with scallop shells round the courtyard.

Scallops are associated with St James in several languages: 'Coquille St Jacques' or 'pelerin' in France, 'Jacobsmuschel' in German. In the past, I reflected, pilgrims were the only civilian travellers. Here's another curious parallel with scallops, which zip around; other bivalves are stationary!

Several days driving westwards, and always ending towards the setting sun: a gleaming goal that became identified with Santiago. From the east, the view of it cannot have changed greatly: a valley full of vines below the city wall. The cathedral, with three domed towers, dominates the city. At the west end, the great Obradoiro façade of the cathedral faces a large square. In honey-coloured stone saints and scrolls mount, like sculptured marzipan. Between the towers, St James looks down on the tourists, from under the wide brim of the famous hat.

The troop of pilgrims mounts the steps and through the double Door of Glory, where St James's feet are polished by caressing hands. The organ pipes splay out across the nave like trumpets. Ahead, down the darkened church, lies the sanctuary of beaten gold and silver, so ablaze with chandeliers and television lights it seems that approaching figures must leave a shadow.

It is a good Catholic tradition that the day before a feast – and the day before that – is also a feast day – for an important saint! Santiago is a medieval town en fête, on foot through its narrow arcades and passages, and in great good humour. Jugglers, sword-swallowers, earring-makers, pipers entertain the crowd – as do pavement artists. A competition is announced with a procession of drums and squealing bagpipes. It is for the best village dance team and brings girls in pretty shawls and bands of men in two-thumbed hats.

First God then food, celebrating in a city crammed for festive eating. Octopus is popular in Galicia (though not liked elsewhere in Spain). On feast days it presides on all the bars, like a pink wig on a stand; the legs, covered with rings, curl away in all directions. A pile of wooden plates stands by it, for *polpo a feria*, octopus with paprika and oil.

Crowds, cigarette smoke and great trays of mussels cram the restaurant. Baked scallops are a 'must' to try: *vieras de Santiago*, crisp-topped with crumbs, and rich

with brandy and tomato. Then *lacón con grelos*, a vast mound of ham hocks with the favourite green turnip tops; a dish to bring tears to the exiles' eyes. And to end, almond *tarta de Santiago* (see recipe).

We slipped into Mass by a back door on the Eve of St James, to a service for the soldiers. At the centre of the cathedral, where two great axes meet, was an open space with a trailing rope. A large brass urn was attended by six hefty clerics. It was as big as any of them.

The organ began to play and the crowd stamped and roared out the marching tune we know as 'My eyes have seen the glory, of the coming of the Lord.' The great *botafumeiro* of Santiago began to rise into the air, swinging across the transept, from north to south, higher on each swing, towards open doors where the crowd pressed in to see it. Belching flame from its caged mouth, it was willed upwards by a sea of faces, then plunged again, trailing clouds of perfume. Once it fell: in front of Catherine of Aragon on her wedding voyage to Henry VIII and England – a bad omen that was fulfilled.

Zamburiñas rebozadas, cuatro en una

FRIED BABY SCALLOPS, FOUR TO A SHELL

The most wonderful scallops of my life were eaten plain fried with garlic and parsley. So large were they that they resembled poached eggs in reverse – an orange roe circling right round the white meat. But nowadays the tiny ones are all most of us can buy. They are served in a top shell.

16–24 small scallops, depending on size
(350 g/12 oz shelled weight)
3–4 tablespoons plain flour
salt and freshly ground black pepper
1 large egg, beaten
3–4 slices of stale bread, crusts removed, crumbed
about 4 tablespoons olive oil
lemon wedges, to serve

SERVES 4

Clean the scallops, removing any frill attached to the base, and rinse them. Blot with kitchen paper. Roll in seasoned flour then in beaten egg. Coat with crumbs.

Fry briefly in plenty of hot oil – about 1 minute each side – and serve in the top shells of large scallops (or 4 small dishes), accompanied by wedges of lemon.

Tarta de Santiago

ST JAMES'S ALMOND TART

Not the cake you find in Madrid, but the real thing, as served in Santiago on St James's day: almonds set off by sherry. The top is dusted with icing sugar, with a stencil of St James's two-handled sword. The layer of quince paste under the almond was suggested by a friend.

FOR A 22-CM /9-IN FLAN TIN

150 g/5 oz plain flour, plus extra for sprinkling
½ teaspoon ground cinnamon (optional)
2 tablespoons caster sugar
100 g/4 oz butter, finely diced
1 small egg yolk, beaten
200 g/7 oz *dulce de membrillo*, sweet quince paste
(sold in Italian delicatessens), or apricot jam

ALMOND FILLING

200 g/7 oz ground almonds from a sealed packet
100 g/3½ oz caster sugar
½ teaspoon ground cinnamon
finely grated zest of ½ lemon
3 small eggs
75 g/3 oz butter, melted
75 ml/3 fl oz sweet *oloroso* sherry
icing sugar

SERVES 8

Make a sweet pastry dough by combining the flour, cinnamon, sugar, butter and egg yolk in a food processor. Chill it for 20 minutes while the oven heats to 200°C/400°F/gas 6 with a baking sheet in it.

Grease a flan tin with a removable bottom. Roll out the dough on a floured work surface to just larger than the flan tin (this is best done between 2 sheets of cling film). Remove the top film and turn the dough face down in the tin, then remove the rest of the film and press the dough into position.

Mix 50 g/2 oz ground almonds with the quince paste or jam and spread over the bottom of the pastry case. Mix the remaining almonds with the caster sugar, cinnamon, lemon zest, eggs, melted butter and sherry. Turn into the pastry case and smooth.

Put the tart on the hot baking sheet in the oven and bake for 10 minutes. Then turn down the heat to 170°C/325°F/gas 3 and cook for 15–20 minutes longer, until lightly browned. Let it stand for 5 minutes then remove the tin and cool on a wire rack. Dust the cold tart with icing sugar.

Shellfish Festival

A breathless warm December day on Galicia's northernmost tip. But the sea was creaming against the sand and the blackest of rocks, despite the calm. I was driving from nowhere to nowhere, and it was 12 o'clock. Too early for a lunch stop, but I wanted a

Horreos are store-houses for cheese, maize and potatoes

beer. The tiny port below seemed the perfect place. The sun sparkled on wet sands but the sea was retreating from the inlet, behind a series of mist-shrouded, tree-decked islands.

The descent was difficult, but I parked precariously and reached the harbour. Little groups were hurrying in the same direction. A canvas bandstand and several stalls. I collected my beer and found I had joined the third annual shellfish festival of O Barquiero. A village lunch!

The band start to play waltz tunes, interrupted by great bangs on the drums. Marching music followed, with a solo on the trumpet of the kind that announces the bull into the bullring. I bought a rough brown casserole, the size of a child's bicycle wheel, for baking the Christmas vegetables, and queued for a lunch ticket: 500 pesetas – 'and all you can eat', I was promised. A bottle of wine and a cup, at another stall, cost 100 pesetas.

The harbour master – he had a gold hat on – was in charge of the proceedings. But the cooking was done by the local ladies. Maribel, in a big front-and-back pinafore, and her team were cooking in the emptied boat shelter. Spanish festivals seem to be a vast extension of domestic entertaining. Home stoves are fired by butane gas and they are just moved for parties.

An ominous squeal came from another corner. The band had competition from the *gaiteras*, three bagpipe players in lace-edged britches with red pompoms. There were drums, too, one big, one small. A repetitive rhythm, on and on. Later the dancing started, neat toe-and-heel steps, too fast to copy.

Lunch was served on the seawall, in a green canvas shelter. A plastic portion-plate per person, heaped with great piles of shellfish from steaming casseroles. *Coquines in vino blanco*, long slim clams in white wine, and other rounder ones in breadcrumb sauce. Fat mussels in a tomato stew, another stew of cockles. Hunks of the flat Galician pie were balanced on top. One, yellow with saffron, had cockles. The other was of mussels with coloured peppers. 'All fished in the rio del Sor', someone boasted, and '500 of us consumed more than 1000 kilos of shellfish!' Pity those women! Besides opening mussels, they had shelled 250 kilos of cockles for 50 pies.

Empanada de berberechos

COCKLE (OR CLAM) PIE

No festival can take place without a pie, and this one smells wonderfully of the sea when cut.

FOR A 35 × 25-CM/14 × 10-IN BAKING TRAY
1 kg/2 lb cockles, rinsed
(300 g/10 oz shelled cockles or clams)
2 large Spanish onions, well chopped
3–4 tablespoons olive oil
0.1 g saffron (20 strands)

CORNMEAL DOUGH
250 g/9 oz yellow cornmeal
15 g/½ oz fresh yeast
1 teaspoon caster sugar
200 ml/7 fl oz warm water
2 tablespoons oil,
plus more for greasing and brushing the pie
2 eggs, beaten
250 g/9 oz plain flour
1 teaspoon salt

SERVES 8

Put the cornmeal into a large bowl (or food processor). Blend the yeast with the sugar until liquid. Add the water, oil and eggs to the cornmeal and beat well, then beat in the yeast. Gradually add the flour, sifted with the salt, to give a smooth soft dough. If working by hand, knead for a minute or two, until fairly smooth and not sticky. Return to the clean bowl, cover with a towel and leave in a warm place for 20–30 minutes.

Meanwhile, make the filling. Cook the onions in plenty of oil until golden. Open the cockles by putting them, in batches, into a large pan with a little boiling water and covering tightly. Leave a minute or two, then take off the shells. Pound the saffron in a mortar or crumble with your fingers, and add a couple of spoonfuls of cockle water. Soak for 5 minutes. Add the cockles and saffron to the onions.

Divide the dough in half and roll out one part, rather bigger than the baking tray. Lift this on to the oiled tray leaving a border still hanging over the edge.

Spread the cockle filling over the dough, leaving a clear margin. Roll out the remaining dough and lay it over the filling. Trim off the edges, just bigger than the tray, and keep them. Fold the outside edge over, rolling it neatly, and press with a fork to bind. Decorate the top with long thin strips of dough trimmings – these often mark the cutting lines. Paint with oil and prick with a fork in the squares.

Bake in a fairly hot oven (200°C/400°F/gas 6) for 20–25 minutes. Cool for a minute or so, then cut into squares. Eat with your fingers – preferably with a sea view! The left-over slices went in a lunch pack.

Chestnuts for the Dead

The smell of chestnuts on the brazier, rich but slightly acrid, signals autumn has come in Spain. There is a seller in most town squares. In Pontevedra, on the coast, the handcarts were modelled on old railway engines. The chimneys puffed smoke and trays of hot nuts filled the stoking compartments.

In the countryside, chestnuts are associated with mourning. Chestnuts and new wine together symbolize death and life. In the old days, All Souls, 1st November, was celebrated by a vigil in the graveyards with lighted candles. Lots of waiting, but hands kept warm by hot potatoes and chestnuts. Now it is just a graveyard visit and 'a feast of walking up and down and eating'. Very Spanish!

In the poorer, southern part of the province chestnut trees cover the hillsides. I drove up from the south, past Viana del Bollo, on its curious black pool, twisting and turning through small trees in country where much mineral water is bottled. Smoke columns stood still in the air, from burning chestnut leaves.

On a dull day I picked up chestnuts, glossy, tuft-topped and like new treasure in their open, spiky caskets. The wind had blown them into dunes, full of twigs and the smaller ones rejected by yesterday's pickers. Last night's fall was fresh and green, and a small wind brought another crop bouncing down into the clear grass. My small bag filled quickly and I

The fat hens and poultry of Villalba are known for their quality

thought – but found it was to fatten up the birds! For stuffing them use 350 g/12 oz peeled cooked chestnuts, the same of diced russet *tabardilla* apple (like Cox's) and soaked prunes. Also good for a 5 kg/11 lb turkey, which is much the same size as a capon. The breasts were rubbed with pork fat, basted later with brandy.

The best of all chestnut desserts is made in Galicia: chestnut purée beaten with butter and chocolate. Was it invented here, or in Italy? These are certainly local ingredients. There are also sugary Galician *marrons glacés*: the best in the world, said Alexandre Dumas. I carried them home for Christmas.

Lomo de cerdo con castañas

ROAST PORK

WITH CHESTNUTS AND COGNAC

1 kg/2 lb boned pork loin (6-chop loin,
skin removed and tied)
750 g/1½ lb peeled, cooked chestnuts *(see page 88)*
(1 kg/2 lb before cooking)
salt and freshly ground black pepper
2 garlic cloves, smashed and peeled
1 bay leaf, crumbled
50 ml/2 fl oz *fino* sherry
2 tablespoons lard or olive oil
50 ml/2 fl oz Spanish brandy or cognac
2 teaspoons paprika

SERVES 6

A few hours ahead, rub the pork with salt and pepper and put it in a crock (or better, a plastic bag) to marinate with the garlic, bay leaf and sherry. Turn once.

Heat the oven to 200°C/400°F/gas 6. Spread the pork with lard, or rub with oil, and put it in an earthenware dish with the marinade juices. Add ½ glass of water. Roast for 1½ hours, keeping an eye on the juices so they don't burn.

Fifteen minutes before the end, baste with the brandy, and again after 10 minutes. Remove the meat and leave to rest for 10 minutes before carving. Meanwhile, add the chestnuts to the dish, sprinkle with the paprika and toss in the juices. Carve the meat thinly and serve with the juices, surrounded by the chestnuts.

Note: the ideal loin roast is the middle ribs.

tried to leave. But I couldn't pass a fat nut – just one more, just another – and another half-hour passed.

Spanish chestnuts have the finest flavour in Europe: most floury, least oily. Roasted at the end of the afternoon, they were my best chestnuts ever, and the easiest to peel: 40 minutes in the oven at 150°C/300°F/gas 2, with no pricking or bursting!

I had joined three jolly women (each of whom owned a pig and whose mother-in-law had wine butts bigger than sofas). We talked of chestnuts: creamy soups with milk, lemon and pepper, and the dried-chestnut soups of summer, with paprika and onion. Before the potato came in the 18th century, chestnuts and turnips were the staple fare here. Now fried *chorizo* sausage is served with chestnuts in its paprika juices. Partridge is a favourite with sausage, chestnuts and sweet old wine. And to accompany game birds, raw peeled nuts are cooked (sometimes in milk) with fresh fennel and a bay leaf or aniseeds to make a delicate purée.

The thing for capons (which used to be king of the Christmas table), I was told, were rolls soaked in milk or wine, plus chestnuts and flour. For the stuffing, I

Castañas con berza

CHESTNUT, CABBAGE AND SAUSAGE PIE

A simple country dish of the kind I like best. The sausages in the original had a touch of anis, and I have included this as the alcohol ration.

1 kg/2 lb chestnuts
1 small green hearted cabbage, about 700 g/1½ lb
600 g/1¼ lb *chorizos*, paprika sausage
or fresh garlic sausage
2 tablespoons oil or lard
salt and freshly ground black pepper
1 tablespoon paprika (if using garlic sausage)
150 ml/5 fl oz stock
2 tablespoons anis liqueur

SERVES 4

Slightly undercook the chestnuts, boiling them for about 15 minutes, then peel, removing all the skin. Meanwhile, oil an earthenware dish and put it to heat with the oven at 170°C/325°F/gas 3.

Wash the good outer cabbage leaves, about a dozen of them, and cut out the hard end in a 'V'. Blanch the leaves briefly in boiling water, drain and run cold water over them. Cut up the cabbage heart roughly and cook for 5 minutes. Drain well, then turn on to a board and chop.

Slice the sausages and give them a brief turn in hot oil in a frying pan – which gives a chance to judge their seasoning.

Spread the chopped cabbage in the earthenware dish, then top with the sausages and chestnuts. Season well, sprinkling with the paprika if not using *chorizo*. Cover with the cabbage leaves and press down gently. Heat the stock and anis in the frying pan and throw over the top (which glazes the cabbage). Bake for about 1 hour.

Castañas en almíbar

CHESTNUTS IN VANILLA SYRUP

A winter dessert, for mixing with other fruit, or home-made *marrons glacés* for Christmas presents. It makes about 4 dozen.

1 kg/2 lb chestnuts
600 g/1¼ lb sugar
1 lt/1¾ pt water
1 vanilla pod
about 6 tablespoons Spanish brandy,
cognac or Anis de La Asturinas (optional)

MAKES TWO 500 ML/1 PT JARS

Bring the sugar, water and vanilla pod gently to the boil, stirring. Simmer for 5 minutes, then leave off the heat to infuse. Meanwhile, cover the chestnuts with water and bring slowly to the boil. Cook completely, simmering for 20 minutes. Remove from the pan in threes and peel, removing the skins too.

Add the chestnuts to the syrup and boil for 8 minutes. Turn off the heat and leave them to infuse. The next day repeat the boiling, and again on the third day.

For *marrons glacés*, drain well, then dry out in a low oven, 50°C/125°F (or a gas pilot light), for 12 hours. Wrap individually in twists of foil. Eat the same winter.

To bottle, remove the chestnuts with a slotted spoon to preserving jars and pour in syrup to cover. Part of the liquid can be replaced with 3 tablespoons brandy or anis to each jar. Good with Spanish peaches in syrup, or sliced oranges.

Brooms and songbirds
on sale in a backstreet of
Santiago de Compostella

Mussels from Galicia are the fattest and the world's best

❧ Mussels and Green Wine ☙

The End of the World was our destination: Cape Finisterre – known to radio listeners by its bad weather reports. The north-west tip of Spain, it juts out into the stormy Atlantic. The Spanish call it La Costa de la Muerte, the Cape of Death. Village cemeteries explain why. There are tombstones here of every nationality.

We never reached it. For driving round the bays to the south of Cape Finisterre we found a mussel heaven at Muros. The best mussels in Spain – in a country that is the world's greatest producer. They grow in the *rias bajas*, deep bays like Norwegian fiords, that bisect this ragged coast. The west coast is Mecca for mussels!

I was not expecting to see a Chinese fleet there. At least, that is what it looked like. Round the corner of the bay and there on the water was a mass of floating houses, platforms round them, rigged front to back from a double central pole. Were they sampans, were they junks? My idea of Chinese boats is hazy. And what were they doing in a quiet Spanish bay, with the evening sun behind them?

The answer was: growing mussels. They were wooden platforms with ropes beneath them, on which the shellfish grow. The French call rope-grown mussels 'bouchots', and oysters, as well as mussels, grow better off the seabed. Imagine the pleasure of pulling up a rope and eating a raw oyster just seconds from the sea!

We stopped for the day and ordered mussels by the plateful. They lay like fat chunks of some exotic fruit, bright orange in their jet-black shells. They were enormous, sweet and tender (though big ones can often be tough). The lip of one shell is the knife to prize free the next one. So good plain, with lemon!

The perfect partner was green wine. The vines were, perhaps, brought here by German monks long ago – the same grape as Portuguese *vinho verde* just over the border. Ours, a Viña Costeira, was light and faintly fizzy, though the best one is still. This is made at the palace-on-the-shore, Fefiñanes, which we visited later.

Vinagreta de mejillones

MUSSEL AND POTATO SALAD

WITH PAPRIKA DRESSING

Simple – and simply delicious! Both mussels and potatoes are at their best in Galicia. Spanish olive oil makes a very light dressing, as it stays in suspension once whisked.

2 kg/4½ lb mussels, opened *(see next recipe)*
500 g/1 lb *cachelos* or best salad potatoes
(Jersey Royals, Pink Fir Apples, Charlottes)

AJADA–PAPRIKA VINAIGRETTE
1 garlic clove, finely chopped
¼ teaspoon salt
3 tablespoons wine vinegar
100 ml/3½ fl oz olive oil, preferably Spanish
1 teaspoon paprika
2 tablespoons cold water
ground white pepper

SERVES 4

Cook the potatoes in their skins in boiling salted water until just done. Drain and leave a few minutes, then peel and slice or not, according to size. Mix with the shelled mussels.

If you haven't a mortar (or can't be bothered to wash it), mash the garlic on the board with the flat of a table knife, working the salt in to form a paste. In the mortar or a bowl stir the wine vinegar into the garlic and then beat in the oil to make a light cream. Add the paprika, dissolved in the water, and pepper to taste. Pour over the potatoes and mussels.

Note: freeze mussel stock. 'The juice of one shellfish is particularly good as stock for a different one.'

Tortilla de mejillones de La Coruña

CORUNNA MUSSEL OMELETTE

The best mussels in Galicia, and therefore in the world, I am told, come from Corunna. Succulent and tender, they are protected inside the *tortilla* – a deep, moist egg cake. The pan must not be too large, or the *tortilla* will turn out like a flat French omelette.

600 g/1¼ lb mussels (175 g/6 oz shelled mussels)
25–40 g/1–1½ oz butter
2–3 shallots or white part of bunch of
spring onions, chopped
6 large eggs
salt and freshly ground black pepper
2 tablespoons parsley

SERVES 2–3

Clean the mussels, discarding any that are open. 'Bouchots' (rope-grown) have no barnacles; rock-grown mussels do, and these must be knocked off with the back of a knife.

Cover the bottom of a saucepan with water (or wine) and when it boils, put in the mussels and cover tightly. Cook over high heat for 1–2 minutes, shaking the pan occasionally, until they are open. Discard the shells and any that are still shut.

Heat the butter in a 20–22 cm/8–9 in frying pan (nonstick is easiest) and fry the shallots or onions quickly. Meanwhile, beat the eggs together in a bowl. Add the shallots or onions, the mussels, seasoning and parsley.

Pour the egg mixture into the pan, spreading the mussels out. Cook for 1 minute over high heat. Run a spatula round the edge of the *tortilla* and shake the pan to and fro occasionally, to be sure the base doesn't catch.

Turn down the heat to medium and cook until the top ceases to be liquid. Cover with a serving plate or pan lid and reverse, turning out the *tortilla*. Slip it back into the pan, just to firm the other side, then serve at once. Also good cold, stuffed into a *bocadilla* (slit bread roll) with a slice or two of tomato.

Note: 'a glass of wine to open a kilo of shellfish'.

CHAPTER 7

Asturias and Cantabria

Misty and apple-growing, this is the north coast and 'green Spain'. The Cantabrian cordillero, 300 miles of mountains, separates it from the plateau. No wonder it has a separate history! Known for beans, milk and cider, traditions here are similar to those of Normandy.

The flags still fly in the casino city of Santander, where the Spanish royal family made seabathing fashionable in the 19th century. Spaced leisurely round two beaches, the city is a starting point for the corridor along the north coast. Here, round curved sandy bays and in villages round small ports, Spanish families can holiday untroubled by trippers, at what must be Europe's last undiscovered seaside.

Cantabrian cooking has some of the Basque virtues. Hake is fished from the Bay of Biscay, and savoury sardines, 'richer than those of Levante', I was told, are served simply in tomato sauce or, in August, roasted and eaten outdoors with the fingers. Excellent small squid, called *raba*, are floured (rather than battered) for frying and served as many as 100 tiny ones to a portion.

For this coast is blessed with the roaring, scouring Atlantic. It makes the locals confident that the *calderetas* (mixed fish stews – see page 100) made in all the little ports are superior to French bouillabaisse 'because Atlantic fish are superior to Mediterranean'. There are mixtures of fish and meat, too, from a peasant economy. Not just salmon and ham (see page 100), but chicken with prawns (in the ancient Asturian capital of Pravía), just as there are in Catalonia.

The Arabs never came here, and for more than 1000 years it was a Celtic kingdom. The difference shows in the kitchen. The parallels with Normandy are obvious: almost identical recipes for spiny lobster and for tripe, the same fondness for black pudding. Both make the drink cider, and cook with it. Both prefer pork fat (lard) to oil, and are less-than-lavish with garlic. Both like milk and butter, while the local *frixuelo* crêpe is like the Breton one. Made with milk for a dessert, this crêpe can also be made with fish stock (to enclose mussels) or with blood (after pig slaughter).

Milk and apples are the two ingredients that passers-by are most aware of. Milk is for drinking and for making pudding (see page 102) with rice, which found its niche in the north, in the 18th century, as a dessert ingredient. *Quesada* is the local cheesecake in the Vega de Pas, below Santander, a grassy and gently rolling valley known for soft (and blue) cheeses. A buttery sponge called *sabaos*, is also made here, so popular for breakfast, it has its own shop!

Below the Picos de Europa, in the lap of the mountains, is a green, wooded land with 100 million apples on the bough in summer. They mostly go for cider. In the mountains above cows graze in the summer and there are 'almost as many cheeses as there are meadows', including the blue Picos, Gamonedo and the strong *afuega'l pittu*. But Cabrales, Spain's greatest

Left: A wooden *horreo* in Asturias

93

Above: Garfish on sale

blue cheese, is made here from ewes' milk. Like Roquefort, the blue veins develop in caves, and the cheese is then wrapped in maple leaves.

Back to the coast again and driving west along the bucketing shore road, I was made aware how much locals also look to the sea to make their fortunes. All the big houses were built by the *indianos*, successful exiles who made fortunes in Mexico or Venezuela, and then came home to spend them. There are hydrangeas, the glossy *Magnolia grandiflora* with white wax flowers, and the occasional palm tree. They were planted as a reminder of the 'Indies' (anywhere abroad), where the exiles had made their money.

On the coast the slag heaps from the coal mines of Oviedo interrupt the green fields. You can't avoid the factories in this area of serious industrialization. (Others are the Basque country and Catalonia.) Spewing bilious smoke, these facories are often stylish and modern, gleaming with red- or blue-coloured overlays.

Beyond Oviedo, *horreos* instantly mark the landscape. They are different from the Galician ones: larger, square and made of wood with galleries, balancing on stone toadstool feet. They make a rodent-proof store for potatoes, and white beans and corn cobs are dried on their wide balconies.

Asturias is famed for Spain's best salmon rivers, so I drove to Cornellana (due west of Oviedo), the salmon capital. Up a long valley, with rippling water, winding through deciduous trees and nut bushes, it reminded me of Wales. And I was told the same story that I have heard in Scotland and Norway, of servants stipulating that they are not to eat salmon more than twice a week! Nowadays demand for these magnificent fish is so great that they have *piscifactorías*. Local recipes were simple: salmon steaks soaked in milk, then grilled, or a big middle piece roasted whole with oil: the skin comes off in one piece.

The Cantabrian mountain range is so long and high that it includes some of the wildest land in the country. There are three sorts of deer in the Bierzo (at the west end), while the high peaks of the Picos de Europa (at the east end) rise over 8000 feet and form one of Europe's largest wildernesses, still wandered by ibex and bears. We once drove up from Potes looking for bears, to Fuente Dé, where the cable car whisks you half a mile into the sky – and were snowed on in July.

Little wonder that stews are popular locally. The *puchero montañes* is a warming combination of mutton,

ham, hen, beans and sausages. And it is for beans that Asturias is best known. 'Beans keep out the rain', and they are ballast for the labouring man in Spain's main mining region. Oviedo also has at least one stew 'for the railway workers', made of beans with oxtail. Better known is *pote asturiano* (see page 98), which comes from the remote Muniellos, in the Bierzo in the west. Local versions add rice, turnips or carrots too, as well as the brown aged fat, *unto rancio*. Better still, it may contain a slice of the local *botiello* sausage.

Octopus in plenty on sale: a northern treat only

94

Croquettas de huevos

EGG CROQUETTES

A small *entremes* or starter at home (though a *tapa* in a bar), these are very creamy in the middle, crisp on the outside – and hot! Excellent with watercress salad, served before ham or roast veal.

500 ml/18 fl oz milk
1 bay leaf, crumbled
75 g/3 oz plain flour
90 g/3½ oz butter
salt and ground white pepper
freshly grated nutmeg
1 large hard-boiled egg *(see note)*, finely chopped
oil for greasing
watercress salad, to serve

FRYING
3–4 tablespoons plain flour
1 large egg, beaten
8–10 tablespoons stale breadcrumbs
olive oil for deep frying

SERVES 5–6

Warm the milk with the crumbled bay leaf. Make a white sauce (a *besamel*) in a saucepan: cook the flour in the butter for a couple of minutes, then, off the heat, strain in some of the warm milk, beating to a smooth paste. Add the remaining milk and simmer 2–3 minutes, stirring gently. Season to taste with salt, white pepper and nutmeg.

Stir in the egg (any addition must be very finely chopped). Pour on to an oiled platter, in a layer about a finger thick, and pat into a rectangle. Leave to go cold and hard.

Cut into fingers, then into about 30 pieces. Make bullet-shapes, rolling them lightly in flour. Coat with beaten egg, then crumbs; they should be well sealed. Deep fry in a basket, in oil at highest heat, in batches of about 8, for 3–4 minutes. Drain on kitchen paper and serve soon, with watercress salad.

Note: 50 g/2 oz cooked peeled prawns or raw ham can replace the egg, or cooked chicken with 1 teaspoon chopped fresh tarragon.

Clams are popular for soup,
in rice and to accompany fish

Chirlas o almejas con arroz verde

CLAM AND GREEN-RICE SOUP

'Can you use long-grain rice for a dish like this?' I asked, explaining it was easier for me to get. 'If you must. But American rice tastes only of flour. Our Mediterranean rice has more flavour.' Emboldened, I tested this with Italian brown rice.

1 kg/2 lb clams, rinsed (300 g/10 oz shelled clams)
1 onion, chopped
2–3 tablespoons olive oil
1 green pepper, seeded and chopped
3 garlic cloves, finely chopped
6 tablespoons chopped parsley
200 g/7 oz *paella* or risotto rice
salt and freshly ground black pepper
1.5 lt/2½ pt fish stock (or water),
incorporating mussel stock if possible
75 ml/3 fl oz dry white wine or strong cider

SERVES 4

Fry the onion in the oil in a large casserole, then add the green pepper, garlic and parsley. Turn the rice in the oil and season with pepper. Add the fish stock (or water) and cook for 20 minutes.

Meanwhile, heat the wine or cider in a large saucepan and add the clams. Cover tightly and cook, shaking the pan to bring top clams to the bottom, until all the clams are open. Add to the rice (discarding a few empty shells), check the salt and serve.

Note: if the stock is not up to much, put the bruised parsley stalks in too. Remove to serve.

Perdices con verduras

—————— PARTRIDGES IN WINE WITH CABBAGE ——————

Good newly made and even better reheated, the cabbage is made slightly acidic by the wine and so perfectly sets off the rich game.

2 plump partridges
100 g/4 oz raw or cooked ham or unsmoked bacon
freshly grated nutmeg
salt and freshly ground black pepper
about 1 tablespoon melted ham or bacon fat
(or more oil)
2 onions, chopped
1 large carrot, diced then chopped
2 tablespoons olive oil
2 garlic cloves, finely chopped
2 tablespoons chopped parsley
1 small green hearted cabbage
1 fresh bouquet garni of 2 sprigs each of
oregano and thyme, plus 1 bay leaf
about 300 ml/½ pt red wine
about 300 ml/½ pt good poultry stock

—————— SERVES 4 ——————

Cube the ham or bacon, seasoning on the board with nutmeg. Tweak out the wishbones from the partridges, running finger and thumb up them, inside the neck skin. Salt and pepper inside and stuff the birds with the ham or bacon. Spread the birds well with fat and put them to roast in a fairly hot oven (200°C/400°F/gas 6) until they are lightly golden, 15–20 minutes.

Choose a small flameproof casserole (of a size to take 4 partridges) and fry the onions and carrot in the oil until softened, adding the garlic and parsley towards the end. Cut the cabbage into quarters — each wedge should be bird-sized. Blanch the wedges in boiling salted water for 3–4 minutes and drain.

When the onion is soft, put the partridges and their juices into the casserole. Pair the cabbage wedges, curves outwards, and fit them between the birds. Add the bouquet garni. Pour in an equal amount of wine and stock, adding them alternately, until everything is well covered. Bring gently to simmering, cover and cook in the oven for 1–1½ hours.

Remove the cabbage wedges and split the birds. Discard the bouquet garni and sieve (or blend) the sauce, then reheat and season in the casserole.

Casadielles

—————— WALNUT PUFF PASTRIES ——————

The Christmas cracker shape of these pastries is distinctive. In the old days they used to be deep-fried in clean oil, then sugared, but now they are baked.

500 g/1 lb prepared puff pastry
200 g/7 oz shelled walnuts
75 g/3 oz caster sugar
2 tablespoons Anis de La Asturianas *dulce*
(see note)
25 g/1 oz butter, plus extra for greasing
1 large egg, beaten for glazing

—————— MAKES 18 ——————

Crush the nuts. (Angelina, who gave me the recipe, does it with a rolling pin, but at home a food processor was perfect.) Work in the sugar, anis and butter, then divide in half.

Roll out half the puff pastry (keeping the rest in the fridge) to a 30 cm/12 in square and cut it into 9 squares. Portion half the filling, making a bullet shape on each square. Brush the edges to left and right with beaten egg. Fold over the top, brush with egg and then cover with the bottom edge. Press the ends together.

Arrange on a greased baking tray, seam down, pressing gently to seal. Seal the free ends by pressing with a fork, then glaze the tops with beaten egg. Bake at a high heat (230°/450°F/gas 8) for 9–10 minutes until well puffed and brown, while you prepare the second batch. Eat warm, on the day they are baked.

Note: anis *aguardientes* (eaux-de-vie) turn up constantly in Spanish cooking. This one is a sweet liqueur: others, like Anis de Chinchón and Anis de Mono, are dry and are drunk with water like pastis. Pernod is the easy substitute.

Bean Queen

She was a bean snob, I decided, Angelina with her elegant upswept blond hair and her oh-so-slim hips in black-and-white houndstooth trousers. Then I discovered they are all bean snobs, all Spaniards. They choose the beans for a dish in the same way a Mexican might choose the correct chilli, or a Frenchman select the wine. And Spaniards are willing to pay big prices for these vegetables. *Fabes de La Granja*, the favoured 'beans from the farm', cost more than milk-fed lamb at Easter! They come from the sierras north of Madrid, and are reminiscent of avocados in texture and colour once cooked.

Fabada is the famous dish of Asturias, made with great flat beans that melt in the mouth and the dry, wrinkled *morcilla*. Smoked locally, this black pudding miraculously swells and returns to life in the stew. 'Heavy on the stomach,' said Angelina, 'with all those *chorizos*. Impossible to eat at night!'

Hare and partridge go into other good Asturian bean dishes, while *fabada con almejas*, with clams and saffron, was a real discovery – like the second beautiful sister in

Spain's best paprika gives a generous flavour to all sorts of bean pots

a family. They were my introduction to beans with seafood.

'The beans must be *fabes de La Granja*,' said Angelina, 'soaked overnight until the skin comes off when you blow on them. When they are done they should be *suave* (smooth), like a person's skin.' She cooks them in the soaking water. When I raised the problems of gas associated with eating beans, it was not one she had met. 'Cook beans slowly,' she said; '4 hours is right. And always cover with water, one or two fingers. Don't stir – even with a wooden spoon. It might break them up.' But reheating wasn't a problem. She thought them sweeter done ahead.

And so I learned to be a bean snob too. I have met about 40 sorts, now, and am still counting. *Fabas* in Asturias, *feizos* in Galicia, *mongetes* in Cataluña, red beans in the Basque country (where they are three times the price of other beans) and *michirones* in Valencia. The latter are broad beans, very sweet when tiny and eaten fresh – and the worst of fart-makers when dried. Broad beans were once the staple diet of Europe, and this is at least one good reason why white kidney beans were so popular when they were introduced after the discovery of America.

Every region adopted and developed its own kidney bean. And there lies the problem. The names are all local. On my kitchen table *fabes de La Granja* look little different from *judiones* from Barco de Avila or *garrafones* from Valencia: all vast, flat and buttery in texture. *Garrafón* actually means a carboy. And 'quite different from *fabes*', I was told. The *alubias* of León and the *judías* of El Barco de Avila may be identical if they are both *redonda*, smallish, rounded and white – or they may not. Both are legally protected names. And always the locals will tell you, there, just in that corner of the world, grows the perfect bean for that local dish. There are often ten to choose from.

Size distinguishes some of them: my smallest white beans were called *arrocinis* (rice beans). And colour helps: beige ones, *pardas* (dun-coloured) or *canela* (cinnamon); black (and red) loved in the Basque country. I bought *fabes de la Virgen*, greenish-grey – a mint tinge – with an 'eye' like a pea, though it was beige. They were wonderful: plump and ripe when cooked, like buttocks straining against the stitching of jeans. I will never eat beans from a can again.

Skim as they come to the boil and cook for 1 hour, until the beans are almost tender.

Cut up the cabbage head finely and bring it to the boil in a saucepan of salted water, then drain it. Remove the meat bones, returning the meat shreds to the casserole. Take out the sausages, slice and then return them.

Crumble the saffron with your fingers into the casserole, with paprika, plenty of black pepper and salt (to taste). Add the cabbage and potatoes; the liquid should cover them comfortably. Simmer until the potatoes are tender, and check the seasonings again. Serve in big soup bowls.

Note: if you cannot buy a ham hock, use 2–3 pork spare ribs, plus a piece of boiling gammon.

Left: Spicy red *chorizo* sausages, ready to flavour traditional bean stews and soups

Pote asturiano

—————— ASTURIAN BEAN AND SAUSAGE SOUP ——————

A traditional bean and pork dish, but with the lightness of fresh cabbage. Fresh meat was also preferred to salt, and unsmoked *morcilla* (black pudding). The particular one used, called *xuan*, is made from the pig's stomach.

250 g/9 oz *fabes de La Granja* or big white kidney
beans, such as cannellini, soaked overnight
200 g/7 oz ham hock, soaked for 1 hour
1 pork belly rib with meat on, about 150 g/5 oz
125–150 g/4–5 oz fresh streaky pork belly, cubed
3 fresh *morcillas* or 350 g/12 oz black pudding
2–3 *chorizos*, paprika sausage or fresh garlic sausage
700 g/1½ lb dark green cabbage
0.1 g saffron (20 strands)
1 teaspoon paprika (2 teaspoons, if not using *chorizos*)
salt and freshly ground black pepper
500 g/1 lb potatoes

—————————— SERVES 6 ——————————

Put the beans to cook in a large flameproof casserole, packing in the ham bone, pork rib, cubed pork belly and whole sausages and adding fresh water to cover.

Fabes con carabineros

—————————— BEANS WITH BIG PRAWNS ——————————

Angelina's dish – and most requested by her neighbours. One glorious *carabinero* (red prawn) is served on top of each portion. They have very rich heads, more so than *langostinos* (caramote prawns); but use any raw prawn with a head. If this is a problem, make *fabes con almejas* with clams instead (*see note*).

1 kg/2 lb *fabes de La Granja* or butter beans
8 large raw *carabineros*, or scampi with their claws,
or 1.5 kg/3 lb big raw prawns

ONION SAUCE
3 onions, finely chopped
2 tablespoons olive oil
2 garlic cloves, finely chopped
2 dried *guindillas*, seeded and chopped
or a good pinch of cayenne pepper
3 dried *choriceros*, soaked for 2 hours,
or 1 tablespoon paprika
5 tablespoons chopped parsley
150 ml/5 fl oz *fino* sherry or white wine
1 bay leaf
salt and freshly ground black pepper

—————————— SERVES 8 ——————————

Starting a couple of days ahead, soak the beans for 24 hours. (With *fabes*, the skin will come off.) Cook in water to cover by 2 fingers for 4 hours: it must not bubble. Do this on the stove if you can manage a low heat, otherwise in the oven at 150°C/300°F/gas 2. Don't stir them. Check occasionally; they must always be well covered with water. This is best done ahead – the beans have a better texture.

Make the sauce by frying the onions in the oil in a flameproof casserole. When they are nearly soft, add the garlic, *guindilla* and pulp scraped from the *choricero* peppers (if using them), then purée with the parsley in a blender. Return to the pan and add the sherry or wine, bay leaf, a little salt, and the paprika and cayenne (if using). Taste: the sauce should be distinctly piquant.

Cook the *carabineros*, scampi or prawns in this sauce for 15–20 minutes, according to size. Take out the bay leaf. Stir the sauce and prawns carefully into the beans. Reheat slowly – 30 minutes in a low oven (150°C/300°F/gas 2). Check the seasonings and serve with the *carabineros* on top.

Note: clams are more traditional. Open 1.5 kg/3 lb clams, in batches, in a large covered pan with a small glass of white wine (or use 500 g/1 lb shelled clams). Shell them, saving the liquid, and add it to the sauce with 0.25 g soaked saffron strands (50 strands).

⚜ Cider Houses ⚜

You can never help yourself, I discovered, in a *chigre*, a cider house. Very frustrating! Not that it isn't etiquette, but because of the mess you may make. For there is a trick to cider pouring. One hand high above the shoulder holds the bottle. The other, as low as you can reach, has the glass – the two as far apart as possible, to get air into the cider. A wide-mouthed glass increases the chance of catching it – not much, for amateurs. These glasses (once cups) are so popular they are used along the coast for everything. Even wine is a two-fingered measure in the bottom.

You must drink your cider very fast, while it has a thin head and is fizzy – and throw the dregs on the floor, if you can't down it immediately. Perhaps this is why it is *muy alegre* – happy-making – for it is only 6 per cent alcohol. Like wine, it is also used for cooking: for *hombriños*, a local name for sardines, or *chorizos a la sidra*.

The 'hurry and drink it' element of an Oviedo cider house is balanced by the need to choose your shellfish. There are windowfuls of wonders outside every *chigre*, a display of scarlet claws and tails to tempt you in. Once inside, I find this is quite the opposite to *tapas*. Not a little taste of anything, but a serious endeavour. I really came to grips with a *centollo*, the spider crab with its bunched legs, menacing posture and half a rock-garden on its back. The Asturians respect quality in shellfish. Crabs fished inshore cost one-third of crabs fished further out, where deeper water and more movement improves their flavour.

A kitchen in Cantabria

Caldereta asturiana

MIXED FISH AND SHELLFISH STEW

A stew of the fish that dart round the rocks: red mullet, grouper and many spiny members. Buy what is fresh, aiming at about 250 g/8 oz prepared fish per person. I bought a small grouper, a piece of cod fillet, a strip of monkfish and some conger eel. What is essential is to drink several *culines* of cider with it.

250 g/8 oz hake or cod fillet
250 g/8 oz monkfish fillet
1 red mullet, cleaned
250 g/8 oz conger eel steaks
250 g/8 oz small squid, cleaned *(see page 165)*
150 ml/5 fl oz dry white wine
250 g/8 oz mussels, cleaned *(see page 91)*
250 g/8 oz large clams, rinsed
1 onion, chopped
2 tablespoons olive oil
3 garlic cloves, finely chopped
1 tablespoon plain flour
2 tablespoons brandy
about 300 ml/½ pt fish stock
8 tablespoons chopped parsley
salt and freshly ground black pepper
pinch of cayenne pepper
250 g/8 oz peppers, seeded and chopped
250 g/8 oz shrimps in their shells or raw prawns
1 bay leaf
1 strip of pared lemon zest
juice of 1 lemon
toasted bread, to serve

SERVES 6

Prepare the fish, cutting it into pieces of even thickness. Cut the squid into 2–3 pieces.

Put the wine in a large saucepan and add the mussels and clams, in 2 batches. Clap on the lid and cook over high heat for 2–3 minutes until the shells open. Discard the shells. Keep the liquor.

Fry the onion in the oil in a saucepan. Towards the end, add the garlic. Sprinkle with the flour and stir in, then add the liquor from the shellfish, the brandy, fish stock, parsley, and salt and black and cayenne pepper to taste.

Choose a small casserole, into which the fish will fit in two layers. Salt and pepper the fish and squid pieces and put in half of them. Add half the chopped peppers, mussels, clams and shrimps or prawns and

cover with half the sauce. Repeat the layers and tuck in the bay leaf and strip of lemon zest. The top layer of fish should be just covered. If it is not, add a little more fish stock.

Cover and put into the oven at 180°C/350°F/gas 4 to cook for 30 minutes. Squeeze the lemon juice over the top and serve with toasted bread. The shrimps can be eaten unpeeled – though personally I discard the heads. Prawns will need peeling.

Salmon a la riberena

RIVERBANK SALMON IN CIDER

The salt in the ham nicely balances the rich fish. A simple spring dish. New peas – and more cider – go excellently.

4 salmon steaks, about 175 g/6 oz each
15 g/½ oz ham fat or butter
1 tablespoon olive oil
100 g/4 oz raw ham or boiling bacon in one piece
about 2 tablespoons plain flour
salt and freshly ground black pepper
175 ml/6 fl oz strong cider
about 100 ml/3½ fl oz fish stock (or more cider)

SERVES 4

Heat the ham fat or butter and oil in a frying pan. Slice the ham into thin scallops and fry briefly, then remove. Coat the salmon steaks in peppered flour (the ham provides much of the salt in this dish) and colour them quickly on both sides.

Move the fish to a heated baking dish into which they just fit – a big soufflé dish is ideal – and tuck in the ham. Add 1 tablespoon flour to the fat in the pan and work in with the spoon, then deglaze with the cider. Pour the juices over the fish. Top up with a little stock or more cider, almost to cover the steaks. Cook in a fairly hot oven (200°C/400°F/gas 6) for 15 minutes. Alternatively they can be poached in a saucepan on the stove.

✧ Rain and Casino Cows ✧

Drizzle has its own name here: Asturias has its own supply of *orbayu*. No wonder the countryside is green! In small villages, like Porrua, a wooden overshoe is still worn against the mud – the *madreña*, a pointed clog with bars under it.

The best milk in Spain comes from Asturias. It used to come from the sweet-faced *casino* cow but, like the native *lacha* sheep, they are being phased out. Here cows can graze in the glorious hay meadows, rich with blue speedwell, purple-pink vetches and bee orchids. Later the hay is cut for winter and pulled away by oxen in carts with medieval wooden wheels.

Up in these high pastures live some of the most primitive communities in Europe. The cattle-minders celebrate Midsummer with a dance that goes back to the early Bronze Age: a view backwards across time.

Down on the farms vast milk tankers, with SAM on the back, are parked in the small farmyards. And round a corner you may well come upon a Danone yoghurt factory.

The rich milk makes traditional desserts such as *leche frita*: not fried milk, but hugely-popular squares of melting, smooth custard fried with a crunchy coating. Crêpes called *frixuelos* or *filloas* are fried and folded in

Above: Poppies and mustard, in Spain's national colours, deck the spring meadows

101

ear shapes, or are served like the Gallegan Carnival *filloas a la crema*, enclosing custard and flamed in liqueur. *Nata con nueces* is rich whipped cream with walnut halves and honey poured over – fattening and absolutely delicious! And there is thick cream aplenty in *bebedizo*, the after-dinner coffee with *coñac*.

Arroz con leche requemado

——— RICE PUDDING WITH CARAMEL TOPPING ———

With its subtle Arab flavouring and the creaminess of good ice cream, the old way to make this milk pudding was to simmer the milk for several hours, to reduce it. The modern version adds butter. I own a *quemador* for this, a round metal plate with a long wooden handle. The plate is heated in the gas to glaze the sugar top. But outside Spain, I use the blow-torch bought for stripping paint!

4 tablespoons medium- or round-grain rice
1 lt/1¾ pt full-fat milk
1 cinnamon stick
thinly pared zest of 1 lemon
75 g/3 oz sugar
25 g/1 oz unsalted butter
2 tablespoons Anis de La Asturianas *dulce*
or another anis liqueur

TOPPING
ground cinnamon
12–15 tablespoons sugar

——————— SERVES 6 ———————

Heat the milk with the cinnamon stick and the lemon zest loosely attached together by a cocktail stick. When hot, add the rice and leave to cook on the lowest possible heat, with a wooden spoon in, stirring occasionally to make sure the bottom doesn't catch. Cook for about 50 minutes, when the rice should start to be visible above the surface of the milk.

Add the sugar and butter and cook for 10 minutes longer. The whole thing should be fairly liquid, as it will thicken when cold. Remove the cinnamon and zest, stir in the anis and ladle into 6 individual bowls or ramekins. Sprinkle with cinnamon, then chill.

Not more than an hour before serving, cover each top with 2–3 tablespoons sugar and give them a blast of heat to glaze: some grills are hot enough for this. (The glaze melts into the pudding if left too long.) Then re-chill until ready to serve.

Tarta de manzanas

——— APPLE BATTER CAKE ———

A cake from apple-and-dairy country in the north, with the typically Spanish flavouring of cinnamon.

FOR A 22-cm/9-IN SPRING-RELEASE CAKE TIN
6 small *tabardillas* or Cox's apples,
peeled, cored and cut in 10–12 segments
175 g/6 oz unsalted butter
2 tablespoons apple brandy or Calvados
150 g/5 oz plain flour
2 teaspoons baking powder
1 teaspoon ground cinnamon
175 g/6 oz caster sugar
3 large eggs
3 tablespoons full-fat milk

GLAZE
4 tablespoons apricot jam
1 tablespoon apple brandy or Calvados
1 teapoon cornflour mixed with 2 teaspoons water

——————— SERVES 6–8 ———————

Use a little of the butter to grease the cake tin, then dust with flour. Heat the remaining butter in a frying pan, add the apples and stir to coat. Cover and cook gently for 10 minutes, stirring once. Chop one-third of the apples (or process roughly) and add the apple brandy.

Combine the sifted flour, baking powder, cinnamon and sugar (adding them to the processor, if using), then add the apple mixture. Work in the eggs and milk and pour into the tin. Arrange the remaining apple slices on top, then bake in a preheated moderate oven (180°C/350°F/gas 4) for about 50 minutes, or until slightly shrunk from the edge of the tin, risen and golden.

For the glaze, warm the jam and apple brandy, and stir in the cornflour mixture. Cook for 2–3 minutes until clear. Brush the cake top with some glaze. Leave to cool for about 30 minutes, then remove the sides of the tin. Rewarm the remaining glaze and brush on the cake. Eat warm or cold, with cream, egg custard or on its own.

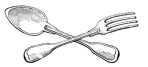

An apple cake in
a cottage window

CHAPTER 8

Basque Country

There is a restaurant in the Basque country, they claim, for every 1000 inhabitants. A small province in the green north, snuggled against the Pyrenees on the road to France, the Basques are self-styled gourmets, and have long been Spain's best cooks.

A tangle of motorways, on the French border, leaps over a countryside of fields dotted with little houses. Like the south of Britain, there are no empty spaces: country – but full of people.

The coast, too, is crowded. Small fishing ports, where steel shrouds clap against the masts, mix with long-established resorts. Bilbao is a major port and industrial centre, an Hispanic Glasgow, full of energy, spewing dirt but making money. In contrast, San Sebastián makes an elegant capital. It has a perfect location on the semi-circular *concha* of white sand, backed by tamarisk trees. Fine buildings and the spaciousness of a 19th-century resort recall more elegant times. There are dishes in keeping: like chops *a la Berritz*, three grilled together. The outside ones are thrown away and only the centre one eaten.

As a nation – the Basques have their own language, near-independence from Madrid, and the title of País (Vasco) – they have always been outward looking. There are Basque provinces in France, and French influence is visible in the food. For example, *piperrada*, the soft, moist, red French-style omelette with peppers, is unlike any other Spanish egg dish. Alone in Spain the Basques make good chocolate, notably Victoria's truffles. They also share the French enthusiasm for the 'new cuisine', creating *la nueva cocina vasca*.

The Basque country is blessed by near-perfect ingredients: the only good beef in Spain, well-hung for enormous *chuletones* (wing rib chops); the first mushrooms in April, eaten with scrambled eggs as *revuelta de zizak*; good chickens; and beautiful vegetables, such as soft artichoke hearts and beans of many colours.

The first to adopt maize and cornmeal from America, the new fashion among the Basques now is for the spicy *pimientos de piquillo* (see page 97), grown round Lodosa, cooked, for example, with rabbit. Game birds wing over from the Pyrenees, and many dishes are shared with Rioja. But they make their own red sausage, a skinny one called *chistorra*, and even lamb sausages.

Red beans are the favourite, though Tolosa is famous for a black bean stew. 'The beans of Tolosa were red, not black, when I was young,' claimed one old lady. There are also special dishes to celebrate fresh white kidney beans, with and without the pod, such as *pochas con codornices* (see page 121).

'The Basques know quality when they see it,' said Palomita Tomé, long-time cook and passionate about food. 'There is excellent cooking in the little villages. People bring a few things to sell. Everything is in season. They eat *chipirones* (small squid) in the north *Virgen a Virgen* (26th June to 15th August, the

Assumption). By November they aren't *chipirones*: they're too large. You can get *chilenos* (squid from Chile), but they have lost their ink. Not good. In Madrid people buy them, and don't recognize that they are imported. In Bilbao people realize the difference and don't eat them.

'Basques pilfer the sierras for things to cook – game, mushrooms. But there has been a change, over 30 years, in the quality of the produce. More additives. Nowadays things are cooked more rapidly but have less flavour. One reason is food is not so immediately seasonal. In prime season things are better. There is also a need to cook ahead. Many dishes need to sleep (*dormir*). Without the rest, I won't guarantee them – big beans, squid, *bonito* – especially dishes cooked with olive oil.'

The brisk Atlantic, which washes into the Bay of Biscay (anglicized from *vizcaína*), produces wonderful shellfish, like the *txangurro*, the spider crab. It is strongly flavoured, and hake is more bland, so 'some mix it with hake, parsley, garlic and brandy, then stuff it back into its own shell. But the authentic way to prepare *txangurro* has no fish with it.'

Hake, the Spanish fish par excellence, is fished in the Bay of Biscay. *Cogote*, hake head, is typical. You may also find potatoes cooked in the same green sauce as that for hake (see page 114). The Basques like the classic fish recipes such as sole with mushrooms, young garlic and white wine. The local white *txacoli*, appley and dry, is also ideal for cooking fish.

But, traditionally, the Basques are deep-sea fishermen and sailors. A Basque, Juan Sebastian Elcano, was the first to skipper a ship round the world (Magellan never made it home). And their shipboard stews are famous: *marmitako* with the white tuna (*bonito*) and peppers, and steaks from its *hijada*, stomach – '¡*Jesús: es 'quisito!*' They catch cod in the North Sea and salt it, for their most famous dish, *bacalao a la vizcaína*, salt cod with pork fat, dried peppers and onions plus, in modern times, fresh peppers and tomatoes.

A *macho* society (it *is* a Spanish word), Basques are famous for bar-hopping and *tapas*: this in the country where bars and discos together equal the number in the whole of the rest of the EC! They are also famous (or infamous) for their gastronomic societies (see page 112), which help keep alive their cooking traditions.

Cooking is the national passion: the invention and promotion of delicacies. *Bocartes* (small anchovies) in sauces, marinated raw anchovies, *gambas en gabardinas* (prawns in light batter – literally mackintoshes) and *angulas* (elvers), which are a 20th-century fashion. In the 1930s they invented *kokotxas*, a triangle from the hake's throat, eaten fried – or in white *pil-pil* (see page 110). It is the identical cut to the American 'cod's tongue', which has a longer history.

The smoky Idiazábal, with its caramel-coloured rind, is the most famous cheese. Many desserts have milk in them: *canutillos* (cream horns), *natillas* (custards) and *leche frita* (see page 101). The pastry tart, *gâteau basque*, which is made with cherries in France, has a custard filling here. Still a village culture, the districts of Vizcaya, Alava and Guipuzcoa are prone to criticize and compete against each other. But a common feature is the hamlet walnut tree, with nuts for *intxaursalsa* (see page 63) at Christmas. It is a delicious cream of walnuts pounded with bread, creamy milk and cinnamon.

Endivias al Roquefort

—— CHICORY WITH ROQUEFORT CREAM ——

Roquefort is extremely popular in Spain, I don't quite know why.

8 small white chicory heads
15 g/½ oz butter
200 ml/7 fl oz single cream
50 g/2 oz Roquefort, in pieces
salt and ground white pepper

—— SERVES 4 AS A STARTER ——

Bring a pan of salted water to the boil, put in the chicory heads and simmer for 10–15 minutes until just tender. Drain in a colander, squeezing lightly.

Melt the butter in a small pan over low heat, add the cream and bring slowly to simmering. Crumble in the cheese, stirring as it melts. Season to taste (it is quite salty). Pour over the chicory and serve.

Fishing boats at Castro Urdiales, part of a Basque fleet of all sizes

Arroz a la vasca

——— RICE WITH EVERYTHING FROM A CHICKEN ———

Simple and economical, this uses all the delicious extras that come with roasting chickens; collect them in the freezer. Four chicken wings (halved) can replace the giblets, or a little cold meat, even stuffing.

500 g/18 oz *paella* or risotto rice, well rinsed
$\frac{1}{2}$ × 1.8–2 kg/4–4$\frac{1}{2}$ lb chicken
4 chicken livers
4 chicken gizzards and 4 chicken hearts
125 g/4$\frac{1}{2}$ oz boneless lean pork
100 g/4 oz raw ham, bacon or streaky rashers
150 g/5 oz *chorizo*, paprika or smoked sausage
5 tablespoons olive oil
3 garlic cloves, finely chopped
150 g/5 oz shelled peas, fresh (preferable) or frozen
2 dried *choricero* peppers, soaked for 2 hours,
or 2 teaspoons paprika (or more)
pinch of cayenne pepper
3 tablespoons sieved tomato (passata)
salt and freshly ground black pepper
1.2 lt/2 pt good poultry stock, hot
200 ml/7 fl oz dry white wine or strong cider
2 red peppers, grilled and skinned *(see page 149)*
or canned pimientos
3 hard-boiled eggs, sliced or chopped
2 tablespoons chopped parsley

SERVES 8 AS A STARTER,
——— 6 AS A MAIN COURSE ———

Take the chicken meat from the bones and cut it into small chunks. Save the better skin and cut it into shreds. Clean and quarter the chicken livers, and open the gizzards and wash them. Chop the giblets, pork and ham. Slice the sausage.

Heat the oil in a *paella* pan or large wide flameproof casserole, with any lumps of chicken fat, and crisp the chicken skin. Fry the chicken wings, larger chicken pieces and sausage over high heat, turning until starting to colour, then add the pork and ham, lastly the garlic and livers, and fry again.

Add the rice with fresh peas, the pulp scraped from the *choricero* peppers (or sprinkle with paprika – 1 tablespoon, if not using *chorizo*), cayenne and the sieved tomato, with salt and pepper to taste. Stir well.

Taste the hot stock and, if it is not well-flavoured, reduce, adding more. Add half to the pan with the wine or cider. When this is absorbed, add the remainder of the stock (and frozen peas if using). Cook the rice for a total of about 30 minutes until done and the liquid is absorbed. In a large flat pan this is easiest transferred to the oven to cook (at 180°C/350°F/gas 4).

Decorate the top with strips of red pepper, hard-boiled egg and parsley, then cover and stand for 5 minutes in a warm place, so the rice grains separate.

Helado Nelusko

——— CHOCOLATE AND ALMOND ICE CREAM ———

I expected this recipe to appear in Escoffier or Larousse (or L. Saulnier's *Le Répertoire de la Cuisine*), so was prepared to discard it, but it was not there. Both the ingredients and method are very Spanish. *Garapiñadas* are a popular snack of almonds in crumbly sugar, toasted but not caramelized.

FOR A 1.5-LT/2$\frac{1}{2}$-PT MOULD (OPTIONAL)
200 g/7 oz dark chocolate
75 g/3 oz caster sugar
250 ml/8 fl oz milk
125 g/4$\frac{1}{2}$ oz toasted almonds *(see page 128)*,
garapiñadas or *guirlache (see page 128)*
6 large egg yolks
4 tablespoons curaçao or Cointreau

MERINGUE
3 large egg whites
2 tablespoons caster sugar

——— SERVES 8 ———

Ahead, make hot chocolate by stirring the chocolate and sugar together in the hot milk. Let this chill.

Pound the almonds (they must be very dry) or process – I used half toasted almonds and half *guirlache* very successfully. Beat the egg yolks until very fluffy and incorporate the almond powder with the chocolate milk. Freeze this – it remains soft.

Whisk the egg whites to soft peaks in a big bowl. Sprinkle with the sugar and whisk until glossy. Fold the frozen custard and liqueur into the meringue. Put it into a mould if you like, then freeze until firm. This can be portioned directly from the freezer.

Note: raw egg yolk custards used to be commoner in ices than they are now. Freezing thickens egg yolks and they never liquefy completely again. However, cook over simmering water, if you prefer, for safety reasons.

Salt cod is the Basque favourite and a national addiction

❧ Salt Cod: a Lenten Fast turned Feast ❧

After the market in San Sebastián, into the bar. And there was yet another new book devoted entirely to *bacalao*: a Basque – and national – passion. 'Yes,' said the owner proudly, showing me. 'My sister-in-law has a recipe in it, *bacalao* with the fruits of autumn' – a sauce with crushed pine nuts and almonds. I called round to shake her hand.

Once a Lent necessity, salt cod is now a passion through the year. The coming of the freezer has changed nothing, for salt cod excites the same sexual nerve as caviar or Stilton.

The Basques acquired the taste four centuries ago – it was newish when Don Quixote ate it. For cod is not a Mediterranean fish. It first came to Europe in a big way in 1481 when, so the latest theory goes, Bristol fishermen discovered the Newfoundland banks – and kept quiet about it! As the big fleets of Britain and northern France moved west to America, the Basque whalers took over the North Sea – and turned to cod. Now Spanish cod boats are away for six or seven months at a time – part of life for many wives to have their men gone in these northern ports.

In the *casa de bacalao* – and most towns have one – salt cod from Iceland and the Faroes is legendary, prized above that of Newfoundland. Fish here is labelled with the fishing ground. Four types of fish are salted, including ling.

The Spanish demand for salt cod is much more sophisticated than the Italian. The dirty, white kite-shaped fish, stacked in the corner like a pile of old newspaper, is still to be found in the south. But the north has a greater choice. So-called white *bacalao blanco* is moist to the finger (though safely salted), easier and pleasanter to cook, as the middle cuts look like fish. Soaked, its weight increases only marginally. *Bacalao inglés* is less salty still; yellower and sold by the fish, it resembles smoked haddock. Soaked, it may be eaten raw (see pages 19 and 149). It was this that opened my eyes to its virtues. Raw *bacalao* has a texture and intensity more exciting than smoked salmon. Different cuts command different prices, and are used in different dishes. Cured flat, the centre is sold as loin. Squares, scallops, throat pieces, shreds, crumbs, from best to worst, all are labelled with the names of classic dishes.

The know-how is in the soaking: to get the palatability of a fresh fish, but retain the magic taste of a cured one. Here is the approved method. 'Cut the fish into squares about 7 cm/3 in and cover with water – at least twice its volume. After 11 hours, turn over the fish with your hand, and cover with fresh water again. Another 11 hours further on, put it in a pot at the back of the stove and let it soak in handhot water for 2 hours. Always soak it for 24 hours, changing the water three times – the last couple of hours in warmish water. Keep this water for cooking – a spoonful or so is often needed.'

Rock-hard and powdery, cut from the stiff fish, *bacalao* will need 36 hours under water. I recommend a bowl in a sink under just-running water (at least for the middle period), for the smell of soaking cod can haunt a house in hot weather. Lion dung was author Gerald Brenan's comparison! It will double its weight, but (unless it is a middle cut) you will lose the extra in discarded skin and bones.

The second method is quicker, but only for dishes which need shredded fish. The *bacalao* is first toasted, which breaks up the fish. It can then be flaked, so soaking is much quicker (see page 19).

Among the proud Basque dishes are *bacalao a la vizcaína*, made scarlet with dried *choriceros* and –

nowadays – fresh peppers, and the mountain *ajoarriero* (see recipe). *Porrusalda*, a soup with potatoes and leeks, is also popular.

Pil-pil is one of the Basques' most famous dishes – and almost the only bad dish I have ever eaten in Spain. By an apprentice hand, it can be a caricature of Spanish cooking: grey fish shapes and garlic swimming deep beneath a sea of oil! Correctly made it is the lightest of white sauces – though it needs Basque cooking talent to make it well. It is normally made with the tail of salt cod, which has the maximum amount of gelatine in relation to the flesh but also with hake (see page 114) and with *kokotxas* (throat pieces).

The taste for salt cod is shared right across the country. Cuenca, on the Castilian plain, makes *atascaburras*, a beaten cream of salt cod with potato and oil. I have had this on Christmas Eve, with walnuts in it. Despite the fresh temptations of the Mediterranean, the Valencians eat salt cod as *giraboix*, with potatoes, green beans and chilli, served with garlicky *allioli*. And Seville invented *soldaditos* (soldiers), the original fish finger!

The Basque fleet encompasses smaller boats on the Bay of Biscay and larger deep-sea vessels

Zurruputuna

SALT COD SOUP

WITH GARLIC AND PEPPERS

'The men got up at five, drank coffee and went to work. Then about eight, they came in for breakfast – a cup of milk and a couple of plates of *zurruputuna*.' One of many garlic and bread soups, it has salt cod as a highlight, spiced with peppers. Four eggs can be poached in it at the end.

250 g/8 oz salt cod, soaked overnight
with a change of water
3–5 tablespoons olive oil
3 garlic cloves, finely chopped
2 slices of stale country bread
1 green pepper, seeded and chopped
3 dried *choricero* peppers, soaked for 2 hours,
or 2 teaspoons paprika
1 dried *guindilla*, seeded and chopped
or a pinch of cayenne pepper
3 tablespoons sieved tomato (passata)
about 1 lt/1¾ pt cod soaking water *(see recipe)*
freshly ground black pepper

———— SERVES 4 ————

Remove any bones and skin from the salt cod, keeping the last fish-soaking water. Heat 3 tablespoons oil in a flameproof casserole, preferably earthenware, and fry the garlic. When it starts to colour, put in the salt cod pieces. Fry them until they have stopped looking gelatinous, then immediately remove them. Fry the bread (or toast it) and the green pepper in the casserole.

If using *choriceros*, scrape the pulp from the skin. Break up the toast and shred the fish on a plate. Return the cod flakes to the casserole with the *choricero* pepper and chopped *guindilla*, or the paprika and pinch of cayenne, plus the sieved tomato and toast. Taste the cod water (to make sure it is not too salty – use more water, if so) and add enough to give a soup consistency. Stir and cook for a few minutes to break up the bread, then check the seasoning.

Bacalao al ajoarriero

SALT COD THE MULE-DRIVERS WAY,

WITH GARLIC

A very old dish, famous throughout Spain, and probably originating in Navarre. This is travellers' food – which perhaps explains why snails and other wild food, like crayfish and even mushrooms, occasionally appear in it – though basically it is cod with garlic and eggs scrambled in at the end. Cooked potato can also be included.

500 g/1 lb salt cod, in 4 slices,
soaked overnight with 3 changes of water
4 tablespoons olive oil
4 garlic cloves, in slivers
2 large eggs, beaten together

TOMATO SAUCE
1 large onion, chopped
2 garlic cloves, chopped
4 *pimientos de piquillo* or 1 red pepper,
seeded and chopped
3 dried *choricero* peppers, soaked for 2 hours,
or 2 teaspoons paprika
4 big ripe tomatoes, skinned, seeded and chopped
75 ml/3 fl oz white wine or *fino* sherry
1 bay leaf
1 tablespoon vinegar, if not using *piquillo* peppers
freshly ground black pepper

———— SERVES 4 ————

Heat 3 tablespoons oil in a small pan with the garlic slivers. When they colour, discard them. Pour the oil over the cod pieces in a flameproof casserole (preferably earthernware) and put into a fairly hot oven (200°C/400°F/gas 6) to cook for 15 minutes. Alternatively, fry the pieces in the garlic-flavoured oil.

When the fish is cooked, remove it. Make the sauce in the same casserole, adding another tablespoon oil. Fry the onion gently, adding the chopped garlic towards the end. When it begins to colour add the chopped peppers, the *choricero* pulp or paprika and the tomatoes. Add the wine and bay leaf and cook to a sauce. Taste for sharpness and add vinegar as needed to accentuate this.

Meanwhile, shred the fish, discarding bones and skin. Drain it on kitchen paper and dry it as much as possible. Incorporate the fish flakes into the sauce and heat through. Add pepper to taste. Add the eggs and scramble everything together for 30 seconds or so.

Men's Clubs and the Story of a Wooden Fork

With good reason I include the all-male *cofradías* in a book about Spanish women and their cooking. There are about 30 of these clubs in San Sebastián alone. Women guests are invited twice a year, on the city's major festivals. They are also allowed to wash up. How do the men manage it? When barriers are breaking down – and when women hold more top jobs in Spain than they do in Britain? Oh, it was argued (wholely to tease?), 'Spain is a matriarchy'. It is true women have great power at home – and men live with their mothers until they marry! 'Men have to have somewhere to get away.' And what do they do, then, when they are alone with other men? Why, they cook!

In the clubs, every member has the right to do so, and afterwards puts money in a box, to pay for what he has taken. They also organize sports and charities and sing! But the business of the club is to talk about, and sample, food. I was instructed about the four basic Basque sauces, their harmonies and colours. Red is *vizcaína* (see page 110), white is *pil-pil* (see page 110), black comes from squid ink (see page 115) and green is famous with hake (see page 114).

Self-styled gourmets, they create food fashions. For example the elver, the famed *angulas*. Eighty odd years ago only modest fishermen round the Bay of Biscay ate them. In nearby France they were sold as pigfood. But the clubs made them a fashion, opening their season in November when the *angulas* arrive.

A mere finger long, and slim like sea-spaghetti, elvers have made a mysterious journey. Freshwater eels breed in the salt Sea of Sargasso and the young travel the Gulf Stream, to the rivers from whence their parents came. Scenting fresh water, they swim up rivers like the Nervion, on the way to the port of Bilbao. Now they are eaten in Galicia and Valencia as well, and are farmed all over Spain because they are so popular.

Highly perishable, they are dipped in a tobacco solution to kill them – 'whichever brand you smoke'. Nicotine, apparently, saves them from insipidity. They are then washed ten times to lose their slime. In the most famous recipe, *angulas a la bilbaina*, oil is heated in an earthenware casserole, with garlic and hot chilli. In go the elvers to be turned a bare minute – 'the oil should not be too hot'. They are eaten with a wooden fork.

Sadly pollution has put paid to most Spanish elvers. The best remaining come from San Juan de la Arena in the Asturias, from the delta of the river Nalón, and some from Cadiz, on the lower Guadalquivir. The softest, whitest *angulas*, I was told, come from France and Northern Ireland. At Aguinaga (on the border) they put Spanish ones (which have a dark thread) in oxygenated water to change the colour, to sell as non-Spanish!

Revuelta de delicías

SPINACH AND SEA TREASURES
WITH SCRAMBLED EGG

The sophisticated San Sebastián version of a common dish on the north coast. Further west it is made with turnip tops and prawns. Soft-set is the best description of these eggs, for a distinction is made between eggs that are stirred while cooking, and *tortillas*, which set to a golden crust.

350 g/12 oz young spinach, stalks stripped
100 g/4 oz butter
salt and freshly ground black pepper
4 *kokotxas* (hake throats, *see page 106*)
or 50–75 g/2–3 oz white-skin sole fillet
($\frac{1}{4}$ × 500/1 lb fish)
3 tablespoons olive oil
100 g/4 oz button mushrooms, cleaned and sliced
100 g/4 oz cooked peeled prawns
8 large eggs
2 tablespoons thick cream

SERVES 4

Wash the spinach. Heat 25 g/1 oz butter in a saucepan and add the well-drained spinach. Cover and cook, turning top to bottom once, until wilted. Turn on to a board and chop coarsely. Season well.

Cut the *kokotxas* into pieces, or a sole fillet into strips. Heat 25 g/1 oz butter and 1 tablespoon oil in a frying pan and cook the mushrooms, adding the fish pieces and prawns. Add to the spinach and mix gently.

Using two frying pans, heat 25 g/1 oz butter and 1 tablespoon of oil in each until frothing. Divide the *delicías* between the two pans. Beat the eggs and cream together, season well and pour in, moving the *delicías* so they do not stick. Turn up to medium-high heat and scramble the eggs lightly, stirring the outside to the middle with a wooden spoon. Divide each pan between two people and serve with crusty bread.

The Bay of Biscay contributes fish and shellfish to a kitchen already well stocked from the countryside

Merluza a la koxkera

————— HAKE OR COD WITH CLAMS —————

To be *koxkera* is to be truly Basque – born in the *calle 31 de agosto*, the last old street in the port of San Sebastián, a golden-housed alley, which runs between the churches of Santa María and San Vicente. Clams are traditional in this green sauce, and any shellfish that traps a little seawater. The sauce is the famous *pil-pil* (see page 110), a white emulsion thickened by the natural gelatine which comes from the fish skins. You will often find it, though, as a flour-thickened sauce – an easier way to make it.

4 very fresh steaks of hake
or 700 g/1½ lb cod fillet, in 4 pieces
salt and freshly ground black pepper
125 ml/4 fl oz olive oil
4 garlic cloves, sliced across into rings
75 ml/3 fl oz good fish stock, warm
175 ml/6 fl oz dry white wine, preferably *txacoli*
250 g/8 oz small clams or cockles, rinsed
or 250 g/8 oz mussels, cleaned *(see page 91)*
8 tablespoons chopped parsley
1 hard-boiled egg, chopped

————— SERVES 4 —————

Salt the fish pieces. Heat the butter and oil in a casserole into which all the fish will fit comfortably, preferably one made of flameproof earthenware. Fry the garlic gently (to flavour the oil) until coloured, then remove and reserve. Add the fish pieces, skin up for fillets. Fry them briskly, 2–3 minutes on each side, adding the shellfish when the fish is turned.

Remove half the oil and grasp the casserole on both sides with gloves. Give it a steady swinging movement, in a small circle (to agitate the fish). On a gas stove keep it moving on the turned-off plate. It takes about 20 minutes for the sauce to thicken and whiten. Return the oil in spoonfuls, still shaking the casserole, to work this in.

Add the fish stock and white wine, working them in gently and bring back to a simmer. Stir in the parsley, check the seasoning and garnish with chopped egg.

Gastaíka

————— RAY OR SKATE WITH CHILLI OIL —————

A distinguished dish. I was advised to buy sections of wing from a 30 kg/65 lb skate for this. And they were good: neater, meatier strips than wings from smaller fish. Whatever the size, the fish always falls beautifully from the bones.

1.5 kg/3 lb skate (or ray) wings, in 6 portions
1 onion, thinly sliced
1 leek with some green, sliced
handful of parsley stalks, bruised
salt

CHILLI OIL

5 tablespoons sherry vinegar or wine vinegar
200 ml/7 fl oz olive oil
5 garlic cloves, finely chopped
1 dried *guindilla* or other chilli,
seeded and finely chopped

————— SERVES 6 —————

Choose a wide flameproof casserole and put in just enough water to poach the wings. Add the onion, leek and parsley, season with salt and give it a headstart of 15 minutes cooking. Add the skate and poach – just 3–4 minutes if thin. Remove the fish to a big warm serving dish.

Put the vinegar in a small pan and boil to reduce by half. Throw it over the fish. Heat the oil in the same pan with the garlic cloves until they colour (seconds), then add the chilli pieces. Pour this over the fish. When the oil and vinegar have mingled, pour them back into the pan, reheat and pour them over the fish a second time. Serve at once.

Note: one of the best stocks for cooking fish – and one of the quickest! Afterwards strain and keep as fish stock.

Huge skate, whose fins or 'wings' are a delicacy in any sauce

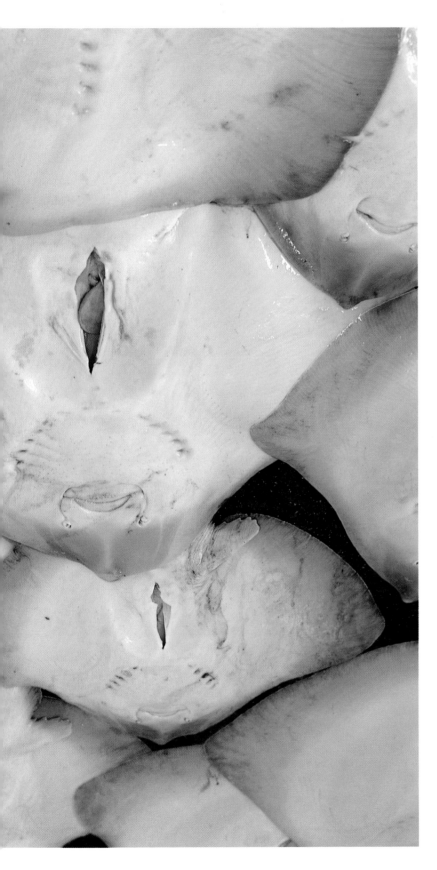

Puddingmania and the New Cuisine

'Oh, many kitchen drawers in the Basque country have a cutting of a fish pudding recipe,' I was told. 'There was a wave of it, a *budínmania*, when *la nueva cocina vasca* became famous' – in the late '70s and early '80s. Some fish, like *cabracho* (the spiny scorpion fish), are nicer without their bones. And 'canned *bonito*' (skipjack tuna) 'has more flavour for *budín*' than the fresh fish. I listened hard, for this was a very good cook speaking. 'Mix it', she said, 'with puréed potato and 2–3 egg yolks, no whites. Cover with mayonnaise and strips of *pimiento* and pickled cucumber.'

The enthusiasm for *nueva cocina* came from France. 'Most of Spain is cut off from France by butter and cream. The Spanish don't use it.' Not true here in the Basque country, where they still covet 'their' provinces over the border and share many cookery traditions. There is good Spanish (or Basque) cooking over the border too, for instance at Les Pyrénées in St Jean-Pied-de-Port. And Firmín Arrambide, the chef there, was keen to help Spanish chefs learn new ways.

La nueva cocina vasca: is it just *nouvelle cuisine* in Spanish? To me it summons up a picture of a *beguiaundi*, a great fat cuttlefish, criss-crossed from the barbecue, with a coal-black sauce round it. Or a pair of stuffed peppers under a black blanket, with pink tentacles of the squid making the only colour.

'It's definitely Spanish. Our chefs caught the bug from big stars like Bocuse, the Troisgros brothers and Outhier in France.' But you can ignore the decorative aspect, or juxtaposition of new flavours, which interest Juán Arzak and Pedro Subijana (famous San Sebastián chefs). The point of it, I learned, was that it was done entirely with local ingredients. Like that black sauce. It comes from line-caught squid, only fished on these shores. Squid panic and expel their ink when caught in nets, and end up in markets elsewhere without any.

La nueva cocina preached things people wanted to hear. Get rid of difficulties and long cooking! Look for simplicity and local things! It has had the happy effect of giving everyone a confidence in their local cooking – though it makes it more difficult to publish Spanish recipes abroad. And the effect has been quite notable. For it has done a great deal to civilize the excesses of oil or lard in peasant dishes right across Spain.

Budín de merluza

PINK SOUFFLED FISH PUDDING

A really delicious light pudding, and a pretty salmon colour, so it is also called *merluza asalmonada*. I like this version because the fish has some texture: versions made in a blender are smooth but anonymous. It is often made with *cabracho* (scorpion fish), a good way to avoid its bones and spines. Vary the composition if you like, adding a proportion of prawns – good in a blended mixture.

FOR A 1.5-LT/2½-PT BREAD TIN

750 g/1½ lb hake or cod fillet
about 700 ml/1½ pt fish stock, water and white wine,
or salted water
½ large onion, finely chopped
1 tablespoon olive oil
2 garlic cloves, finely chopped
750 g/1½ lb ripe tomatoes,
skinned, seeded and chopped
2 tablespoons finely chopped parsley
½ teaspoon sugar
salt and freshly ground black pepper
40 g/1½ oz butter, plus extra for greasing
1 slice of stale bread, soaked in 2 tablespoons milk
4 large egg yolks
3 large egg whites

SERVES 6

Heat the fish stock or other liquid, then slip in the fish (making sure it is covered). Cover and, when it returns to the boil, remove from the heat.

Meanwhile, fry the onion in the oil in a saucepan. When it colours, add the garlic, chopped tomatoes and parsley. Cook until the sauce thickens. Press the sauce through a sieve (or blend) and season with sugar, salt and pepper. Grease the bread tin well with butter, line the bottom and long sides with grease-proof paper or foil, and grease again well.

Remove the fish from the poaching liquid and shred it with 2 forks, discarding skin and bones. Heat the butter in a wide saucepan and gently warm the shredded fish, forking in the crumbled bread. Add the tomato sauce and heat through. Check the seasoning again and then beat in the egg yolks off the heat.

Whisk the egg whites with a pinch of salt in a large bowl to soft peaks, then lightly fold in the fish mixture. Turn into the prepared tin. Stand in a small roasting tin and pour boiling water round to come

two-thirds up the sides of the bread tin. Cook in a moderate oven (180°C/350°F/gas 4) for 50 minutes.

Wait a couple of moments, then run a knife round the pudding and turn out on to a serving plate. Best served hot (with a cream-and-parsley or tomato sauce if you wish), but can also be eaten cold. Chill, then spread with a thin mayonnaise just before serving.

Note: one woman suggested 8 tablespoons of tomato ketchup and 8 tablespoons of cream as a shortcut for the sauce.

Solomillo con salsa de berros

STEAK WITH WATERCRESS SAUCE

Steaks in the Basque country are enormous, well-hung and well-grilled. Cream sauces are popular: Roquefort (see page 106) and this one, with peppery watercress.

4 rump steaks or entrecôtes,
300–350 g/10–12 oz each
40 g/1½ oz butter
salt and freshly ground black pepper
4 tablespoons Spanish brandy or armagnac

WATERCRESS SAUCE
15 g/½ oz butter
2 shallots, finely chopped
150 ml/5 fl oz white wine
or 100 ml/3½ fl oz dry white vermouth
300 ml/½ pt meat juice
or well-reduced meat stock
bunch of watercress, picked over and chopped
125 ml/4 fl oz thick cream

SERVES 4

Melt the butter in a saucepan and cook the shallots. When soft, add the wine, meat stock and watercress and boil to reduce by half. Purée (in a blender), then add the cream and reduce again. Add salt to taste.

Heat the butter and fry the well-seasoned steaks to your taste. Pour the brandy over and flame it, scooping the juices back over the steaks. Serve at once, with the sauce.

Quality is appreciated in the Basque
country and ingredients are superb

Reinettas en salsa de limón

BAKED APPLE WITH LEMON SAUCE

A pleasant contrast of hot, slightly caramelized apple pieces and a rather tart lemon sauce. Thick cream is served as an accompaniment – a reverse of the usual truth that lemon juice cuts the fat!

6 *reinettas* or Cox's apples
about 100 g/4 oz caster sugar
butter for greasing
about 175 ml/6 fl oz thick cream, whipped

TART LEMON SAUCE
75 g/3 oz sugar
75 ml/3 fl oz water
2 strips of lemon zest and juice of 2 lemons
2 teaspoons cornflour
25 g/1 oz unsalted butter
1 egg yolk

SERVES 6

Peel and core the apples and cut into 6–8 wedges, according to size. Toss them in sugar and arrange (core side upwards) on a heavy baking sheet greased with butter. Sprinkle more sugar over them, then bake in a hot oven (220°C/425°F/gas 7) for 10 minutes, until the sugar starts to caramelize on the sheet. Give the apples a stir to coat well.

Meanwhile put the sugar and water for the sauce in a pan with the strips of lemon zest. Bring slowly to the boil, then boil for 5 minutes. Leave off the heat to infuse. Dissolve the cornflour in a little lemon juice. Pour the hot lemon syrup on to it and return to the pan. Stir over low heat until thickened. Discard the zest pieces and add the remaining lemon juice. Bring back to the boil, then add the butter and egg yolk. Stir off the heat.

Centre the apple wedges on 4 plates, pour the lemon sauce round and pass whipped cream.

CHAPTER 9

Aragon and Navarre

Aragon and Navarre have their heads in high mountains, but feet in the warm river valley. Huge Aragon, once a proud kingdom, straddles the Ebro valley that runs parallel to the Pyrenees. Navarre borders Rioja, a small province which makes fashionable fruity wines.

The great, snaking, wooded pass of Roncevalles, full of rocks, looming trees and potential ambushes, forces its way through the Pyrenees into Navarre. The west route into Spain, there are signposts in France, three days' drive away, to Santiago de Compostella. It is a place full of ghosts: Roland's lost army, massacred 1200 years ago, and pilgrims to the shrine of St James, who came here in medieval times.

is related to the original blanc-mange (found across Europe, with almond milk and minced chicken). This dish is made with bread, milk and sugar, enriched with chicken fat. It is still popular as a dessert.

Aragon has crops, too, which no one else cultivates, such as borage with its bright blue flowers with black points and hairy stalks. 'It takes a morning to wash it.' Stalks and leaves are boiled and served as a vegetable, with potatoes and oil. The leaves taste of cucumber and can also be made into sweet fritters (see page 161).

Two million pilgrims a year travelled to Santiago 500 year ago. They shaped the road system to run west, not towards Madrid, as it tries to now. The hillsides here are full of monasteries, usually in inaccessible places. Pilgrim dishes remain too, like *bacalao ajoarriero*, a white dish of salt cod, eggs and garlic, which has tomato added in modern versions (see page 111).

Old ways endure still, but for how long? *Migas*, fried breadcrumbs crisp and hot from the pan, are served with chocolate sauce or grapes – and in Aragon with pork *torreznos* (see page 42). 'Very fatty and so *good*!' I was told. Behind it are older dishes. *Migas* were once just flour, stirred and stirred in the frying pan. They do this still, with golden cornmeal, to make *gachas* in Zaragosa. *Regañaos* is a primitive pizza, a flat bread with *pimiento* in it, topped with sardines. And *sopa cana*

Cooking here is simple: grilled chops are popular. *Costillas a la baturra* they are called: 'cooked by a country bumpkin'. But rustic cooking also embraces spit-roast lamb and goat, served in hot hunks with melting golden garlicky *allioli*. These mountains rear some of the best lamb in Spain, and simplicity suits *ternasco*, lamb roasted young and small with garlic lending its savour to new potatoes, and *cochifrito*, tender lamb strips in lemon juice.

The region is called the *zona de chilindrones*. Quite why these stews should be named for a card game, no one knows. But I learned how to play it: a simple Patience, for two or four people. The stews are flavoured with peppers, once with dried *choricero*. The best is lamb *chilindrón de cordero* (see page 125).

Mountain foods include freshwater crayfish, flavoured with the same peppers, and rabbit with snails (which eat wild rosemary and so form a walking bouquet garni), *conejo con caracoles*. Equally famous are the fine brown trout. *A la navarra*, they are cooked in red wine with thyme, and are perfection fried in the pan with raw ham: one version is on page 124). Teruel, across the Ebro, makes one of the finest raw *serranos* in Spain. Another favourite ham dish is *magras con tomate*, ham slices in fresh tomato sauce.

The Pyrenees is a truly formidable barrier, both high and wide, air icy with the tang of old snow. We drove once more to the rim, up to the Val d'Arán. Forty years ago it was cut off from Spain for six months of the years,

Borage in Aragon is an unusual (and hairy) vegetable

120

until the tunnel was built. Now a ski area, every *borda* (barn restaurant) has gourmet ambitions, and offers home-cooked stews on Villeroy and Boch plates.

Game birds are netted flying through the mountain passes. *Perdices al chocolate*, partridges in chocolate sauce, came from Aragon, and is now popular across Spain. Turtle doves are cooked on the grill, basted with lard, vinegar and red wine, and quail are roasted in fig leaves. Quail are at their fattest when hunting starts on 15th September, and their return is joyously celebrated in a stew of fresh kidney beans, *pochas con codornices*. 'They must be the fresh beans, not dried ones – even *fabes de La Granja*.'

History dominates here as much as geography. The Arabs came and left dishes like *pollo en pepitoria*, fried chicken with a delicate sauce of saffron, garlic and pounded nuts, as well as almond sweetmeats like *ghirlache* (see page 128). One is constantly reminded that Aragon was once a powerful kingdom, ruling the south of France and land as far away as Sardinia, Naples and Sicily. And Sos del Rey Católico – a dust-coloured hill with a very plain palace – is the birthplace of King Ferdinand, for ever remembered for uniting Spain by marrying Isabella of Castile – 'the Catholic Kings'.

Some French influence is visible in Navarre: dishes with Bayonne ham and many vegetables. *Pote con coles* is a solid cabbage soup, rather like *garbure* in neighbouring French Béarn. And Navarre red wines can be reminiscent of beaujolais nouveau. At Roncal a fine hard cheese (with rice holes) is made; it mostly goes to France. Junket, *cuajada*, is sold everywhere in earthenware pots and eaten with honey.

But it is the fruit that I best remember. Zaragosa to Teruel, mile on mile of orchards, with plums, cherries and apples. The *melecotones* (peaches) of Zaragosa must be the world's largest. They were memorable baked in red wine, tops just clear and crusted in baked sugar. The chocolate-coated candied fruit are also delicious! Fruit is also made into *retacías* (ratafias) liqueurs made by adding fresh juice to a spirit.

Some of the best *rosados* (rosé wines) come from Navarre, and Aragon makes purplish reds in Cariñena and somewhat lighter ones in Somontana. Sloes from the mountain slopes are the main ingredient of *pacharán*. It is a mild anis-flavoured brandy, drunk 'on the rocks'. Zoco, the principal brand, make a red one for export. It is Spain's most popular liqueur.

Lentejas de Ordesa

LENTILS WITH LEEKS AND MUSHROOMS

The sweet alcohol makes a pleasant final addition to this dish. If using something like Pernod (which is not sweet) for the anis, I add a pinch of sugar

500 g/1 lb green lentils, soaked for at least 6 hours
1 piece of ham bone *(see note)*
2 tablespoons olive oil
1 onion, chopped
2 leeks, white and edible green, sliced
250 g/8 oz mushrooms, preferably wild,
cleaned and sliced
2 big ripe tomatoes, skinned, seeded and chopped
2 sprigs of fresh thyme
1 sprig of fresh rosemary
1 *morcilla* or 200 g/7 oz black pudding
salt and freshly ground black pepper
2–3 tablespoons moscatel wine
or anis liqueur (or Pernod)
pinch of sugar (optional)

SERVES 6

Put the drained lentils in a pan with the ham bone (or bacon, if you choose this option) and add water just to cover. Skim if necessary and simmer for 1 hour.

Meanwhile heat the oil in a large frying pan and soften the onion, adding the chopped leeks and mushrooms towards the end. When these wilt, add the chopped tomatoes and herbs and cook until soft. When the lentils are done, remove the bone (if using – or shred the bacon) and add to the frying pan with the sliced *morcilla* or black pudding if using. Cook for 10 more minutes. Before serving season to taste, adding the wine, or liqueur, with a pinch of sugar if it is not sweet.

Note: ham bones, sawn into rings, are available in most Spanish markets. A piece can be popped into a stew like a stock cube. Outside Spain I use a piece of unsmoked boiling bacon (about 200 g/7 oz) to replace both this and the *morcilla*.

Chilindrón de cordero

LAMB STEWED WITH PEPPERS

Named for a card game, this dish has a long and famous history in Navarre, and is about what peppers – the queen of hearts – will do for lamb. Old recipes use only dried *choricero* peppers. 'No tomato,' I was told. 'This is a stew of lamb and peppers – about two dried peppers each. Extract the pulp after soaking them. And no water. There's lots of onion and this gives all the liquid needed.' I love these spare recipes with tightly-balanced seasoning: impossible, though, to get the right dried peppers elsewhere.

1.5 kg/3 lb boneless shoulder of lamb, cubed
2–4 tablespoons olive oil
salt and freshly ground black pepper
2 onions, chopped
2 garlic cloves, finely chopped
4–6 big ripe tomatoes, skinned and seeded
2 big red peppers, grilled and skinned *(see page 52)*,
or canned pimientos
2 tablespoons finely chopped parsley
1 bay leaf
good pinch of cayenne pepper

SERVES 4–5

Heat 3 tablespoons oil in a flameproof casserole and fry the seasoned lamb, in 2 batches, over high heat until browned on all sides, then remove from the pan.

Fry the onions, adding more oil if needed, adding the garlic at the end. Chop the tomato and red peppers finely (or process), then add with the parsley, bay leaf and cayenne. Cook for a few minutes to make a sauce, then season and return the lamb. Simmer for 1 hour, covered, over very low heat. It makes its own liquid, but check occasionally that the heat is low enough.

Taste for seasoning, thinking particularly about pepper and cayenne: it should be just spicy. Surprisingly, you may even have to boil off a little liquid – it's pure lamb essence.

Note: also good made with chicken. Diced raw ham (or bacon) – about 100 g/4 oz – is usually included too.

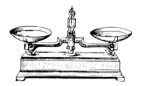

Pichones con pasas y piñones

PIGEONS WITH RAISINS AND PINE NUTS

Serve with the good alcoholic red wines of Cariñena. The dish is also good made with partridges, when it will serve 8.

4 pigeons, cleaned
125 g/4 oz muscatel raisins,
preferably from Malaga
salt and freshly ground black pepper
4 tablespoons olive oil
2 onions, chopped
3 garlic cloves, finely chopped
1 tablespoon plain flour
2 ripe tomatoes, skinned, seeded and chopped
(or 4 canned ones)
2 tablespoons finely chopped parsley
200 ml/7 fl oz Cariñena or red Côte de Rhône
about 300 ml/10 fl oz good meat or poultry stock
4 tablespoons Spanish brandy or cognac
1 bay leaf
freshly grated nutmeg
50 g/2 oz pine nuts

SERVES 4

Pour boiling water to cover over the raisins. Reach into the neck of each bird and run finger and thumb nails up the wishbone to the top; pull it out. Salt and pepper the birds inside and out. Choose a flameproof casserole into which they fit snugly. Heat the oil and spend 20–25 minutes browning the birds on all 3 sides. Remove and keep warm.

Add the chopped onions to the pot, and fry gently until soft, adding the garlic towards the end. Sprinkle with the flour and cook for 1 minute. Stir in the chopped tomatoes, parsley, wine, stock, brandy and bay leaf, and season with a little nutmeg.

Snug the birds back into the casserole and simmer until tender, about 1½ hours, though tough wild birds in Spain may need 2 hours. Keep an eye on the liquid level – spare liquid from the raisins can be used to top up the pan. Meanwhile dry-fry the pine nuts over low heat in a frying pan for 2–3 minutes.

Remove the birds and sieve the sauce (or blend, first discarding the bay leaf). Return the birds and sauce to the pot, adding the drained raisins (seeded if necessary) and pine nuts. Simmer for 10 more minutes, then check the seasonings. Green cabbage is the best accompaniment.

⋐ A Day in the High Hills ⋑

We climbed the Col of Leyre: the first limestone crest that edges the Pyrenees from Navarre. Crawling through the scrub and up the cramped rock chimneys, towards the sky above. It was full of wheeling griffon vultures.

At the top we turned back, to see where we had come from: a man-made lake and the monastery of Leyre, where we were staying. The monastery has been there for 1000 years, in total quiet and almost unchanged country. The previous evening we heard the monks sing Vespers, plainsong that would have been familiar anywhere in Europe 500 years ago. The sun through the west door illuminated a splendid 12th-century apse, unusual with three equal arches.

I ate my first cardoons that night at supper, white stalks, blanched in a head while growing (like celery), by tying black plastic bags round them.

Above: Pink columbines in a grassy corner of Navarre

This is how the kitchen cooked them. Cut the stalks in lengths: they need a lot of washing. Cook them in a pot with plenty of boiling water and the pulp of $\frac{1}{2}$ lemon, to keep them white, for about 40 minutes. Pass them through flour, then eggs beaten with salt, and fry them in plenty of oil. Make a little white sauce by frying onion in the cooking oil, then add flour, some cooking water and a little milk. On Christmas Eve the dish also has ham in it, and is also eaten in other parts of Spain.

From our hilltop we viewed a range of valleys. The Pyrenees is made up of many rows of mountains, slopes filled with pines and high sward for grazing. There are wild things here in plenty, crayfish and trout. I slept on a thyme bank and woke to find a small rabbit by my face. How good *that* would be cooked with *that*, I thought.

123

Pâté del Alto Aragón

PORK PATE FROM THE MOUNTAINS,
WITH APPLES AND NUTS

An economical coarse pâté with lots of interesting flavours and textures. If pork fat is a difficult purchase, use half lean boneless pork and half lean pork belly.

FOR A 1.5-LT/2½-PT BREAD TIN

300 g/10 oz pork liver or chicken livers
about 125 ml/4 fl oz milk
100 g/4 oz pork fat, finely diced
1 onion, chopped
150 g/5 oz mushrooms, preferably wild,
cleaned and sliced
2–3 russet dessert apples, chopped
400 g/14 oz boneless lean pork, cubed
100 g/4 oz cooked chestnuts *(see page 88)* or hazelnuts
4 small eggs
1 sprig of fresh tarragon (12 leaves)
½ teaspoon cumin seeds, crushed
salt and ground white pepper

SERVES 6

Soak the livers in milk for 2 hours. Drain well and slice.

Put the pork fat in a frying pan over low heat and sweat until it gives off fat. Add the onion and fry over medium heat until it starts to soften, adding the mushrooms towards the end, then the chopped apple. Cook until starting to wilt.

Put the meat through a mincer (or use a food processor) followed by the liver, vegetables from the pan (including the pork fat scraps) and the nuts. Beat in the eggs and season with the tarragon, cumin, salt and pepper. Fry a spoonful in the unwashed pan to check seasoning.

Pour into the bread tin, cover with foil and stand in a bain-marie, pouring in boiling water to come halfway up the sides of the tin. Cook in a moderate oven (180°C/350°F/gas 4) for 1¼–1½ hours. Check with a skewer that the centre is cooked – it should come out clean. Serve with toast and eat within 48 hours; it doesn't mature.

The rim of the Pyrenees lends a sense of vast space to Navarre and Aragon

Truchas con serrano y hierbabuena

TROUT WITH RAW HAM AND MINT

A simple recipe for trout with raw ham. I was surprised mint and ham went so well together.

4 trout, cleaned
1 handful of fresh mint
125 ml/4 fl oz dry white white
salt and freshly ground black pepper
4 thin slices of raw ham
(75 g/3 oz packet prosciutto)
2 tablespoons bacon fat,
from frying streaky rashers
boiled potatoes, in rounds, to serve
about 2 tablespoons good olive oil

--- SERVES 4 ---

Ahead, extend the belly cavity of each trout, cutting up on one side of the backbone with a knife. Bending them makes the little rib bones pop up; snip these off with scissors. Stuff with several sprigs of crushed mint. Pack the fish head to tail into a dish where they fit closely and pour the wine over them. Leave in a cool place for at least 6 hours.

Pat the fish dry with kitchen paper (reserving the marinade) and season inside. Roll up the ham and stuff into the trout with a mint leaf on either side. Fry the trout over medium heat in the hot bacon fat, 5 minutes each side, when the skin will be crisp.

Serve accompanied by well-seasoned potatoes with the hot marinade poured over them, and sprinkled with good oil. Garnish with more mint if wished.

Conejo con patatas

RABBIT STEWED WITH POTATOES
---

2 wild rabbits, about 800 g/2 lb 10 oz each
250 ml/8 fl oz water
2 tablespoons wine vinegar
4 tablespoons Spanish brandy or cognac
6 tablespoons olive oil
salt and freshly ground pepper
2 sprigs of fresh thyme
1 bay leaf
500 g/1 lb onions, thinly sliced
2 fat garlic cloves, finely chopped
400 g/14 oz canned tomatoes
250 ml/8 fl oz red wine
600 g/1¼ lb potatoes

--- SERVES 6 ---

Ahead, wash the cleaned rabbits free of any blood inside and soak in water and vinegar overnight. Pat dry and split the front legs from the ribs. Cut free the flaps from the saddle and cut all the thin end pieces into flat portions. Put all the pieces in a flat dish and sprinkle with brandy. Marinate for 2 hours or till ready to cook.

Heat the oil in a wide frying pan (there should be enough to float the rabbit, as it is wettish). Salt and pepper the rabbit and fry the back legs and saddles until golden on all sides – 15–20 minutes. Remove from the pan to an earthenware casserole and heat the oven to 180°C/350°F/gas 4. Fry the remaining rabbit pieces more briefly and add to the casserole with any remaining marinade. Tuck in the thyme and break up the bay leaf.

Fry the onions slowly in the frying pan until soft, then add the chopped garlic. Add the tomatoes (canned in these modern times), breaking them up, with the wine. Bring gently to the boil and pour over the rabbit. Cook in the oven for about 1 hour until it is approaching tender.

Cut the potatoes into chip shapes and add to the casserole, distributing them, and pushing them under the sauce. Return to the oven to cook for 30 minutes longer until the potatoes are tender. Covering helps if the liquid is low.

Left: Fresh peas from the Ebro valley

Tudela: of Asparagus and Jews

'Synonymous with asparagus: the *tortilla de Tudela*.' 'No, it is *cogollos* (lettuce hearts). What about the *cogollos de Tudela*?' Then *menestra* – a stew of young vegetables – then an almond candy. If all these beautiful things came from Tudela, on the Ebro, then I had to go there. It is the centre of the great vegetable garden of the north, which stretches from the lower Rioja down the valley.

The riverbank gives its name to one of the nicest sauces for hake, *merluza a la ribera navarra*, with green peas and asparagus tips. So popular is it that many restaurants will serve it for *merluza a la koxkera* (see page 114)! Navarre is also known for fresh white kidney beans – *pochas* – and many recipes for young beans in the pod, usually with ham or a little tomato. Alas we have forgotten such things exist and can only do such recipes with sugar snap peas!

I went in search of Tudela's past citizens. The Arabs were here, and the Jews. There is strong evidence of the former in the town: brick houses in the Mudejar style. In the countryside the lower plains of Navarre have

mile on mile of cultivated almonds, not relegated to the hills as they are in Andalusia. And in the cake shop on the corner of the colourfully painted town square, the Plaza de los Fueros, I counted 12 different almond cakes including a *turrón de Tudela*. It was marzipan with toasted nuts inside.

Perhaps the citizens had infidels in mind when the horrors of hell were carved on the cathedral Judgement door. Though there is less evidence of them, Tudela is equally famous for its Jews. In the 12th century Benjamín de Tudela was a noted rabbi. Little is left of the *judería* here; they are better preserved at Hervás and Gerona. In agriculture and commerce – and, of course, the *cocido* (see page 56) – what a lot Spain owes to both its *descreídos*!

When the Jews were expelled, in 1492, at Queen Isabella's instigation, they were allowed to take nothing but their house keys. The story is told, in Cordoba, of families walking round now, trying keys in old doors. And one, at least, turned. Its owner bought the house, believing it had belonged to his forebears.

Esparragos con huevos

ASPARAGUS WITH POACHED EGGS

Eggs and asparagus are common in *tortilla* (omelette) and *revuelta* (scrambled) – or just plain.

1 kg/2 lb asparagus, washed
salt and ground white pepper
4 large eggs
1 tablespoon vinegar
2 tablespoons olive oil
1 tablespoon plain flour
2 tablespoons chopped parsley

SERVES 4 AS A STARTER OR SUPPER DISH

Cut the hard bases off the asparagus and peel the stems as necessary. Simmer the trimmings for 15 minutes, then discard. Use the salted asparagus water to cook the stems very gently until just tender – 12–15 minutes for green asparagus, longer for blanched shoots.

Meanwhile poach the eggs in simmering water with the vinegar (see page 55), and keep warm.

Heat the oil in a flameproof casserole and stir in the flour. Cook for a minute. Off the heat stir in 250 ml/8 fl oz of the asparagus cooking water and bring back to a simmer, stirring. Season to taste, add the asparagus stems and eggs, and rewarm the stems. Serve sprinkled with parsley.

Note: I was given the tip to slit slightly any asparagus stalk that was thick, so that it cooked in the same time as the tip.

Cogollos de Tudela

LETTUCE HEART AND ANCHOVY SALAD

Buy a pointed, hearted lettuce per person, such as Little Gem, wash it as necessary and put it in a bag in the fridge to chill. At serving time, cut each lettuce into 4 wedges, dribble with vinaigrette and arrange a split canned anchovy fillet in a cross on each one. A popular summer starter.

Cordero a la pastora

—— LAMB WITH NEW VEGETABLES AND MILK ——

This 'shepherdess's' recipe uses an abundance of new vegetables and milk – unusual for Spain.

1.4 kg/3 lb lean boneless lamb shoulder, cubed

2 tablespoons olive oil

12 baby or 6 large spring globe artichokes

1 tablespoon plain flour

75 ml/3 fl oz white wine

12 sprigs of fresh mint, or more

4 sprigs of fresh thyme

1 bay leaf

6 bruised parsley stalks

salt and ground white pepper

250–350 ml/8–12 fl oz full fat milk

4 tablespoons thick cream

2 tablespoons chopped parsley

800 g/1¾ lb boiled baby new potatoes, to serve

MARINADE

15 white peppercorns

2 cloves

3 garlic cloves, finely chopped

2 tablespoons vinegar

2 tablespoons olive oil

—————— SERVES 6 ——————

Marinate the lamb ahead. In a mortar crush the peppercorns and cloves to powder, then add the garlic and make a paste with the vinegar. Add the oil and work this into the lamb with your hands. Leave overnight.

Put the oil in a flameproof casserole over very low heat and add the lamb, tossing to make sure it is all oil-coated. Cover and leave to cook while you prepare the vegetables. Trim the artichokes, cutting off stalks and removing outside leaves and the tips down to the tender leaves if they are large. Quarter large artichokes (the chokes should still be small). Blanch the artichokes briefly in boiling water.

Uncover the casserole: the meat will have stiffened and made stock. Sprinkle with the flour and stir in, adding the wine to make a sauce. Tuck in plenty of mint, the thyme, bay leaf and parsley stalks. Salt the stew well and add pepper.

Stir in the artichokes. Cook over low heat until everything is tender – about 30 minutes. As the liquid disappears, replace it with milk – I used it all.

Remove the visible stalks (parsley, thyme and mint), then add the cream. Shake to mix the sauce, without letting it boil again. Stir in the potatoes (or serve separately). Check the seasonings and garnish with the chopped parsley, including a leaf or 2 of chopped mint.

Note: asparagus can be substituted for the artichokes, as can new peas and broad beans.

Cheerful *chorizo* salesman, with sausages for tapas and for frying and plenty of *tocino*

Guirlache

—— ALMOND AND ANISEED CANDY ——

Hardly known outside Spain, this is the least sweet version of the famous *turrón*. The aniseeds are unusual. It is sold commercially in a block, but I make little rounds to serve with ice cream.

250 g/8 oz almonds, half blanched, half unblanched

250 g/8 oz sugar

1 tablespoon lemon juice

½ teaspoon aniseeds, roughly crushed

1 teaspoon almond oil or a flavourless oil

—— MAKES 48 ——

Toast the almonds – 30 minutes in an oven at about 150°C/300°F/gas 2 – shaking the pan occasionally. They should become biscuit-coloured, smell pleasantly and be very dry.

Put the sugar and lemon juice in a small pan over high heat. As the sugar melts and colours round the edges, pull it towards the middle with a wooden spoon. Continue until it is all coffee-coloured. Tip in the almonds and stir once, then add the aniseeds. Spoon on to oiled foil, four nuts at a time (mixing the colours) to form little rounds.

Alternatively, spread out on the foil, keeping the nuts close together. Let it set for a couple of minutes, then use the foil to fold it over lengthways. Press it together with a rolling pin and pat with the side of the pin to make straight edges all round. Wrap the spare foil round and store as it is, in an airtight box. Chop off strips to eat.

✿ Olite Festival: Kings and Castles ✿

Olite Castle, once home to the kings of Navarre, would look familiar, even to those who have never visited Spain. For these are the towers and little turrets copied by Walt Disney for every fairytale castle. They are so well restored that they have a Lego-land feel about them, but their profile lends enchantment to the square.

It was late September in this small town in the Navarre foothills and it was en fête for its saint's day. The first impression was that everyone was wearing white, with a red neckerchief or red scarf attached at the waist. There were scarlet berets too – normal gear for Basque policemen. Even a baby in a pram had espadrilles laced with red ribbon.

Great stout gates cordoned the exits from the main square. The bulls had clearly been through earlier. But now it was all bands and dancing, a tune, followed by a recurring chorus. '¡Ya! ya! ya!' 'Now! Now! Now!' we shouted each time it came round, left then right hand punching in the air.

Not one but three bands were on duty, drums banging and blowing mightily. Here came the chorus again! Spectators rose from their perches and we revolved once more upon the spot.

The *gigantes* and *cabezudos* arrived, three tall kings and queens, their stilts covered with faded cotton robes. The *cabezudos* had vast heads of papier-maché. It dis-torted their proportions to Disneyland dwarves. One had a blown-up pig's bladder on a stick, which he bobbed round ankles, making people jump. I knew it was a medieval trick, but had never seen it.

The band passed round a *porrón* (glass drinking-kettle) between numbers. A thin spout of wine arched towards the mouth: a wettener, no more. There seemed little drunkenness, just immense good spirits. The crowd drank beer and ate *tapas* of bread with *lomo embuchado* (cured pork loin) or *chorizo de Pamplona*, which looks like salami and is the best of the *tapa* sausages.

Two bands set off round the town, each with a troupe of dancers. Now I noticed costumes. Teenage trios wearing the same – black or batman capes. What hours the young can dance! As they passed beneath the walls, they called to the people smiling in the balconies above. Throw it! Throw it! And glasses of water, sometimes buckets, were emptied down on the dancers to cool them. Occasionally it was a bottle of wine. Then, to general cheering, a boy positioned himself beneath, arms wide, mouth open to catch the red wine spout, and down the gullet.

CHAPTER 10

Catalonia

On the east coast, where the Pyrenees and the Mediterranean meet, Catalonia embraces the Costa Brava, a hinterland of mountains and vineyards, and a star in Barcelona. In many ways a northern city – efficient and interested in making money – it has an ebullient, southern style.

Salvador Dalí put bread loaves all over the outside of his house at Figueres. And why not? Made of yellow plaster, they are dotted regularly against a deep strawberry: the Catalan round loaf, twiddled at three corners, then slashed between them. He has vast brown eggs around the cornices, too. Don't go in summer. The Spanish adore his eccentricities and queue to enter.

Barcelona is the only city I know that has blue pavements: a pattern of snails and pumpkin leaves, designed by Gaudí (I saw the originals) along the Passeig de Gràcia, the major fashion street. Gaudí's buildings round the city are all disturbing. On La Pedrera the stone balloons look like the fantasies of a pastry cook: elsewhere it drips like a sauce. The towers of the Sagrada Familia are shaped like hock bottles, topped with bursting rockets. The inlaid ceramics in the Parque Güell have the colours of an *amanida* (arranged salad). Food is important in Barcelona. It is the universal hobby, in a city with 10,000 eateries.

All Catalan meals start with *pa amb tomàquet* – ripe tomato and good olive oil pressed on to very lightly toasted bread. Simple but excellent topped with *serrano* ham. Local ways with vegetables are sensitive, including many decorative salads. Called an *amanida*, the salad takes its name (like our word) from salt and means

seasoned. The *amanida catalana* often includes sausage and cured fish together.

The meat is good, and well barbecued. The best is *al sarmiento*, meaning over a fire of vine prunings (true of all Spain's wine provinces). This fire of intense heat means fast cooking, unlike most charcoal, which cooks quite slowly. Mixed grill is a *graellada*, splendid when it's fish and shellfish together, and this is often served Catalan style with *allioli* (garlic, oil and egg yolk sauce). Indeed, *allioli* (see page 138) accompanies many things here.

The coast is famed for fish stews and *sopa de musclos*, mussel soup with tomato and anis *aguardiente* (eau-de-vie). Snails and cuttlefish are much enjoyed, the latter often with peas.

Salt cod goes into salads such as *esqueixada*, made with strips of red pepper and tomatoes. *Xato* (pronounced 'château') is a dish I rate highly. It combines flakes of raw, soaked *bacalao inglés* (see page 110), which are translucent and salty, with two other cured fish – canned tuna and canned anchovy fillets – in an escarole salad with olives and a light dressing of *romesco* sauce (see page 140). The subtle, smoky *escalivada* (see page 144) is an unusual cooked vegetable salad.

The Ebro reaches the Mediterranean in Catalonia, a great delta growing rice. There are local rice dishes like *el rossejat*, rice first fried until coloured, then cooked in fish stock. This is served with *allioli* stirred into it, like the Murcian *arroz en caldero* (see page 154). In L'Empordà, *arròs negre* (black rice) was invented, a striking dish coloured with the ink of cuttlefish.

Barcelona also has a *paella*. *La parellada* was created for a dandy, Julí Parrellada, at the beginning of the 20th century: his house is now the Barcelona Atheneum. Without bones, shells or any other interruptions, its popularity has spread – it is called *paella ciega* in Majorca – you can eat it with your eyes shut!

Barcelona was once the capital of a kingdom (House of Aragon) that ruled southern France, and as far away as Southern Italy and Sicily. There are dishes and foods with Spanish names across Languedoc still. Catalonia leans towards France, though the weight of Spain is towards Africa. There is often a French way of looking at things – the ç with a cedilla (pronounced S), for instance, as well as white sauces and *jamón de pato* (cured duck breasts).

Catalonia has sauces, too, to challenge the Basque ones. *Samfaina* is made with tomatoes, peppers, courgettes and aubergine on a fried onion base. *Salmoretta* (see page 154) is similar but fishy. And there's *allioli* with garlic, and *romesco* (based on nuts and chillies).

In Catalonia the *picada* reaches perfection. The idea of a condiment puréed in a mortar will be familiar if you have read to Chapter 10, for the *picada* is used throughout Spain, and is of Moorish origin. In Catalonia there is almost a standardized version, with a nice balance of garlic, bread, nuts and parsley, to which fish livers are added if to be used in a fish dish. It serves the double purpose of thickening a visible amount of liquid and added seasoning at the end of cooking.

Vic is known for sausages – *salchichón* of the salami type (but with larger fat flecks) – and the surrounding hills for a smell of piggeries. But Catalonia's chief sausage is the fresh white *botifarra*, famous with beans as *mongetes amb botifarra*, and eaten with *rovellon* (wild mushrooms) in autumn. There is also a black one – and even a sweet *butifarrón dulç* with sugar and lemon. From the mountains come dishes such as rabbit with herbs and hare with chestnuts. *Escudella i carn d'olla* is a slow-simmered pot in the same tradition as the Madrid *cocido* (see page 56). It provides a soup first, then the *carn d'olla* or meat (which, in this case, is one vast dumpling). A century ago it was eaten daily, except in Lent and Semana Santa. These are the seasons for *panadones*, pies of spinach, raisins and pine nuts.

'*Tienes pasta?*' 'Have you any cash?' As in our slang, dough is synonymous with money. Visiting Italians made pasta part of the diet here. Old rice dishes now have pasta versions. *Fideos rossejat*, for instance, consists of short spaghetti lengths fried, then cooked in fish stock and served with *allioli*. *Fideos* are also eaten with sausages. Cannellonis are stuffed with liver, pork and veal (or ham, brains and foie-gras), and I came across an unusual version that also had canned tuna added to the béchamel topping.

The parallels between Barcelona and Italy are clear. Italian chefs were fashionable in the 19th century, and made Barcelona one of the best restaurant cities in Europe. Now Barcelona airport upstairs is like an Italian art gallery – miles of marble flooring screened by a double glass window with scaffolding in the vortex. Spain in the 1990s has that buzz of creativity and going-somewhere that made Italy such an exciting place in the 1970s.

Miles of orchards in Lerida produce fruits for dessert. Cream cheese is eaten with honey (*mato con miel*), and *menjar blanco* is an almond milk pudding that once contained chicken. In *crema catalana* there is the best (and possibly the original) crème brûlée. Redolent of cinnamon and lemon, the net of grilled sugar is now copied in top French restaurants. Festive fritters include *bunyols* and the All Saints *panellets*, little cakes based on sweet potato and pine nuts.

The general ebullience and desire to break the mould, evident in the art world, turns up in food too – birds with fruit, for instance: gosling with pears for Christmas and duck with figs. There are dazzlingly-brave combinations – though not the eccentricity of the Italian Marinetti. Hot apple rings with anchovy, for instance, or peaches stuffed with ham and then baked in a sauce with chocolate. Catalans are not the inventors of surf and turf: it dates from the Romans. But *mar y muntanya* is a live tradition: pork with mussels, chicken and scampi (see page 142) or chicken with lobster – in an elaborate sauce with puréed nuts and chocolate.

The region makes some of the best white wine in Spain, on French models, and often with French grapes in Penedès and Allela. There are good cabernet sauvignons from Jean León and Raimat – and cherry-red *rosados* from Ampurdán. And to celebrate it all, glasses of sparkling *cava*. For Sant Sadurní de Anoia is the world's biggest producer of wines by the champagne method.

A wealth of vegetables in La Boquería

Tarragona makes communion wine for the whole of Europe – and Chartreuse (it was exiled here from France from 1902 to 1940). It also makes fine *vi rancio*, dark, strong and rounded, like an old dry sherry. The Costa Brava is also famous for *cremat*, a drink of flamed rum (together with brandy – or moonshine made from sugar locally) poured into hot coffee.

Rap amb all cremat

MONKFISH WITH CARAMELIZED GARLIC

Garlic is capable of a vast range of tastes, including the mild fresh green shoots of spring, the aggressive crushed raw clove, and the seasoning of this sauce, which is caramelized or 'burnt'. The shellfish texture and taste and texture of monkfish are ideal for this fish stew.

700 g/1½ lb monkfish tail (or other white fish)
about 90 ml/3 fl oz olive oil
350 g/12 oz ripe tomatoes, skinned, seeded and chopped
700 ml/1¼ pt fish stock
salt and freshly ground black pepper
700 g/1½ lb waxy potatoes, cut in rounds
1 bay leaf
2 tablespoons chopped parsley
allioli (see page 137), to serve

CONDIMENT
6 garlic cloves, cut in rounds
2 slices of stale bread, crusts removed
1 dried *guindilla*, seeded and chopped
or a good pinch of cayenne pepper
3 tablespoons chopped parsley
4 tablespoons *vi rancio*, dry *oloroso* or other sherry

SERVES 4

Heat the oil and cook the garlic pieces, standing by with a slotted spoon to remove them the moment they turn deep golden (not burnt, which would make the sauce bitter). In the same oil brown the bread slices (which should not be too thick) until deep gold. Fry the *guindilla* too and save them together.

Cook the tomatoes in the remaining oil, reducing it to a sauce. Add the hot fish stock, bring to simmering, season and add the potatoes and the bay leaf. Simmer until almost done – about 20 minutes.

Meanwhile, pound the garlic in a mortar (or blend) with salt, the parsley, *guindilla* (or cayenne), bread and some black pepper, working to a paste with the wine.

With care stir the garlic paste into the sauce to make a dark cream – fishermen call this chocolate.

Cut the fish into fingers and season. Add to the sauce and cook for another 5 minutes or so. Check the seasonings and serve very hot, sprinkled with parsley and accompanied by golden *allioli*.

Note: the potatoes must be completely cooked before adding a softer white fish, such as cod etc.

Pechugas de pollo Villeroy

CHICKEN BREASTS IN CREAM-AND-CRUMBS

Once French, this is now such a Spanish classic that Lhardy's in Madrid sells it prepared, to cook at home. The sauce is also good for coating brochettes of mussels and other shellfish for grilling.

4 boneless free-range chicken breasts, without skin
3–4 tablespoons plain flour, for coating
2 small eggs, beaten
8–10 tablespoons stale breadcrumbs
olive oil for frying
4 lemon wedges, to garnish

VILLAROY SAUCE
65 g/2¼ oz butter
50 g/2 oz plain flour
250 ml/8 fl oz good poultry stock (or fish stock, for shellfish), hot
250 ml/8 fl oz milk
freshly grated nutmeg
salt and ground white pepper

SERVES 4

Make the sauce ahead: melt the butter, then stir in the flour and cook for 1 minute. Taste the stock and, off the heat, stir it in; simmer for 2–3 minutes, stirring gently. Add the milk, bring to simmering and then add nutmeg, salt and pepper to taste. Cool with a butter paper on the surface, then chill.

Coat the chicken breasts with the sauce using the back of a spoon, turn down on to a floured tray and dust lightly with flour. Then coat the chicken all over with beaten egg and breadcrumbs. Chill well.

Heat a generous quantity of olive oil in a wide pan. Fry the breasts for 10 minutes on each side, turning once, and serve with lemon wedges.

Barcelona's Market

Food is entertainment in Barcelona. The market of La Bouqería faces on to Las Ramblas, the principal pedestrian walkway. It is a show with several acts. There is a wide arch over the entrance, with a border of orange and yellow glass rondels on blue. Metal crosses hang on either side, like orders of merit.

Inside, a huge pile of strawberries scents the market. They are in season for Easter and San José – 19th March and Father's Day. I watched a woman arranging piles within some cabbage leaves.

I had come from the north and winter, so the spring produce was most appealing. Tongues of lamb's lettuce, still bearing water drops, and new peas. Peas are also sold podded, conical piles in a plastic bag corner: and £2 for 250 g/8 oz. There are tiny black potatoes from La Isla. Were they Spanish? 'No, from France.' Fat white heads of asparagus were labelled Navarra – this is March – and were bigger than Churchill's cigar. There was also fine green wild asparagus. Chanterelles were 3680 pesetas a kilo (almost £10 a pound). There were beautiful pears, individually displayed in yellow papers, and green cauliflowers.

Local produce included a hot, slim chilli called *bitcho*, Spanish sugar cane, in a length for sawing, *pasas de Málaga* (huge muscatel raisins), kumquats and custard apples. There were imports, too: tamarind pods, physalis lanterns and enchanting baby pineapples. Even the eggs looked tempting!

The market women wear white embroidered pinafores with shoulder frills – very decorative. I get a strong sense of craft pride. In Spain the care goes into fish that the French devote to butchery. I watched a woman working delicately with a huge cleaver. It was like a Chinese one, but with a round front corner. I must get one! She took out the top fin from a hake, cutting a delicate V on either side in two movements. Then she sliced it into cutlets. The result was elegant: the neatness of something in a packet, but without the question mark as to its origin.

The market has the buzz of a good restaurant, the bustle of anticipated eating. Luxuries include *chanquetes* – invisible fish if not heaped – and *espardenes*, an orangey, jellied seaslug. Some cuttlefish are mottled, like pebbles at the bottom of a rock pool; others are round, white and gleaming, ready with their skins

cleaned off. The pink skin on the squid show how fresh they are; it will go grey later. Under the spot lights the sardines make a brilliant glitter. The hall looms darker above them. The octopus are brown, as though rusty. Mixtures of small fish are also sold for soup: long pink

Frilled pinafores: *langostas* and *centollos* in La Boquería

things, with baby groupers and scampi, one on its back with legs flapping.

Market wisdom dictates which are the best stalls. These are packed with knots of women. The olive stall offers dozens to choose from. Big *obregóns* and tiny *arbequines*, some still red, not much bigger than marrow fat peas. There are black *Aragón extras* and *negras perlas* – biggest and fattest of the black ones. Small green *manzanillas* and *aliñados* are olives for work days, the latter marinated and crushed. The stall also sells capers and dried *romescos* with the olives.

I watched two nuns choosing sausages. The *chorizo extra* has the bumps and lumps of a gut expanding, but the Catalan *fuet* is skinny – and well moulded on the outside. A fresh *longaniza* was curled round and round in a brown earthenware bowl with cream markings. The Catalan sausage is the pink *botifarra blanca* that goes white on cooking – a mammoth banger. Sausages for slicing included a *chorizo* from Rioja, with marbled meat, and a brick-red *chorizo de Pamplona*, with paprika in it. A *morcon ibérico* (bits of the black pig) is like a grenade, marked by its string in two directions.

I want to gather up everything. It would need a wheelbarrow!

Crema fría de melón con virutas de Jabugo

——— ICED MELON SOUP WITH RAW HAM SHREDS ———

Two classic partners – melon and ham – rearranged to make a refreshing soup. The region of Balaguer is famous for its Piel de Sapo melons, which are also exported, but if you can't find them honeydews can be used. Allow roughly 500 g/1 lb per person.

**1–2 ripe Piel de Sapo or honeydew melons,
well chilled**

50 g/2 oz raw Jabugo ham, or prosciutto, shredded

——————— SERVES 4 ———————

Halve the melon(s), discard the seeds and scoop the flesh and juices straight into a blender. Purée, then chill well. Ripe melon needs nothing more. Taste before serving (consider sugar, salt, pepper). Serve in bowls, over ice if you like, garnished with shreds of raw ham.

Lechuga a la catalana

——— BRAISED STUFFED LETTUCE ———

A starter which makes a supper dish for 2 when served on slices of fried ham.

2 small Cos or Webb's lettuces
2–3 tablespoons olive oil
1 big onion, finely chopped
2 carrots, finely chopped
2 very ripe tomatoes, skinned, seeded and chopped
2 tablespoons chopped parsley
salt and freshly ground black pepper
1 bouquet garni
100 ml/3½ fl oz dry white wine
100 ml/3½ fl oz poultry stock (optional)

STUFFING
white of 2 small leeks
4–6 garlic cloves
50 g/2 oz canned anchovy fillets, drained
25 g/1 oz softened butter
2 egg yolks
freshly grated nutmeg

——— SERVES 4 AS A STARTER ———

Heat 2 tablespoons oil in a small flameproof casserole into which the lettuces will fit neatly and fry the onion and carrots, adding the chopped tomato flesh and parsley when the onion softens. Season and set aside.

Put the lettuces in a colander, pour boiling water over them in turn, then drain well. Chop the leek white, garlic and anchovies very finely (the food processor works well). Work in the butter, egg yolks and a little nutmeg. Salt lightly.

Squeeze the lettuces gently in kitchen paper to blot, then split them lengthways. Put the stuffing between the leaves, starting with the outside leaves and working towards the middle. Reshape them again and lay on the bed of vegetables, tucking in the bouquet garni and moistening with the wine. Cook very gently for about 1 hour, checking occasionally whether stock is needed (it depends on pan size). Check the sauce seasonings before serving.

Pésols a la catalana

——— PEAS WITH FRESH HERBS AND PORK ———

A dish of fresh peas from L'Empordà, it is a pleasant change from beans with ham – *habas a la española*. The pork was fresh, though cured meat could be substituted.

2 kg/4 lb peas in the pod, shelled
1 small strip of streaky pork belly
salt and freshly ground black pepper
3 sprigs of fresh mint
3 sprigs of fresh marjoram
2 tablespoons olive oil
3 spring onions, sliced
4 green garlic shoots, or 2 small leeks, sliced
2 tablespoons sweet anis liqueur,
or Pernod plus a pinch of sugar
2 tablespoons moscatel or orange juice
pinch of grated orange zest (optional)
2 tablespoons water

——— SERVES 4 ———

Rub the belly strip well with salt and pepper, then dice it. Make a bouquet garni with the herbs. Heat the oil in a flameproof casserole over high heat and fry the pork belly, bowling it around until it begins to colour. Add the sliced spring onions and green garlic or leeks and cook until they start to wilt. Add the peas and the bouquet of herbs with a little salt, which brings out the juice of the peas. Add the anis, moscatel or orange juice (plus a few raspings of zest if using an orange) and the water.

Cover the casserole with foil (a sheet of brown paper said the original recipe), then a lid and put over very low heat (or in the oven at 150°C/300°F/gas 2). Cook until the peas are tender – about 40 minutes – making sure they have enough liquid. Check the seasonings and discard the herbs before serving.

Tarragona and Allioli

Pontius Pilate was born in Tarragona, Caesar Augustus commanded from a tower that still stands here, and St Paul came to convert the city. Principal actors in one drama. *Allioli* was also present, first recorded here by Pliny. The name comes from the Latin: *allium* is garlic, while *oleum* is oil. The correct Catalan spelling has two ll's, pronounced L here (though not in Castilian). In other provinces the sauce is called *ajoaceite*.

'Don't eat it before a wedding, when you will be kissing a lot of people.' This is really the only advice you need about *allioli*. It is easy to make, simple, delicious, and VERY healthy if you make the classic one – whisking crushed garlic with olive oil, both of them known to lower cholesterol!

In its pure form *allioli* is white and shiny: 'like a lemon sorbet'. It is best made with Spanish oil, with its high acidity, which holds the emulsion stable. *Allioli amb ous* includes egg yolks, as do Provençal aïoli and Languedoc's aïllade.

Warning! You can't purée garlic with bought mayo! It splits! One easy way to make sure there are no lurking pieces of garlic is to chop the cloves, then crush to a paste with a pinch of salt, on a board, using the flat of a knife. Garlic never seems to dissolve enough in a blender, though a herb mill (like a coffee grinder, but with moving parts that go into the dishwasher) is excellent. Crushing garlic is the first step in the typical Catalan *picada*. This is a very common way of making a sauce in Spain – other things are added for a condiment that finishes off the sauce.

Tarragona has not one, but two famous sauces. To sample them both, a perfect menu here might be *calçots* (grilled young onions) served with *romesco* sauce (see recipe page 138), followed by grilled fish and *allioli*. The alternative is *arrossejat* (rice cooked in fish broth) with *allioli* followed by *romesco de peix* (see recipe page 138).

Along the coast here grow pines, hazelnuts, almonds and olives. *Romesco* sauce embraces all of them. It was born in the barrio del Serrallo of Tarragona, and is equally wonderful served with fish, roast chicken or rabbit.

The basis is the dry *romesco* pepper, called a *ñora* in Castilian, which lends piquancy and sweetness to the ground nuts. The sauce also includes bread and garlic, which indicate an ancient origin.

Allioli

———— GARLIC, OIL AND EGG SAUCE ————

EGG YOLK ALLIOLI

6 garlic cloves, finely chopped

½ teaspoon salt

2 teaspoons lemon juice

1 large egg yolk

250 ml/8 fl oz olive oil, preferably Spanish,
including half virgin oil

ALLIOLI FOR FISH

1 small bulb of garlic, finely chopped

salt and freshly ground black pepper

1 small potato (50 g/2 oz), boiled in its skin

125 ml/4 fl oz fish stock

1 large egg yolk

125 ml/4 fl oz olive oil, preferably Spanish

———— SERVES 6 ————

For egg yolk allioli: a mortar is still the best place to make this. Crush the garlic with the salt in a mortar (or with the flat side of a table knife on a board), mashing it to a smooth paste.

(If necessary move it to a bowl.) Work in the yolks, then the lemon juice. The oil must be at room temperature. Add it, drop by drop, working it in with the pestle, 'always in the same direction' (or whisk it in), until an emulsion forms. Continue adding the oil until it is all incorporated, to make a thick sauce.

Because there is little acidity in the mixture, *allioli* splits more easily than mayonnaise. Not to worry! This is called *allioli negat* and is often stirred into fish stews and sauces.

For allioli for fish: pound the garlic with a pinch of salt in a mortar to a paste, or blend. Peel the potato and work it in, alternating with the fish stock, then the egg yolk. Add the oil – drop by drop, like mayonnaise if working by hand. Season with salt and pepper.

Musclos gratinats

GRILLED MUSSELS WITH SPINACH
AND ALLIOLI

An easy prepare-ahead dish with simple things.

1 kg/2 lb mussels, cleaned *(see page 91)*
4 tablespoons white wine or dry vermouth
25 g/1 oz butter
500 g/1 lb spinach (300 g/10 oz chopped frozen)
salt and freshly ground black pepper
4 tablespoons thick cream
egg yolk *allioli (see page 137)*

SERVES 4 AS A STARTER

Put the wine into a saucepan and, when it boils, add the mussels, in two batches. Cover tightly and cook over high heat for 1–2 minutes, shaking the pan occasionally, until the shells are open. Discard the top shells and any mussels that are still shut.

Melt the butter in a pan and put in the spinach. Cover and cook, turning top to bottom, until well wilted. Remove and chop it. Return to the pan, season well, add the cream and beat it. Put a spoonful over each mussel.

Spread a spoonful of *allioli* on top of each mussel with the back of a spoon. Grill for 60 seconds, until just coloured, and serve at once.

Romesco de peix

SHELLFISH STEW WITH HAZELNUT
AND CHILLI SAUCE

One of the great shellfish soup-stews of the Mediterranean, the *romesco* sauce is a subtle blend of chillies with hazelnuts and garlic.

I used a cod steak, small monkfish and flat fish, and a red mullet. Buy about 2.3 kg/5 lb whole fish if you can, and reckon to get 1 kg/2 lb heads and bones. Good fish stock is essential so, even if you start with a commercial stock, still simmer in it the prawns heads and unsightly fish trimmings (belly flaps etc) for 30 minutes. Traditionally all the tomato is blended, but a little left sliced enhanced the dish.

1.1–1.2 kg/2½–3 lb assorted filleted fish,
plus their heads, bones and debris
1.2 lt/2 pt fish stock
about 6 tablespoons plain flour
salt and freshly ground black pepper
2 tablespoons olive oil (optional)
250 ml/8 fl oz dry white wine
2 sprigs of fresh thyme
2 sprigs of fresh oregano
500 g/1 lb scampi with their heads or big raw prawns
250 g/8 oz small clams or 500 g/1 lb mussels,
cleaned *(see page 91)*
4 small squid, cleaned *(see page 165)* – optional
6 tablespoons coarsely chopped parsley

ROMESCO SAUCE
25 g/1 oz almonds, toasted *(see page 129)*
25 g/1 oz hazelnuts, toasted with the almonds
4 tablespoons olive oil
1 slice of stale bread, crusts removed
2 garlic cloves, finely chopped
2 *ñora* chillies, or an extra dried chilli,
seeded and chopped
1 dried *bitxo, guindilla* or other chilli,
seeded and chopped
2 tablespoons chopped parsley
2 tablespoons lemon juice
500 g/1 lb ripe tomatoes, skinned, seeded and sliced
salt and freshly ground black pepper

SERVES 6

Simmer the fish heads, bones and debris in the fish stock for 30 minutes, to make a concentrated stock. Meanwhile, make the sauce: heat the oil in a flameproof casserole to very hot and quickly fry the bread, garlic and chopped *ñora* chillies, if using. Pound the toasted nuts (or use a blender), adding the bread in pieces, the garlic, *ñoras*, other chillies, parsley and lemon juice. Blend in half the tomatoes and season.

Coat the fish pieces in seasoned flour. Add 2 tablespoons oil to the casserole (if needed) and fry the fish over high heat, moving the pieces around. Pour the sauce over them and add the wine. Taste the stock and reduce if it is not good enought, adding more. Add enough stock to the casserole to cover everything and bring to simmering, adding the thyme and oregano.

Put in the scampi or prawns. (Scampi with heads go in whole: otherwise they should be shelled and deveined.) Bring back to simmering and then add the clams or mussels. When they open, add the squid and remaining tomato flesh. Simmer for 10 minutes. Taste for seasoning and add the parsley.

A back street in
Tarragona, ancient
capital of the eastern
coast

Anchovy Coast: the Costa Brava

The French were second to discover the Costa Brava. Just over the mutual border, sandy bays and rocky outcrops earned the coast the name of 'wild'. It had been popular with Spain's artistic community since the beginning of the century.

Mountains cut off Cadaqués from inland. The Dalí family had a villa there, where Federico García Lorca was their guest. André Derain and Picasso worked here – and Cubism may have been born in the latter's studio, which overlooks the port. There is nothing particularly square about the view, beyond the way little houses pile up to the dominating church.

I spent a week spotting *modernista* villas: a beauty here at Cadaqués, the Casa Serinyena. Built round the turn of the century, these villas combine bravura with cosiness. The urge to decorate put blue ceramics round the windows and up the house spines of this one. Down the coast there are a few villas in every seaside stop – several at Sitges.

The food here is timeless, and superb fish stock is the base of many dishes. Made from the Mediterranean rascasse, this is truly a scorpion fish: a spine that merely pierced my index finger put it out of action for two days. The local soup, called *bullabesa*, is much like the French bouillabaisse. The Spanish claim theirs came first.

Suquet is the favourite fish stew: a wonderful mixture of fish and shellfish with tomato and potato. *Sarsuela* (local spelling) is an even more ambitious medley of fish with saffron and anis-scented brandy. Colours and shapes proliferate in it: the name, roughly, means operetta. I'm told the dish is called *ópera* when it also contains lobster. There is also the divine *romesco de peix* (see page 138), the most sophisticated because of its sauce. Family lore is that '*suquet* is best for children, because they can mash the potatoes into the tomato-fish broth.'

L'Escala, on the promontory, is famous in Spain for its large salted anchovies – as is the whole coast, as far as French Collioure. The anchovies are left in salt for a few days, to remove the bitter-tasting blood. Then the head and stomach are removed with one twist of the fingers: a smelly job, if ever there was one! They are then split and arranged in layers with salt in a barrel and left to ripen to the dark colour we associate with canned anchovies. Almost every *amanida* (salad arrangement) seems to include them, while anchovy toasts are served with the smoky *escalivada*.

In contrast, many *tapas* bars sell the fresh *boquerones*, simply filleted and macerated in vinegar and lemon juice for a couple of days. The result makes them white – and very different!

Escalivada amb anxoves

— BARBECUED VEGETABLE SALAD —

WITH ANCHOVIES

Firm vegetables are barbecued to soften them – and literally blackened: the Spanish name is from a verb meaning to cook in the ashes. They are then peeled and eaten cold. The rather crisper fennel slices are a successful modern addition to the dish.

4 small aubergines, about 250 g/8 oz each

4 red peppers

4 onions, 75–100 g/3–4 oz each

1 big bulb of fennel, sliced thickly

about 4 tablespoons virgin olive oil

salt and freshly ground black pepper

50 g/2 oz canned anchovy fillets, drained

— SERVES 4 —

Best barbecued outside, nevertheless this is still good cooked in the oven. Heat it to 200°C/400°F/gas 6. Bake the aubergines, peppers and onions together on a baking sheet for about 1 hour, turning them over once. Then cool and remove the outside skins.

Grill the fennel slices, brushing them with oil and turning them. Arrange the fennel pieces on 4 plates, putting them to left and right. Slice the other vegetables; aubergines reduce to a quarter of their former volume. Arrange the strips together in the centre of the plates and dribble with virgin oil and seasoning. Arrange a few anchovy fillets over the top (or on some lightly toasted bread) and serve.

The Costa Brava in a stormy moment, that justifies its soubriquet of 'wild'

Pollastre amb escamarlans o gambes

CHICKEN WITH SCAMPI OR PRAWNS

A delicious combination of delicate flavours. The dish needs raw shellfish to work – the scampi we buy are always blanched, but are not sold cooked, so may be the better choice. Or 500 g/1 lb squid can be substituted.

1.2–1.4 kg/2¾–3 lb free-range chicken
8 big scampi or 500 g/1 lb large raw prawns
5–6 tablespoons olive oil
4 tablespoons dry anis or liqueur, or Pernod
1 large onion, chopped
salt and freshly ground black pepper
2 garlic cloves, finely chopped
500 g/1 lb ripe tomatoes, skinned,
seeded and chopped
1 fresh bouquet garni of 2 thyme and
2 oregano sprigs, 1 bay leaf, 1 leek strip
and bruised parsley stalks
150 ml/5 fl oz dry white wine
(or a dry *oloroso* sherry – but not with Pernod)
about 100 ml/3½ fl oz chicken or fish stock,
or water, if needed

CONDIMENT
25 g/1 oz almonds, toasted *(see page 129)*
2 garlic cloves, finely chopped
3 Marie (or Rich Tea) biscuits
2 tablespoons finely chopped parsley

SERVES 4

A farm chicken is cooked with scampi for the local dish

Cut the chicken into bite-size pieces, discarding unsightly skin and the worst bones. Heat 2 tablespoons oil in a flameproof casserole and add the shellfish. Fry them over medium heat for 4–5 minutes (or according to size). Move them to a warm dish. Warm the liqueur in a ladle, then flame it and spoon it over the shellfish until the flame dies. Reserve them (but don't put them in a warm oven!).

Add 3–4 more tablespoons oil to the casserole and fry the onion and seasoned chicken over medium-high heat. Move them fairly steadily so the onion doesn't catch, then add the garlic. When everything is coloured, add the tomato flesh and bouquet garni, and cook down to a sauce.

Add the wine, with a little stock or water if needed almost to cover the chicken. Cover and simmer for about 20 minutes.

For the condiment, pound the garlic cloves with a little salt (or blend), then work in the nuts and crumbled biscuits. Work in the parsley.

Discard the bouquet garni and stir the condiment paste into the sauce. Return the shellfish (peel them at this point if you feel you must) and their juices and warm through. Check the seasonings.

Note: it isn't orthodox, but one woman finished the dish with a little cream and cayenne, instead of the nuts and biscuits.

Right: A vegetable shop in Cadequés caters for the summer visitors

❧ The Spring Onion Festival ☙

The idea seemed eccentric. Celebrate spring by eating onions? I could suggest other ways. This was before I ate a *calçot*.

The return of warm weather is the time for *la calçotada*. These feasts are famous in Valls and Cambrils. But driving across the province of Tarragona, they seem to be universal. Farms advertised the onions for sale, and restaurants had hoardings outside about making bookings. There were also *calçots* in every market: nice spring onions (but milder and sweeter), fatter than a finger and a good hand's length, well trimmed for domestic consumption.

The feast is different. Grilled in the open, they arrive in bundles on a long pantile (which keeps them warm).

No trimmed leaves: the herbiage is like something in a wheelbarrow. I watch my neighbours distastefully grasp the leaves above black objects, trying to avoid the ashes, and strip off the outside layer. Then they dipped them in *romesco* sauce (see page 138) and, facing heavenward, held them high, dribbling the onion into a waiting mouth. It was a messy business, so bibs are provided by the management.

Then they started to eat faster, cramming in the onions, grubbing for the next one; counting how many were left in the communal pile, and what the share was; skipping on the peeling, hurrying on the chewing. How fast can you eat to get a new one? Then, thankfully, replenishment comes from the grill again.

୬୫ Mushroom Picking in the High Pyrenees ୧୨

We climbed in search of lammergeyers, a bearded vulture – and Europe's largest bird of prey. There were rumoured to be two breeding pairs in this part of the Pyrenees. 'You will know it, if you see it, by the *ailas inmensas*' – a wing span of 2.5 metres/8 feet.

A day, in late September, without seeing another car, snaking upwards, then up again, to a high cliff where, on one side, all the Pyrenees stretched out in the sunshine. We set up a watching point. Griffon vultures wheeled in flights overhead, lazily inspecting me as lunch, for I wore a carrion-coloured shirt.

At the back of the cliff sloped a pine wood. I have never seen so many mushrooms: Russulas, red, green, black, white, so many it was like a Disney cartoon. And which were safe? I needed guidance. Then I suddenly realized the woods were full of people. Serious men, not quiche-eaters, pick mushrooms in Spain. My new companions were only interested in one mushroom.

A stunning golden-yellow underneath, and so big they had become cup-shaped, the *rovelló* was reminiscent of a communion chalice. A penknife through the stalk produced a single drop of blood, like some medieval miracle. This was *Lactarius deliciosus*, the bleeding milk cap.

It is Spain's best-loved mushroom, and the picking season is a social event. They are known as *niscalos* in the Guadarrama, outside Madrid, *miscalos* in Extremadura, and *esne-gori* in the Basque country, but supremely they are a Catalan mushroom. As we descended to the valley, the roadside was full of mushroom-sellers with their baskets. We ate them in Martinet, high in Lérida, done with garlic and parsley.

Sopa de setas

WILD MUSHROOM SOUP
---

200 g/7 oz fresh *ninfas* (fairy-ring mushrooms) plus
100 g/4 oz fresh *cabrillas* (chanterelles)
or 500 g/1lb cultivated mushrooms plus
25 g/1 oz dried ceps (Italian porcini)
2 tablespoons olive oil
25 g/1 oz butter
2 onions, finely chopped
6 green garlic bulbs and stalks, or 2 young leeks,
chopped with their green
500 g/1 lb ripe tomatoes, skinned, seeded and chopped
1.5 lt/2$\frac{1}{4}$ pt poultry stock
5–6 slices of stale French bread, toasted
salt and freshly ground black pepper

CONDIMENT

25 g/1 oz almonds, toasted *(see page 129)*
2 garlic cloves, finely chopped
0.1 g saffron (20 strands)

--- SERVES 6 ---

Trim the earthy stalk tips from the mushrooms and wash them well. Chop larger mushrooms (fairy-ring mushrooms are quite tiny), so they are all the same size.

Put the oil and butter in a large saucepan and fry the onions and chopped green garlic or leeks. When they begin to take on colour, add the chopped tomato flesh and leave it to soften for about 10 minutes. Add the mushrooms and the stock. Simmer for 15 minutes, then process roughly.

Pound the chopped garlic in a mortar with $\frac{1}{4}$ teaspoon salt (or use a blender), adding the saffron and the almonds, and diluting with a little stock from the pan if necessary. Add this paste to the soup and float the toast on top. Cook for 3–4 minutes longer. Check the seasoning, adding pepper, and serve.

Right: A hunter of wild mushrooms

CHAPTER 11

Levante

'Where the east wind blows.' Levante takes in most of the east coast, including Valencia, Alicante and a good many of the sunshine beaches. Valencia is synonymous with oranges but it is for *paella*, Spain's most famous dish, that the region will for ever be remembered.

A shower of rice greets the happy wedded couple (naturally) in Valencia. They emerged from the church into the quiet Plaza de la Paz behind the cathedral, and a cloud of pigeons descended on the bride, white feathers and lace veiling all fluttering together.

Rice is the most visible record of Arab occupation – they were driven out by El Cid in 1094 – though the yellow, copper-green and blue hand-painted Manises pottery is another. Rice grows in the Ebro delta and beside the Guadalquivir too. But here, round Lake Albufera, is the *zona de los arroces* and the home of *paella valenciana*.

Paella's history is a short one, for Spain's most-celebrated dish is less than 200 years old. It was invented by men, combining fish and meat in rice for the first time. It is also an outdoor dish – and a lunchtime one – made on a dying fire. Every village here has its *tío*, uncle-expert, who will hold forth on how to make it. I soon found mine. Lake Albufera is famous for eels and they have uncles, too, an *allipebrotero* to give his counsel on the proper pepper sauce to cook them in.

The uplands that back the coast have also given the region some filling dishes. I met them in the form of *michirones* (broad bean stew) in Valencia, but it also has other *hervidos* (stews), and north of Castellón in the Maestrazgo heavy stews are based on potatoes, cereals and wheat. This region is also known for good meat – and makes *cecina* (beef hams). And, as always, there are stewed salt cod dishes, like *giraboix*, with green beans and cabbage.

On the coast orange trees everywhere earn it the name of *costa de azahar*, of fragrant, heady blossom. The problem is to dodge the industry that also comes with a major port. I found a route through the rice fields, up the river Júcar through groves where the fruit hung like lamps on the trees. 'When are they picked?' I asked, used to the idea of flowers in the autumn and fruit at Easter. 'In all seasons.' This is agribusiness, not nature. The preferred orange here is the navel, and not the valencia, though that is the world's most-eaten orange. There are lemons too, chiefly the juicy Verna. Here they grow 80 per cent of Spain's crop.

Driving south, the bluest of blue seas and continual sand stayed at my left elbow, and beaches where the sun turns all bodies (whatever their shape) into gold. I stopped at Gandía, famous as the home of the Borjias. They are remembered locally for their saint, not their pope. Here *fideuá* was invented, a wonderful noodle (*fideos*) version of *paella*, with seafood in it. There are also sea-dates, the brown mussels for the best of mussel soups.

Reaching Alicante, it would be easy to mistake it for North Africa, bare mountains in the background.

Every roofline is broken by tufted palms and the light has an exceptional clarity. There are a million date trees here, Europe's only major grove and the most northerly. You can see them from the road from Elche to Orihuelo, though there is no way to count them. The dates were round, plump and yellow. I bought them on the frond, and freshly picked.

Murcia is the third kingdom of the coast, proud of its Arab past. Moors ruled here until 1609 and the land is the richer for it, one vast, irrigated vegetable garden. Peppers (introduced from America) are the thing they are now proud of. But Arab dishes are still eaten, like *zarangollo*, a slow-cooked hash of onions and courgettes. The local pie, *pastel murciana*, has much in common with the Moroccan *b'stilla*. The filling is veal, ham and *chorizo*, inside a shortcrust shell. But the top of *filo* pastry rises, flower-like, in concentric circles. 'Do you make it at home?' 'Oh no, we buy it.'

Every market has new surprises. In Murcia it is the superb capers. Their pickled leaf tips are used in several salads. Capers are canned here for the whole of Spain, though they grow in the Balearics. Another acid taste (and Arab invention) is *escabeche* (see page 22), fish lightly pickled in vinegar.

This is a coast of *marismas*, pools and salt marches, mirroring the sky. It has been famous for salt since Carthaginian times. The Mar Menor is a small sea, pollution-free, divided from the Med by the sports colony of La Manga.

The fish and shellfish here are astounding. For they absorb salt and iodine from the water, and gain incomparable flavour. The famous dish is *mújol a la sal* (see page 150), grey mullet baked in a salt jacket and cracked open at the table. There are also *salda gorda*, fat prawns from salt water. I ate *dorado*, gilt-head bream – cooked quite simply – and perhaps the best fish of my life.

Salt from San Pedro del Pinatar, behind the Mar Menor, is used to make *arencs*, salted and pressed sardines, and the thinly sliced, mahogany *mojama*, cured blue-fin tuna, a delicacy since Arab times. There is *huevos de mújol*, grey mullet roe, too, the 'caviar' of the Mediterranean.

From Alicante to Valencia, the coast is famous for muscats, their tawny plumpness fed by the sun. Kumquats grow here, as well as fat greengages called *yemas* (yolks) and a wealth of other fruit I had never seen: a plum, white and juicy within, called *chinchols*, which quickly marks with brown, and a flat, white-fleshed peach called a *paraguaya*. Desserts are sweet too – from Arab days. There's *tocino de cielo* (see page 158), heavenly in name and nature, and a *pan de Ala* of pressed figs with almonds. And Valencia's festival season brings *dulces de sarten* – sweets from the frying pan – little cakes of sweet potato, and *bunyols* (see page 158).

Ajotomate

—— TOMATO SALAD WITH TOMATO DRESSING ——

One of the oldest salads on the east coast, it uses tomatoes at different stages of ripeness.

4 salad tomatoes – 'rock hard'
1 very ripe beefsteak tomato, or about
300 g/11 oz ripe tomatoes, skinned and seeded
4 garlic cloves, finely chopped
½ teaspoon salt
200 ml/7 fl oz good olive oil
1 tablespoon sherry vinegar
freshly ground pepper
½ teaspoon cumin seeds, finely ground (or paprika)

—— SERVES 4 ——

Cut the salad tomatoes in rounds and put in a salad bowl. Purée the garlic with the salt – in a mortar or on a board with the flat of a knife. Purée the ripe tomato flesh with the garlic (in a blender), adding oil and vinegar to make a smooth emulsion. Taste and check the seasonings. Pour over the sliced tomatoes, dress with a little cumin (or paprika) and stand for 30 minutes before serving.

Note: a wonderful tomato salad that needs no garnish. However, I met a festive variant which doubled the recipe, then garnished it with 16 black olives, 2 tablespoons large capers, tuna from a 100 g/3½ oz can and a chopped hard-boiled egg.

Esgarrat

RED PEPPER AND CURED FISH SALAD

My favourite red pepper recipe – and one of the best ways to eat salt cod. Better, I think, than *mojama* (cured tuna), which is the more expensive alternative. Canned tuna can also be used.

250 g/8 oz *bacalao inglés* (moist centre fillet pieces
of salt cod), or a tail piece of salt cod
4 tablespoons good olive oil
2 garlic cloves, finely chopped
6 large red peppers

SERVES 4

Well ahead, simply soak *bacalao inglés* for 3–4 hours and drain it, patting it dry. If you can't get this, then soak an equal weight of stiff salt cod for 24 hours, changing the water 3–4 times, then remove skin and bones and flake the flesh. Mix the oil and garlic and marinate the fish flakes for 24 hours.

Put the peppers on the hot iron (*la plancha*), or under a grill, and turn them regularly until charred on all sides. Leave until cool enough to handle, then strip off the skin (on a plate to catch the juices) and remove the seeds. Cut into long strips and mix these, and their juices, with the fish and dressing.

Note: bacalao inglés is for eating raw, salted, but less dry than the salt cod sold in Italian delicatessens. It is nearer to salt herring – which is a possible substitute.

Bajoques farcides

COLD STUFFED PEPPERS
WITH RICE AND TUNA

An unusual version of a very well-known recipe, it goes well before grilled meat, or makes a simple, filling lunch. In Spain it is made with slim pointed green peppers, but I have adapted it to *morrones*, the fist-shaped ones. I was advised to use Calasparra rice, the best in Spain.

4 small green peppers (or 8 slim pointed ones)
olive oil for deep frying
1 small onion, chopped
2 tablespoons olive oil
2 garlic cloves, finely chopped
150 g/5 oz *paella* or risotto rice
2 tablespoons *fino* sherry or dry vermouth
2 tablespoons sieved tomato (passata)
or tomato sauce
0.1 g saffron (20 strands), crumbled and soaked in a
little of the stock for 5 minutes
1 bouquet garni
400 ml/14 fl oz chicken or fish stock
200 g/7 oz can tuna, drained
mayonnaise, to serve

SERVES 4–8

Deep fry the peppers whole, putting them in at top heat, for 10 minutes, until they have lost their plump football appearance (pointed ones need about half the time). Remove with a slotted spoon and drain on kitchen paper.

Make the filling: in a wide shallow pan fry the onion in 2 tablespoons oil until soft. Add the garlic, then the rice and stir. Add the sherry, tomato sauce, saffron and its liquid, and the bouquet garni. Add a third of the stock and let it simmer until absorbed, then add the rest in 2 batches. Simmer the rice for a total of about 20 minutes, until all the stock is absorbed. Leave it to sit for a couple of minutes, then add the well-forked tuna.

Slit the peppers from end to end and remove the stalk and seeds. Stuff with the rice mixture and reshape the peppers. When cold they will halve neatly. Arrange in a circle, green side up, and pile the mayonnaise in the middle.

Valencia is famous for its tiling
and hand-painted pottery

Mújol a la sal

WHOLE FISH BAKED IN SALT

A very easy dish, suddenly made accessible because granular salt is sold for dishwashers in large quantities. It is now one of the great recipes of the east coast. The fish is baked in a salt jacket, which keeps it very moist, without making it excessively salty. Two smaller fish work just as well as one (about 600 g/1¼ lb will serve two). Much of the salt can go in the dishwasher afterwards.

**1 whole grey mullet, gilt-head bream or codling,
about 1.25 kg/2½ lb, uncleaned
about 2 kg/4½ lb granular salt
lemon wedges or *allioli* (see page 137), to serve**

SERVES 6

Make a bed of granular salt in a small roasting tin into which the fish just fits neatly – I saw this done in a small fruit box. Put in the fish, uncleaned (or it will leak), and build a snow mountain over it with salt, so there is no visible grey.

Heat the oven to top heat (240°C/475°F/gas 9) and put in the fish. Cook for 25 minutes (20 minutes for smaller fish) – the salt will cohere into a solid mass, the sign that the fish is done. It will wait in a warm place for another 10 minutes.

Shew it to the table as it is, cracking open the salt there. Best then to portion it on a side table. The skin and fins lift away with the salt crust. Take three portions off the top of the backbone. Turn it, discarding the stomach, and portion the other side. Serve with lemon wedges or *allioli*.

Note: discard any coloured salt, then use the rest. Dishwasher detergent is a powerful cleaner and copes with all smells!

❧ Real Paella ☙

The men were going to cook *paella*. Would I join the party? It was to celebrate a marriage. But the hosts (except one) were unemployed – the owner of the bar and the men who spent their day there. We were in working-class Malvarossa, the last back street of Valencia, on the beach edge. No one swims here because of pollution from the port. But the sand drifts through the bar door, open 18 hours a day.

Breakfast comes with a tot of something, and the cooks were pacing themselves when I arrived. Manolo was the bar owner and chief chef, middle-aged and vast. 'You will recognize him by his glass eye,' I was told. He was fortifying himself with *ponche* (herbal brandy) from a silver bottle. Second (and silent) cook was José, with a neat crescent of ginger beard and respectable jeans like a carpenter's. For ten people they had bought: 3 kg/6½ lb squid, 3 kg/6½ lb small clams, 2 kg/4½ lb *rojas* (large red prawns) and 3 kg/6½ lb scampi, plus the necessary extras, like chickens, rice and saffron.

The *paella* pan on the stove was the cheapest sort, with green handles and a dimpled bottom. It seemed as big as a bicycle wheel and gas burners in concentric rings, attached to an orange butane bottle, were needed to heat it. In it were chicken pieces in a ring, scampi and prawns, squares of white translucent squid: all arranged with the precision of a stained-glass window. The smell

of oil was awful, the kitchen a windowless hole, like so many in Spain. I fled, but I went back to taste the fish broth and saffron as it went in.

Non-cooks started drifting towards the table, dragging chairs, at the arrival of *sangría*. In an unglazed jug, this was not the namby-pamby lemonade stuff made for tourists, but the real thing: wine, citrus juice and a heavy slug of Soberano brandy. It signalled the closing of the bar, metal shutters crashing downwards. Non-guests were encouraged towards the door.

There were three dishes of *mariscos* to start. The first was cooked by José-the-honest, non-drinking long-term bar companion, for whose marriage the feast was given. It was clams *a la marinera* in a sauce of garlic, plenty of paprika and a Moriles wine that was much like *fino* sherry.

This was followed by prawns *a la plancha*, unctuous, rich and the colour of steak, grilled rare. There was a suggestion of black where they came off the griddle, and of blood as they spluttered open. The big heads were an embarrassment on the table, which was quickly littered. Then came boiled scampi, beautiful with their long pink claws – three well-balanced dishes, I noticed.

Opposite me sat José-with-the-crash. His shirt was plentifully spattered. Did he own another, I wondered? Newly out of a detoxification unit, his face was half

bashed, though whether from a recent accident, or a birthmark that had caught the sun and peeled, I dared not ask.

José-with-the-beard brought out the *paella*, wrapped up in sheets of 'el Mercantil Valencio', and placed it on more newspaper, to wait 10 minutes for the rice grains to separate. He remarked (the second time he spoke) that of ten at table, five were called José (counting me, for Pepita is a diminutive of Josephine). Our fifth was José-minus-the-legs. So very little was left, one wondered what he sat on. He had recently been to London to attend a conference on the handicapped and been introduced to Princess Margaret. But the simultaneous translation had broken down, and he had slept throughout.

Andréas, with bright eyes and exuberant curly beard atop two bird-like legs, was the last man. His wife was a junkie and his child had gone away with grandma. This had made him a philosopher.

It was news to me that three sorts of beans are needed for *paella*: *garrafón*, big and flat like butter beans, *talvillas* (young white kidney beans in a pod) and flat green *ferrauras*. 'Unknown outside Spain,' I was assured by the philosopher (though they looked like tender runner beans). He moved on to bricklaying and ended up with Handel, without my quite following how he got there.

The newspaper came off! Of course it is the seafood that catches the eye, but the rice is the real star. Plates were loaded for the 'two girls' (the bride and me), while a dirty two-year-old appeared from under the table and was given rice (but no seafood). But she got the crisp bit underneath in the middle, the *soccarat*, which is what I fancied.

More drinks. A concoction from José-with-the-beard of kiwi syrup and gin, whisked with egg white and diluted by *cava* (local champagne) – and then another with Moscatel and something. Of the ten assembled to eat the great *paella*, five took a plateful, five barely put their forks in the pan. But for everyone it was a day to remember.

Was it the greatest *paella* in the world? I couldn't fault it. It was cooked with the classic ingredients, in exactly the right place, by people who had done it a thousand times before. It was also done with love for a special occasion – enjoyed for a day and slept off. The shutters were down for the whole of Monday.

Paella pans ready waiting

Lake Albufera: Ducks, Rice and Eels

The rice harvest was late in September, because the weather was good. Normally it brings rain to Valencia (again in spring) – and floods. *La gota fría*, it is called: the cold drops. It's the floods that make rice viable in this flat coastal strip in the bay of the east coast.

I drove out beside Lake Albufera, one of Spain's largest natural freshwater lakes. The names of the villages I passed were familiar to me: the *paella* rollcall of honour. First Catarroja (now industrialized), then El Salar and El Palmar, later El Perellonet, El Perelló, Silla, Sollana, Sueca.

From the tree shade of the shore a soft grey sheet of water spread out to the mountains. The Arab 'mirror of the sun' and space to breathe after Valencia city! To the south, banks of reeds shelter migrating birds – duck with orange was an early dish here. The lake is also famous for its eels. Rice grows in the black mud and, when I eventually reached the western edge, the ripe rice stretched out, golden like the proverbial cornfields.

Paella was invented in this countryside, a peasant rice dish, and a Lenten one. Eels, snails and green beans with rice were its origin, put together outdoors by men cooking. El Palmyr is one of the few lakeside villages approachable by car, for punts and ancient motor boats are the local transport. Little bridges with square, dark cobbles cross a series of green canals between islands of swaying bamboo. The traditional cottages are thatched with rice straw, *barracos* steep-roofed against the rain. There are not many left.

On to El Perelló, on the coast, where I fell into conversation with Señor Manoli on the beach, and was delighted to find his wife was the *maestra paellera* (best cook) of the coast the previous year. I admired her trophy and was amused to discover she was born in León in the north.

'*Paella valenciana* is the most famous dish, but it is not really home food. It's for Sundays out. In these villages we make *paella* with chicken and rabbit, but no fish.' The chicken feet were essential for good stock.

Though the things that go into rice catch the attention of foreigners, locals care more about the rice. It is this that wins the prize. 'Rice is the principal actor,' I was told. 'There are good dishes with rice served with nothing in it. *Paella* is a dry dish. When it is done the grains must be separate. That is why it is important to wash the rice first.' I had already met *soccarat* (the crust underneath), but I found its name was that of the next village on the coast.

And life before *paella*? 'Rice has been here since Arab times. It used to be cooked in casseroles in the oven. And that meant the baker's oven, since homes had none in this heat.' In Catalan it is called *arròs passejat* – walked rice. One of the famous ones is the rice dished out to the Jijona factory workers. *Empedrat*, it is called – 'cobbled' – just rice and beans, but the latter look like paving stones.

Elche is famous for a *paella* like a pie – rice with a crust, *arròs amb costra* in the local dialect. Beaten eggs are poured over the half-cooked rice with a mixture of chicken and ham, *chorizo* or *morcilla*. This protects it in the oven.

Soupy rice dishes come from a different tradition. These often contain bits of pork, like *arròs amb fesols i naps*. With dried beans, I find, and the yellow swede (not turnips). Not what you expect in the heat!

We got on to saffron and fish soups, the oldest rice dishes on this coast. But the yellow colour of much rice comes from *ñoras*, the pepper called *romesco* in Catalonia (see page 138). They are important when the rice is *arroz abanda* – rice apart (ie eaten alone first). The famous dish is from Castellón de la Plana, and made with rascasse, which is then eaten with *allioli*. Murcian *arroz en caldero* (see page 154) is related to it.

'The rice is cooked in the rich broth that was used for the fish. *No* water.' I was rebuked. 'Valencian water is only for soup. To cook rice it must be good *caldo* (broth).' However he relented, and told me the story of a Valencian family bottling town water (well-known for its bad taste) to take to Madrid, to add that authentic local 'something' to *paella*.

Left: Ancient boats are the means of travel between the rice fields

Arròs amb forn

OVEN RICE WITH PORK AND TOMATO

You won't find this recipe in any book, but it is the fore-runner of *paella* – and much easier to make, for it is made in a flat casserole in the oven. It never contains fish, but is made with pork, except in Lent, when it features garlic!

400 g/14 oz *paella* or risotto rice

4 pork belly ribs, cut with the meat

salt and freshly ground black pepper

1½–2 tablespoons paprika

6 tablespoons olive oil

8 thickish rounds of potato

350 g/12 oz *morcilla* or black pudding

1 whole bulb of garlic, loose skin removed

200 ml/7 fl oz *fino* sherry

1 lt/1¾ pt good stock (taste before use)

0.25 g saffron strands (1 teaspoon of best Manchego)

1 large onion, chopped

1 garlic clove, finely chopped

4–6 fat tomatoes

SERVES 4

Rub the pork ribs well with salt, pepper and paprika. Heat 3 tablespoons oil in a large pan and fry the potato rounds and meat until golden on all sides. Sausages and potatoes will take about 25 minutes, ribs and black pudding (in 4 chunks) about 15 minutes.

Heat the oven to 180°C/350°F/gas 4 with the garlic bulb in it. Warm the sherry with the stock, and put the crumbled saffron to soak in 4 tablespoons hot stock for 5 minutes or so.

Meanwhile, heat 3 tablespoons oil in a saucepan and soften the onion, adding the chopped garlic towards the end. Cut 4 tomatoes in half across the middle, taking a good slice off each side. Dice the ends and the other tomatoes, add them to the saucepan and cook gently to a sauce. Add 1 table-spoon paprika plus the saffron and its liquid.

Rinse the rice in a colander, stir it into the sauce and heat gently. Turn into a wide flat earthenware casserole and spread it out, seasoning generously. Bed the pork and black pudding or sausages down into the rice, slicing them when in position. Press the potato and tomato slices into the spaces and put the garlic bulb in the middle, opening it out a bit. Pour in the stock and put the dish into the oven for 30 minutes.

When the rice is tender, cover the pan with foil, turn off the oven and leave, with the door open, for 10 minutes, so the rice can absorb the last drop of moisture. To serve, give everyone their share of pork, sausage, tomato and potato, then stir the rice before spooning it out. If you like garlic, mash a cooked clove or two into the rice as you eat.

Arroz en caldero

RICE WITH PEPPERS AND ALLIOLI

FOLLOWED BY FISH

The popular lunch in Murcia is just the rice course, made in a little witches' cauldron, with a suave creamy mousse of *allioli*. No fish! However, the double course is very splendid. The *ñora* pepper was once the base of both the rice and the fish sauce.

400 g/14 oz *paella* or risotto rice

1 bulb of garlic, in unpeeled cloves, smashed

2 *ñoras* or 2 cm/¾ in canned Mexican *jalapeño* peppers, chopped (or 2 teaspoons paprika)

6–8 tablespoons good olive oil

1 ripe beefsteak tomato, skinned and seeded

0.1 g saffron (20 strands)

1.5 lt/2½ pt fish stock, from the bones etc. of the fish

salt and freshly ground pepper

allioli for fish *(see page 137)* to serve

FISH

1.4 kg/3 lb fish fillet, such as grey mullet,

or several types, cut in serving pieces

SALMORETTA SAUCE FOR THE FISH

1 ripe beefsteak tomato, skinned,

seeded and chopped

3 tablespoons olive oil

3 garlic cloves, finely chopped

2 tablespoons chopped parsley

100 ml/3½ fl oz fish stock *(from the recipe)*

juice of 1 lemon

1 teaspoon paprika

SERVES 6

For rice alone, create a very quick base: fry the garlic (and *ñoras* if using) in oil, then remove. Fry the chopped tomato, then add it to the pulverized garlic, peppers and saffron in a blender, plus 1 lt/1¾ pt fish stock, salt and paprika (if using). Easy!

For two courses, start by preparing the fish, cutting it into steaks and seasoning. Heat the oil in a *paella* pan and fry the garlic and chopped *ñoras* until the garlic colours, then reserve. Stiffen the fish in plenty of oil, then remove.

Fry the chopped tomato (and sprinkle with paprika, if using), reducing it to a sauce. Peel and pound the garlic, with the *ñoras* or *jalepeño* and saffron in a mortar or small blender. Stir the paste into the tomato. Return the fish to the pan and add the fish stock and a little salt. Poach for 5–6 minutes, depending on shape. Remove to a serving dish and keep warm. Reserve the stock for the *allioli* and the *salmoretta* sauce.

Press the stock through a sieve (or blend). Return 1 lt/1¾ pt to the pan, taste and adjust the seasoning. Add the well-rinsed rice. Cook for 18–20 minutes: the rice must still have some bite when ready. Make the *allioli* and serve together as the first course.

For the *salmoretta* sauce, fry the chopped tomato in the oil in a small saucepan. Pound the garlic cloves in a mortar with the parsley (or blend) and add the fish stock and lemon juice, with paprika and salt. Beat well and serve in a sauce boat with the fish as the main course.

A moment of rest from cooking

Pollo all y pebre

— PEPPERED CHICKEN —

'The lake is famous for peppered eels,' said Señor Manoli, 'but nowadays it's difficult to find the quality. They're both insipid and greasy. The problem is the pesticides used for the rice – they drain into the lake. You'll do better with peppered chicken.' This version is 'brave and manly'.

1.5 kg/3½ lb free-range chicken,
in bite-size pieces, plus backbone
3 tablespoons olive oil
6 garlic cloves, unpeeled but smashed
1 tablespoon paprika
salt and freshly ground black pepper
2 *ñoras*, or 1 cm/½ in canned Mexican *jalapeño*
pepper, seeded and chopped
1 dried *guindilla* or chilli, seeded and chopped
350 ml/12 fl oz chicken stock, hot
0.1 g saffron (20 strands), crumbled
and soaked in a little stock for 5 minutes
freshly grated nutmeg
1 teaspoon lemon juice
pinch of sugar

CONDIMENT

50 g/2 oz almonds, toasted *(see page 129)*
4 garlic cloves, unpeeled but smashed
1 tablespoon pine nuts, toasted in a dry frying pan
2 tablespoons chopped parsley

— SERVES 4 —

Heat the oil in a flameproof earthenware casserole with the garlic cloves until they colour, then discard them. Fry the garlic for the condiment and reserve. Season the chicken with paprika, salt and pepper and fry over high heat (including the backbone) until coloured, then remove and reserve. Pour off all but 1 tablespoon oil.

Add all the chopped chillies, stirring rapidly, then immediately add the hot stock, saffron and nutmeg. Boil for a couple of minutes, then return the chicken.

For the condiment, pound the garlic (discarding skins) with a little salt (or blend) to a paste with the nuts and parsley. Work in a little stock and add to the casserole. Cook gently for 15 minutes or so, then discard the backbone. Check the seasoning: it should be very piquant. A lack of Spanish peppers (which have a depth of flavour) can be balanced by adding the lemon juice and sugar. Plain rice makes the best accompaniment.

Creepy Crawlers: Snails in Valencia

Women who sell apples don't have to pursue them, with a grab and a whoop, to prevent them walking off the table. But this snail-seller moved quickly to recover one that had made it further on the road to liberty. Snails don't have a good press in non-Latin countries, but this one was quite endearing. The movements of its head were like those of a cat pricking its ears.

There were great baskets of snails on sale: dark-shelled *paellitas*, *vaquetas de oliva* with grey and black whorls, and similar *cristianos* and *sonetas*. The biggest were great, gross black ones called *moros*, and the tiniest cream *avellanets*. 'Those are best in a tomato sauce with *pimiento* and a few bits of raw ham (or *chorizo*).'

Bags of hot peppers were on sale too – much as parsley comes with fish. There were sacks of fresh *guindillas*, Spain's hot chilli, and red and green *pimientos* shaped like a heart. She also had *cayenna*, our familiar dried supermarket chilli, a child's finger long, as well as a tiny, very hot one, sold in Britain as bird peppers.

I asked about the recipes. 'The two larger types of snail are much less good to eat. Roast them on the grill. But in the interior of Valencia you can buy the *vaqueta*. There's a snail! They are very expensive, 800–1000 pesetas for a dozen – if you can find them. For *paella* and rice dishes.' For a good rice dish she was emphatic it must be *vaquetas* or *xonetas* (mountain snails), not the *negros* (blacks) or *moros* that she was selling. Indeed, I was assured later, one of the nicest *paellas* was snails with runner beans (*ferrauras*) and butter beans (*garrafones*) – eaten outside in the shade of a broad-topped fig tree or under a hanging vine.

This was September. Was it specially good for snails? No, spring was the time for snail festivals – even a freshwater snail feast, as the river dried out at Os de Balaguer in Lérida!

But the famous festival – *la cargolada* – marks the return of warm weather. The snails are cooked outdoors on a grill, 200–300 at a time. At the last moment a torch is made from a piece of lard, wrapped in greasy paper, and the fat is dribbled along them, so a tiny drop enters each snail shell. They are eaten from the communal dish. Everyone has their own bread slice, for a plate, and piles it high with golden *allioli*. And the empty shells are collected, to count at the end like cherry stones.

La repetellada is more elaborate because the snails are cooked on a metal sheet, covered with branches of smelling things – thyme, wild rosemary, very dry fennel stalks. There may be a second tray and more boughs on top. Then the whole things is fired – 'for 15–20 minutes the flames rush through it, and the smell makes everyone hungry.' More bread and *allioli*? 'Yes, and a good *porrón* (a drinking-kettle) of red wine.'

Lola's caracoles

—— SNAILS WITH PIQUANT SAUCE ——

The spicy sauce is used for other things, like tripe – and is excellent for heating cooked prawns.

60 snails
plain flour
salt
vinegar
handful of fennel stalks or parsley stalks

SPICY TOMATO SAUCE
350 g/12 oz onions, chopped
3 tablespoons olive oil
½ bulb of garlic, finely chopped
1 leek, chopped
1 green pepper, seeded and chopped
500 g/1 lb ripe tomatoes or
400 g/14 oz canned tomatoes, chopped
3 *guindillas* or dried chillies, whole
1 bay leaf
freshly ground black pepper
1 teaspoon lemon juice
2 tablespoons chopped parsley

—— SERVES 4 AS A STARTER ——

Snails should be purged for a week, in case they have eaten something toxic to humans. Shut them up in a box or bucket with a lid to prevent them walking away. Weight it – there is snail power! After 3 days feed them by sprinkling flour into the bucket.

The day before cooking moisten them by splashing a little fresh water into the bucket. The ones that climb up the sides are alive. Any motionless in the bottom are probably dead: discard them.

Fat luscious snails in Valencia market

them into a pot with very lightly warmed water. Bring slowly to the boil and they seem to get caught unawares. Discard this water, which will be scummy.

Drain them and put again to boil in salted water with handfuls of herbs: wild fennel, or bruised parsley stalks will do. Cook for a good 30 minutes.

Make a tomato sauce in a big saucepan: fry the onions in the oil until soft. About halfway through, add the garlic, leek and green peper. When the onions are ready, add the tomatoes and the whole chillies (seed and chop one if you really like things hot!). Add the bay leaf and a little salt. Cook gently for 10 minutes, then add a ladleful of stock from the snail pan and cook down to a sauce.

Sieve the sauce (or not, in which case the tomatoes must be skinned at the beginning, and the chillies and bay leaf removed): a blender produces the wrong consistency. Return to the saucepan, taste, add the lemon juice and correct the seasoning. If the sauce is not piquant enough, the chillies can be returned, and then removed before serving.

Add the snails and simmer for a further 30 minutes. Serve in individual casseroles, sprinkled with the parsley, and accompanied by bread.

Clean the snails with salt and vinegar to get rid of the black spittle which they usually have. After half an hour, rinse them under fast-running water for several minutes, or wash them in several waters. When the black has all gone, drain them well.

For easy eating, they must be tricked into expiring with the maximum of body outside the shell. Put

❧ Turrón, Nuts and Other Sweets ❧

Xixona – Jijona: obviously Arab. A brown village on the edge of the Sierra de la Carrasqueta, in rocky hills the colour and texture of toasted almonds – almost as though the main ingredient of *turrón* was mined here, not made. For Jijona is celebrated for a type of nougat which has been made in the town for four centuries. The whole of Spain eats it at Christmas and, increasingly, throughout the year.

The finest Marcona almonds are at least half the weight of all *turrón*. Riding the village bus from Alicante, through the village of Muchamiel (lotsahoney), I reflected there must be lotsascrub in the mountain and lotsabees around too, for honey is the other main constituent of this nougat.

The *turrón* made here is soft and sticky; the meringue-covered nuts go into the grinder, then are beaten until creamy, to make a coffee-coloured, almond-scented paste. (A domestic recipe is given on page 25.) The other version is studded with whole toas-

ted nuts – like the white El Almendro from Alicante, and the Lérida *torta imperiale* (the best in Spain). There is also a dark caramelized version, *ghirlache* (see page 129), in Aragon.

The Spanish sweet tooth and taste for nuts is also indulged with the drink called *horchata*. Alboraya, just outside Valencia, is the world capital of *chufas*. 'An Arab from Saudi owns the lot,' I was told. 'His supply is sent weekly on a plane.'

The *chufa* is an underground tuber, an irregular little brown pebble to look at, textured like a peanut shell. It is produced by a type of sedge – toughish hummocks of grass (not unlike rice), growing in the fine black sand. It is harvested in summer by burning off the grass.

The taste is between almond and coconut, and it is made into a long refreshing drink, and sometimes an ice cream. It is sold in cafés in Valencia. To make *horchata* the *chufas* are ground, steeped in water and strained: 1 kg/2 lb nuts, 800 g/1¾ lb sugar flavoured with a little lemon zest, and water makes 5 lt/8 pt. A good profit, as the nuts are only 200 pesetas a kilo. But good cafés make it daily and throw it away if not consumed.

I find *horchaterías* are a Jewish-Arab tradition. In Madrid they may also make *persianas* (venetian blinds) or *zapatas* (rope-soled shoes). Poor trades; the men switch to making *horchata* in summer – and *turrón* at Christmas.

Bunyols de vent

—— HOT ORANGE PUFFS A WIND COULD LIFT ——

'They're a gift!' she said. They are, too, the lightest of little choux puffs with very Spanish ingredients.

75 ml/3 fl oz milk
50 ml/2 fl oz water
1 tablespoon strong black coffee
(the end of a *solo* cup, usually sweet)
15 g/½ oz butter
1 tablespoon sunflower oil
pinch of salt
75 g/3 oz plain flour
finely grated zest of ½ orange
2 small eggs
1 teaspoon orange flower water
oil for deep frying
caster sugar for sifting

—— SERVES 4 ——

Put the milk, water, coffee, butter, oil and salt in a saucepan over heat. When boiling point is reached, shoot in the sifted, measured flour. Beat vigorously with a wooden spoon to obtain a fine dough. When it comes away clean from the sides of the pan (about a minute) take from the heat. Don't skimp here – it must be reasonably dry.

Beat in the grated orange zest. Let it cool a minute, then beat in the eggs in turn, to make a smooth paste. Lastly beat in the orange flower water.

Heat clean oil for deep frying. Make small balls with 2 teaspoons, using one to scrape the mixture off the other into the fat, 6–7 together, as quickly as you can. Fry them, rolling them over with a slotted spoon, so they expand evenly – 1–2 minutes. Drain on kitchen paper, while you fry the rest. Don't keep them waiting long. Eat powdered with sugar.

Tocino de cielo

—— SWEET TEMPTATION ——

'One dessertspoon is the most you should eat,' she said, 'so it doesn't matter that everything about it is sinful – yolks and sugar.' It is one of those sweets one has no curiosity to try, but then proves to be irresistible. The name means, literally, a slab of heaven.

FOR AN 18-CM/7-IN RING MOULD
75 g/3 oz granulated sugar for the caramel
175 g/6 oz caster sugar
½ cinnamon stick
pared zest of ½ lemon
150 ml/5 fl oz water
6 yolks plus 1 whole egg

—— SERVES 8–10 ——

Put the sugar for the caramel in a small saucepan with 1 tablespoon water and heat until it caramelizes, pulling the toasted sugar in from outside to middle. When the syrup is a good toffee colour, pour it immediately into the mould: it helps if this is warm. Using gloves, quickly tip the mould to and fro until coated.

Put the caster sugar in the same pan with the cinnamon stick, lemon zest and water. Dissolve the sugar slowly, then boil – for about 10 minutes – until it will make a weak thread when dropped from a spoon (102°C/215°F on a sugar thermometer). Remove the cinnamon stick and zest.

Whisk the yolks with the whole egg until creamy, then slowly pour in the hot syrup, whisking all the time. Strain the custard into the mould.

The cooking operation is very delicate, and even a bain-marie in the oven risks splitting the custard. Stand the mould on a trivet (of the type used for steaming vegetables) in a saucepan and pour boiling water beneath it. Cover the pan with foil, then a lid and steam for 20 minutes. Cool then chill. Run a knife round the custard, invert a plate over the top and turn out to serve. Cut small portions.

The date palms at Elche lend the east coast an aura of North Africa

Paparajotes

———— FRITTERS WITH LEMON OR BAY LEAVES ————

The lovely lemon tree has deliciously scented leaves as well as fruit and these are used to flavour simple fritters. You can do the same thing with bay leaves (even dried ones). Children at teatime can easily devour a dozen fritters each – the best way to eat them – but an adult portion for dessert is about 8.

about 70 fresh lemon or bay leaves
250 g/8 oz plain flour
50 g/2 oz caster sugar
250 ml/8 fl oz milk
2 tablespoons not-too-dry white wine
or (better) moscatel
3 small egg whites
fresh sunflower oil for deep frying
vanilla sugar for sprinkling

———— SERVES 8 ————

Wash and dry the leaves. Mix the flour and sugar together in a bowl, and make a well in the middle (or use a food processor). Pour in the milk and wine and beat in the flour to make a smooth cream. Whisk the whites to soft peaks and fold in the batter.

Heat clean oil for deep frying. Hold each leaf by the stalk and quickly dip it in the batter. Fry about 8 at a time (a portion), flipping them over with a slotted spoon when they start to colour round the edges – about 2 minutes overall. They puff like cigars. Drain on kitchen paper. If serving a batch at a time – the best way – take the oil off the heat, until you are back to cooking. (Otherwise it overheats and the first fritters of the new batch overbrown before the last ones are dipped.)

Sprinkle with vanilla sugar and eat by picking them up by the stalk and pulling the fritter off the leaf (discard it) with your teeth.

Refrescos

———— REFRESHING DRINKS ————

In the glare of the day, or sitting out under the trees at night, waiting for the first breeze to break the heat, nothing is more refreshing than an iced lemonade. However, the beach drink of the coast is *palomita*, red wine with Casera (fizzy lemonade).

Sweet fritters for the children's tea: lemon leaves, bay and even borage leaves can be used

Granizado

———— ICED LEMONADE ————

Unlike Italian *granita*, this is not frozen lemonade, but is poured over slushed ice. Break ice cubes inside a towel by hitting with a rolling pin, then put in the processor.

———— MAKES 20 GLASSES ————

Wash 10 juicy lemons and thinly pare strips of zest. Put these in a bowl and cover with 1 lt/1¾ pt boiling water. Leave to infuse until cold.

Remove the zest strips and stir in 350 g/12 oz sugar, with the lemon juice. Keep this base in the fridge. Dilute with an equal amount of water. To serve, fill a tall glass with ice slush, then top up with lemonade and add straws.

El pixer

———— ICED COFFEE LIQUEUR AND LEMON PUNCH ————

An indefinable fruit flavour, rather like passion fruit: you'd never guess what it is made out of.

———— MAKES 35 GLASSES ————

Put 4 tablespoons sugar into a saucepan and heat until they caramelize. Immediately take from the heat and add some of the measured water – 1 lt/1¾ pt. Stir until dissolved. Pour into a punch bowl and add 750 g/1 lb 10 oz sugar, the finely pared zest of 2 lemons and the juice of 1, plus ½ teaspoon ground cinnamon and the remaining water. Stir until dissolved, then chill well.

Before serving add a 75 cl bottle of coffee liqueur (like Tia Maria), cold from the fridge, and 1.5 lt/2½ pt icy water. Serve in a wine glass over 2 ice lumps.

Carajillo

———— BRANDIED COFFEE ————

A hot one . . . 'The perfect drink to start an evening when you are rather tired,' said a Valencian friend, 'because it gets you drunk and wakes you up at the same time.'

———— SERVES 1 ————

To a *solo* cup of coffee – small, strong and black – add a little sugar, then a slug of sweetened Spanish brandy. Anis de Chinchón, strong and not sweet, is very good.

CHAPTER 12

Balearic Islands

Spain's biggest Mediterranean islands are Majorca and Minorca (literally the major and minor islands) and Ibiza. The latter was the one part of Spain never occupied by the Fascists. One reason, perhaps, why it became the Mediterranean's first hippy colony in the 1960s.

I once got locked into Palma cathedral. Never mind! I had my *ensaimada* with me in a paper. The cathedral is vast and late Gothic: slender soaring pillars (with chandeliers round them) and light, with coloured glass and a wide rose window. A moment of panic as I struggled with the outside lock in the pitch-blackness of a double-porch. Then comfort, as I bit into that glorious breakfast pastry, many layered, its flaky softness coiled under a dusting of icing sugar. Workmen arranged my exit.

Eight in the morning is the time to see Palma de Mallorca, when the city is untroubled by the tourists that will engulf it later. And March is the time to be there, to experience the elegance that once gave it its bon-ton image. The bay is very beautiful – and a major sailing port in summer, which still brings the King to the Marivent Palace. March to April is the opera season, and in a shop on the arcaded Avenida Jaime III I saw a windowful of male opera gear, white silk scarves matched to different shirts and styles of dinner jackets. The Hotel Formentor, in the north of the peninsula, is part of this same elegant tradition, built in 1929 as the first of the 20th-century luxury resort hotels. In summer some such retreat is needed: tourist beds on the islands outnumber those in Greece!

I hadn't expected the island to be so beautiful. First the bay of Palma, dominated by the cathedral hulk and buttresses, then the interior of the island, where agricultural life goes on as usual. I passed a field of almond blossom (obviously in a frost pocket). The Sierra de Tramonte forms a ridge down the west of the island and rises to almost 4500 feet in places. Though pink in the morning light, it is grey and without vegetation. The rough stony *garrigue* grows a profusion of herbs, which are the basis of domestic and commerical green herb liqueurs. In the valley are gnarled olive trees, some over 1000 years old. Ancient and grey, often split down the middle, they are as old as those on the Mount of Olives. I watched a woman picking up *muertas* – ripe black olives left to shrivel and drop. Beyond the ridge is the west coast road, with incomparable views of blue sea and the villas of the discerning.

Majorca is known for solid soups and vegetable dishes. *Sopa mallorquina* is almost solid with bread, more like a juicy pudding, though I ate a very good one with three sorts of greens – *bledes* (chard), cabbage and spinach, plus stock (and bits) from pork and rabbit. Perhaps the pleasantest of these dishes is *tumbet*, with layered, lightly fried aubergine and potato in tomato sauce (see party version page 166).

Minorca's popular soup is *oliagua* (see recipe), one of the few dishes not to start with a fried *sofrito* of onion and tomato. For these vegetables, with potato, are the basic fare. *Trempó* is the local salad – mixed tomato, peppers and onions, sometimes with fruit. Many recipes include bread, a good way to use up a stale loaf (though Majorca has a dark saltless bread that lasts). There are also flat breads called *cocas*. Sugary ones are eaten for festivals and they are made in many flavours, though I find them less good than pizzas.

Pork is basic, and the use of lard for cooking. There was local uproar at the time I was there because of an EC threat to outlaw the family *mantance* (pig-killing). Much pork goes to make the raw, red sausage, *sobrasada*, so soft that it is bread-spreadable. In the western market town of Soller, eggs are fried and served on slices of *sobrasada*, then covered with a milky sauce with puréed peas in it. Sausage also enriches *escaldums* (see page 171) and *perdices de capellán* (chaplain's partridges), which are veal escalopes rolled up with ham and sausage filling.

At Alcudía, a port with sugar-brown city walls built in the 14th century, I joined the party of a local *cofradía*. Sucking pig in Majorca is roast plain or stuffed with its own spiced liver, apples and cherries. But this was the festive *mero con lechona a la malloquina*. From beneath the roast piglet's splayed legs came the tail of a grouper. Pork and fish together. The *mero* was huge, the flesh slashed and stuffed with lemon. Is it a fantasy that one can taste the milk in the pig meat? It was tender, even when well-roasted as is the tradition. Beneath it were layered vegetables – potatoes, tomatoes, onions, spinach – in a sauce that contained raisins, pine nuts and paprika.

Fishy glories start with cultured pearls, made here by Majorica at Manacor, also celebrated for its trotting races. Their sheen comes from the belly scales of certain fish, including herrings and bleak (technically guanine). Black pearls are the ones I covet, and I'd like to wear them to the Baile de Piñata (Carnival ball) on the first Sunday of Lent. The famous *bolero*, I learned, comes from an 18th-century ballroom dance in Palma.

Fish is often eaten simply, such as sardines barbecued on the beach over old rosemary bushes from the stony *garrigue*. Sauces are traditional, like that in Ibiza's *burrida de ratjada*, ray with a sauce of pulverized almonds. The fish stews, *calderas*, have great variety and freshness. Most start with a *sofrito* of onion and tomato and lightly fried fish is added. Peas are very popular, especially with cuttlefish.

Summer is celebrated with spiny lobster in all the islands. The most glamorous dish is *caldereta de langosta*, with a tomato sauce containing peppers and bread, spiked with the local herb *aguardiente*. I was amused to find it was assumed this was *salsa americana*. I met other good lobster dishes, one called a *greixera* – the name of a flattish brown casserole, and therefore of many local dishes. The lobster was baked and shelled, then layered with about one-third of its bulk of cooked spinach mixed with eggs and milk, flavoured with cinnamon and lemon juice and topped with breadcrumbs.

Flat Minorca, to the British eye, still has many British traces: Windsor chairs and English tallboys in private houses – and willow-pattern dinner services still on wedding present lists. The British had a long and benign occupation. Ex-English words have become local argot – *boinder* is a bow-window, *potato* instead of *patatas*. There are turkeys, and flat, unSpanish soda biscuits called *crespells*, plain or with a layer of jam. I was also given lemon meringue pie, which my hostess said was an old Minorcan recipe. The popular governor, Richard Kane, introduced dairy cows to replace goats, planting *enclover* to feed them, and so formed the local cheese. The square, orange Mahón is semi-hard, and is now found in good restaurants in London.

A stew pot standing on *la plancha* – the iron sheet used for grilling

Calamares rellenos a la menorquina

SQUID STUFFED WITH PINE NUTS,
MINT AND RAISINS

Joaquina, who cooked me this recipe, was a young blond woman, with several babies, in Binibeca. When I returned the next year, I heard she had died, having another.

4–8 squid, about 500 g/1 lb
½ small Spanish onion
4 tablespoons olive oil
1 slice of stale country bread
25 g/1 oz pine nuts, toasted in a dry frying pan
75 g/3 oz raisins, preferably muscatels from Malaga, simmered 10 minutes in boiling water
12 fresh mint leaves
2 tablespoons chopped parsley
1 egg
salt and freshly ground black pepper
about 2 teaspoons plain flour

SAUCE

½ small Spanish onion, chopped
1 garlic clove, finely chopped
350 g/12 oz ripe tomatoes, skinned, seeded and finely chopped
125 ml/4 fl oz dry white wine
1 bay leaf
salt and freshly ground black pepper

SERVES 4 AS A STARTER, 2 AS A MAIN COURSE

To clean squid, use the tentacles to pull out the body. Cut off and keep the tentacles, with the fin flaps from either side of the body. With salted hands rub off the skin; flexing will pop out the spinal structure. Rinse inside and out.

Make the stuffing by chopping the onion finely (briefly in a processor) with the tentacles and pointed fins. Heat the oil in a flameproof casserole in which the squid fit neatly. Over high heat fry the bread. From this point all the stuffing ingredient can be added to the processor, or chopped separately and then combined.

Add the bread and pine nuts. Pip the raisins (if using muscatels) and add with the mint, parsley and egg. Season well with pepper and a little salt.

Stuff the squid and stitch them through the top with a cocktail stick to hold the stuffing inside. Flour the squid very lightly and fry them briefly in the casserole, turning until coloured.

Make the sauce round the squid if there is room. Fry the onion there, then add the garlic and tomato. Let this wilt a little, then stir in the wine and bay leaf. Simmer gently, covered – 30 minutes for large squid, 20 for small ones. Check the seasonings and serve the squid sliced in rounds.

Oliagua amb escarrats

TOMATO AND GARLIC SOUP WITH ASPARAGUS

The name means 'oil soup' and it centres on the vegetable in season: cabbage, tomato or just parsley with garlic. I was given it with fine wild asparagus. With cultivated asparagus a practical solution is to cook the hard asparagus ends first, then discard them and make the soup with the asparagus water.

1 onion, finely chopped
8 garlic cloves, finely chopped
½ green pepper, finely chopped
700 g/1½ lb ripe tomatoes, skinned and thickly sliced
4 tablespoons olive oil
750 ml/1¼ pt vegetable water
salt and freshly ground black pepper
pinch of cayenne pepper
250 g/8 oz thin wild asparagus
or 500 g/1 lb green asparagus
12–16 thin slices of French bread
or good quality country bread

SERVES 4

Put the onion, garlic, green pepper and tomatoes in a flameproof casserole and add a glass of cold water. Cook very gently, covered, until the onion has softened, without letting it colour – a good 30 minutes.

Add the oil and stir in. Add the vegetable water, bring to the boil and season with salt, black pepper and cayenne. Press much of the solids through a sieve or blend (in this version). This is really best done ahead and allowed to mellow.

Bring to simmering (when a slight skin forms on the surface), then add the asparagus, cut in manageable lengths. Simmer for about 15 minutes (wild asparagus can take longer).

Dry out the bread slices in a low oven or toast them. Put 3 or 4 in each soup plate and ladle the soup over them.

Motllo d'alberginies de Mallorca

AUBERGINE TIMBALE FROM MAJORCA

A party version of the famous *tumbet*, with the aubergines moulded round the edge and the whole thing turned out. It is more commonly served as a simple layered dish, topped with crisp crumbs. We agree it is best assembled in the morning, to bake later.

FOR A 2.5-LT/4-PT SOUFFLE DISH

1 kg/2 lb aubergines
salt and freshly ground black pepper
500 g/1 lb green peppers
25 g/1 oz lard or butter, softened
2–3 tablespoons grated stale bread
2–3 tablespoons plain flour
about 125 ml/4 fl oz olive oil
1 big bunch of parsley, chopped
500 g/1 lb potatoes, in rounds
250 ml/8 fl oz sieved tomato (passata)
or extra tomato sauce, to serve

TOMATO SAUCE

1 Spanish onion, chopped
50 g/2 oz streaky bacon, chopped
2 tablespoons olive oil
4–5 garlic cloves, finely chopped
750 g/1¾ lb ripe tomatoes, skinned, seeded and chopped
4 tablespoons chopped parsley
1 bouquet garni

SERVES 6

Two gifts from the Moors to Spain's kitchen – aubergines and lemons

Cut the aubergines in rounds 5 mm/¼ in thick and salt them. Leave for a good 30 minutes, while you make the tomato sauce. Fry the onion and the bacon in the oil until soft. Add the garlic, chopped tomato flesh, parsley and bouquet garni. Moisten with ½ glass of water and simmer for 20–25 minutes. The sauce should be thickish.

At the same time grill the peppers until charred on all sides. Leave to cool in a plastic bag, then peel the skins off on a plate, to catch the juice. Remove the stalks and seeds and chop the peppers.

Smear the soufflé dish, particularly the bottom, with half the fat or butter. Dust with breadcrumbs, tipping out any that don't stick.

Rinse and drain the aubergine slices, pressing gently with kitchen paper to dry them. Flour them and fry in a generous quantity of very hot oil (they can absorb it so treacherously). Blot and fry the potato slices until well browned on each side.

Arrange a ring of aubergine slices on the bottom of the soufflé dish, overlapping them, with one in the middle. Make one row overlapping round the sides, bending them at the bottom, so they have something to sit on. Sprinkle the bottom with 2 tablespoons parsley, and add a quarter of the peppers and of the freshly made tomato sauce, then more parsley. Layer

166

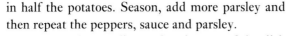

in half the potatoes. Season, add more parsley and then repeat the peppers, sauce and parsley.

Using the better slices, edge the rest of the dish with aubergine. Then layer all the awkward ends into the dish and sprinkle with parsley. Repeat the peppers, sauce and parsley, and then the potato layer, seasoning again. More parsley, then top with peppers and tomato sauce. Sprinkle the top with bread-crumbs and dot with the remaining lard or butter.

Bake in the oven at 190°C/375°F/gas 5 for 45 minutes. Run a knife round and turn out on to a hot dish. The mould is rather firm, so a couple of table-spoons of sieved tomato (or tomato sauce) are wel-come. Pour a little round the mould (and the rest into a sauce boat). Cut in wedges, giving each serving 2–3 tablespoons sieved tomato. Good cold with *allioli*.

⚜ Mahón and Mayonnaise ⚜

Horatio was here, Nelson, and the British fleet for nearly the whole of the 18th century. The harbour is one of the best in the world, an inlet a couple of miles long (I walked it) and 200 yards or so wide, with a cliff to the west offering shelter. On that day there was a stiff breeze blowing, of a kind that makes sailors want to be at sea. It was easy to imagine the harbour full of ships-of-the line and British frigates.

The English must have been so happy! Decent, white and clean, there is something here reminiscent of Devon. Sash windows (inconceivable in the Medi-terranean) and well-painted solid shutters are preva-lent in Mahón, and in El Castell at the harbour entrance (Georgetown in the British era). I saw six-panelled Georgian doors that would not have been out-of-place in Woodstock or Greenwich. Halfway down the harbour, on the eastern shore, is San Antonio, a red villa with a lookout tower, where Nelson reputedly lived with Lady Hamilton. It is certainly in the perfect semaphore position.

The harbour was lost briefly to the French – and thereby hangs the story. There is an engraving in the museum of the party when the British got it back again, full of wine, dancing and babies. There must be a lot of Minorcans with English great-grand-parentage.

In 1756 the French took Mahón – and the legend of mayonnaise was born. Did a Frenchman invent it, or did the English miss it entirely? An English engin-eer, John Armstrong, wrote a good account of the island's food in 1752 without remarking on it. The French took it back to France in triumph.

A widespread local legend associated it with Maré-chal Richelieu. It is said his chef served it to enliven the local greenstuff during the siege of San Felipe castle. But Elizabeth David lends support to a local origin in *French Provincial Cookery:* 'It seems likely by the 1750s the sauce was already known in Spain and Provence.' The probability is that it is *allioli* without the garlic. The local dialect name is *maionesa* (from Maó) and Spaniards often favour a spelling, *mahonesa*, that emphasizes the local origin.

Mayonnaise is a southern sauce, and sensitive to cold. Spanish oil, with its high acidity, is ideal for it, and probably why it was born here. The oil blends at once and never separates. An acidity of 0.8 per cent, I was advised, is perfect for mayonnaise: in Spain acidity is marked on oil labels in big numerals. It is a sauce in which virgin oil is not successful. This goes in, if at all, after the emulsion is formed, to add to the flavour.

Start by diluting salt with vinegar (or lemon juice – even top chefs can't agree on the perfect recipe). Vine-gar is better, though, for it will kill off any salmonella bug lingering in the yolks.

Then drip in the oil slowly. Sod's law applies to this (like meringues): the recipe is simple and works for everyone – but not when you are in a hurry! One egg will go on absorbing huge quantities of oil without the emulsion breaking; the sauce just gets thinner. Real mayonnaise should be thick, even cuttable! It then can be diluted to pour, or take other flavours. Once made, good Spanish mayonnaise also doesn't separate: witness mayonnaise in warm soup.

Ybarra is the local make, and a steady export. But my attempts to find purely local recipes that use it were rather frustrating. Invariably the answer was '*todo*' – with everything. I give the best ideas below the recipe. I was reminded, though, that Ernest Hemingway liked it, mixed with a little tomato sauce and a spoonful of pap-rika, over a tail of monkfish.

Mahonesa

MAYONNAISE

Here is the classic recipe, and the way I find it is often made now. Temperature is important for a successful emulsion. Warm the oil gently if it seems chilly. Below are the best local serving suggestions, two easy, two lavish.

juice of ½ lemon or 1 tablespoon white wine vinegar
salt
yolks of 2 large eggs, at room temperature
(plus 1 egg white, if making in a blender)
300 ml/½ pt Spanish olive oil, preferably one with
0.8% acidity, at room temperature,
or 3 parts plain oil (even sunflower or corn oil)
plus 1 part good virgin olive oil

OPTIONS
1 garlic clove, chopped (then crushed with the salt)
2 tablespoons finely chopped parsley

MAKES ABOUT 300 ML/½ PT

Put the lemon juice or vinegar and a pinch of salt in a bowl (or blender) – the acid element is important as the sauce won't emulsify without it. (A smigeon of crushed garlic can go in here, if it matches your recipe.) Add the egg yolks (use 1 whole egg plus 1 yolk in a blender) and whisk (or work) to a cream. (Parsley goes in here, in a blender.)

Add the oil (start with the plain one), drop by drop if working with a whisk, until the mixture emulsifies. Add more oil, in larger quantities as the mayonnaise thickens, until it is all absorbed. Virgin oil can be used once the sauce has emulsified. Taste and correct the seasonings.

This mayonnaise is quite thick and can be thinned with 1–2 tablespoons boiling water if it is to be kept.

For Mahón potato salad: mix chopped parsley and a little more vinegar into the mayonnaise and coat rounds of cold potato. Decorate with anchovy fillets and lemon slices.

For Mahón mussel salad: steam open the mussels and remove the shells, then serve in a pile, covered with mayonnaise and parsley. Garnish with a radiating ring of mussel shells, bedding them a little under the salad.

For hot baked lobster: split the lobster (they use the spiny one without large claws) and barbecue it in the ashes, dribbling the flesh with a little wine and vinegar. Serve hot with mayonnaise.

For cold lobster: boil the lobster in seawater with big handfuls of herbs – or a sliced onion, parsley stalks and a couple of bay leaves. Once the water has returned to boiling, allow 30 minutes for a 1 kg/2 lb lobster. Cool and split, then serve with mayonnaise. The local accompaniment will include shredded lettuce, tomato and, invariably, hard-boiled egg slices.

Of Gin and Gravy

It was probably for the sheltered box-hedge garden that George Sand chose Valldemossa in 1838. Why else should she winter in the ex-Charterhouse, a great enclosed stone pile? She found it draughty (there is a break here in the sheltering mountains) and wore trousers. The locals hated her (and she took her revenge by disparaging them in *Un Hiver à Majorque*). The presence of consumptive Chopin (and her children) was more comprehensible. I inquired about what she might have eaten. Pickled hocks are the village speciality, as prepared by the monks of the Eremita de la Trinidad.

The beauty of the coast here is that it falls directly into the sea, a blue marked only by a few sailboats. There are no seabirds, for the fish moved out long ago. Robert Graves moved to Deía and wrote *Goodbye to All*

That here, after his experience in World War I trenches. His favourite, I am told, among local dishes was rabbit with onions cooked down to a confit. An Austrian Archduke, Luis Salvador, planted Mediterranean-smelling gardens nearby at Son Marroig – and made an intimate record of the islands. He was an early preserver of natural beauty. Now a staggering 45 per cent of the island of Majorca is protected.

Waves of invaders have occupied these islands, off Spain's eastern coast, before the present tourists. Bronze Age people left *taulas* (T-stones) and conical stone piles in Minorca. Greeks, more helpfully, planted olive trees and the flat-topped Aleppo pine (which gives

Pink roses up a cottage wall –
loved by Spaniards and British alike

pine nuts) in all the islands, and left a sweet cheesecake called a *flao*. I imagine the islands offered no resistance, but simply absorbed the newcomers.

The Arabs left Moorish baths in Palma, villages with names starting with Bini (son of) in Minorca, and a sweet tooth. I know nowhere else in Spain that has shops called *Sucrerías* (sugar-sellers). There are jams of every sort (I bought apple with pumpkin) and they are credited with *ensaimadas*, a delicious sugared spiral roll, Arab in its layers and lightness, though made with pork lard. It is first choice for breakfast in much of Spain's eastern coast.

There are main courses with sweet sauces, such as *pollo con salsa de granada* (chicken with pomegranate sauce) and *sobrasada con miel* (sausage in honey) – of Arab inspiration: I know a similar recipe in Andalusia for chicken. Even stuffed aubergines (an Arab introduction) have a potato-stuffed version with cinnamon, butter and honey! Spinach, too, is Arab. *La espinaga* is a piquant pie that includes eel.

In Minorca the French bâton lies beside the English tin loaf in the local bakery. The French may have influenced the excellent sweet tarts, and I came across a lamb stew called *rogout de cordera*. To balance this, there are beans served in *grevi* – a sauce made with meat juice. The British Navy also bequeathed a taste for rum and gin. The gin is seriously strong, the famous name being Xoriguer: either *pomada*, with lemon, or herby. It is drunk almost neat, *gin en pallofa*, with ice, lemon and (little) soda water. And the rations are naval!

Cocarrois de Mallorca

CHARD (OR SPINACH) PASTIES
WITH RAISINS AND PINE NUTS

A little closed pizza, with the edges making a wavy 'crown' (hence *rois*) on top, this is a Cornish pasty gone Spanish. It is also related to the chard tarts of Tuscany, with their sweet pastry and identical filling.

1 large egg
50 g/2 oz lard or butter
50 ml/2 fl oz sunflower oil
juice of 1 large orange
1 tablespoon caster sugar
350 g/12 oz plain flour

FILLING
750 g/1¾ lb spinach or leaves from 1 kg/2 lb chard
(425 g/15 oz prepared leaves)
25 g/1 oz pine nuts
50 g/2 oz raisins, simmered for 10 minutes
salt and freshly ground black pepper
½ teaspoon paprika
1 teaspoon oil

SERVES 6 AS A STARTER OR SNACK

In a large bowl beat together the egg, lard and oil with a wooden spoon until creamy. Add the orange juice and sugar, then little by little beat in the flour until smooth. (The old method works well in a food processor.) Pull the dough together and chill while you prepare the filling.

Wash and drain the leaves. Wilt the spinach in the water clinging to the leaves in a covered pan, turning the top to bottom. Cook chard leaves in boiling water for 10 minutes. Drain as well as possible, pressing to extract excess water, then chop.

Toast the pine nuts in a heavy frying pan over low heat, tossing, for 3–4 minutes, until coloured and smelling richly. Drain the raisins (and seed, if they are muscatels). Chop coarsely with the pine nuts, then mix with the spinach and add a little salt, pepper, paprika and the oil. Mix well.

Roll out the dough on a lightly floured surface and cut circles round a saucer (15 cm/5 in across) – or make 12 balls, then roll out each one. Put the filling in a bullet shape in the centre of each one. Dampen round the edge with a finger and draw up the sides to meet along the top. Squeeze together, then use finger and thumb to crinkle it to and fro. Push in the ends slightly, so there is no empty pastry. Move to a lightly oiled baking sheet and bake in a moderate oven (180°C/350°F/gas 4) for 30 minutes. Eat warm or cold.

Escaldums d'indiot o de pollastre

——— TURKEY, OR CHICKEN, FRICASSEE ———

This is turkey fricassee, converted for Spain, with puréed nuts, and enriched with a little of the smooth local sausage. It is served with roast potatoes as a New Year dish.

1.2 kg/2½ lb boneless turkey breast, or free-range
chicken, in frying pieces
salt and freshly ground black pepper
1 teaspoon paprika
3–4 tablespoons olive oil (or half lard)
1 large Spanish onion, finely sliced
1 celery stalk, sliced
1 bulb of garlic, cloves smashed then peeled
350 g/12 oz ripe tomatoes, skinned, seeded and
chopped
1 bay leaf
5 sprigs of fresh oregano, leafy tips
3 cloves, ground to powder, or a good pinch of
ground cloves
75 ml/3 fl oz *amontillado* sherry
150 ml/5 fl oz poultry stock
2 tablespoons chopped parsley, to garnish

CONDIMENT

25 g/1 oz pine nuts, toasted in a dry frying pan
(or toasted almonds – *see page 129*)
2 slices of *sobrasada* sausage or 50 g/2 oz smooth liver
pâté (such as Brussels)
1 teaspoon paprika (if using pâté)
1 tablespoon melted butter (if using pâté)

——— SERVES 5–6 ———

Season the poultry pieces with salt, pepper and 1 teaspoon paprika. Heat the oil (and fat) in a wide flameproof casserole and fry them over medium-high heat, in 2 batches, moving them around and removing when coloured.

Fry the onion and celery, adding the whole garlic cloves towards the end (these mellow with cooking). Add the chopped tomato flesh, bay leaf, oregano and ground cloves and cook gently to reduce the tomato to a sauce. Add the *amontillado* and stock, and return the poultry – it should just be covered. Simmer for 30 minutes. This can be done ahead, so flavours blend.

For the condiment, pound the nuts in a mortar (or blend), adding the *sobrasada*. This is a raw pork-and-paprika sausage, very soft and fatty, and it both thickens and enriches the final sauce. Alternatively use the pâté with paprika and melted butter, working to a smooth paste. Add a little stock from the casserole and stir into the sauce. Taste for seasoning and simmer for 10 minutes. Serve sprinkled with a little parsley.

Dos ponches

——— TWO PUNCHES ———

A milk-and-rum punch with overtones of the British Navy, the first punch is served in Majorca for Carnival balls and grand occasions. Some older families have beautiful china punch bowls and fine silver spoons with long mother-of-pearl handles to serve it. The second punch is made with the local white rum, and is an enticing deep-pink colour.

PONX D'OUS – RUM, MILK AND EGG PUNCH
2 tablespoons dark rum (or brandy)
2 small egg yolks
2 tablespoons caster sugar
250 ml/8 fl oz milk, hot or icy

——— MAKES 2 GLASSES ———

PONCHE DE SANGUINEAS – ICED WHITE RUM
WITH BLOOD ORANGES
250 ml/8 fl oz white rum or Bacardi
1 lt/1¾ pt water
350 g/12 oz sugar
3 ripe citrons (or lemons)
1 teaspoon orange flower water (with lemons)
juice of 4–6 blood oranges

——— MAKES 16 GLASSES ———

For milk punch: beat the yolks and sugar until white and the sugar has completely dissolved. For a hot punch, stir in the hot milk and rum to form a cream. Strain into 2 glasses and serve at once. For cold punch, use cold milk and serve the drink in wine glasses over ice.

For blood orange punch: put the water and sugar into a punch bowl. Add the thinly pared citron (or lemon) zest and the fruit, sliced very thinly, and stir to dissolve the sugar. Leave for 24 hours to infuse, chilling thoroughly. Strain, pressing the fruit slices well if using lemons. Add the orange flower water with lemons, as citrons are highly perfumed. Add the orange juice and rum from a bottle in the fridge before serving. Serve in a wine glass over a couple of ice lumps.

List of Recipes by Region

Andalusia

Zoque (Red gazpacho) 13

Ajo blanco con uvas de Málaga (White almond and garlic soup with muscat grapes) 14

Gazpacho de primavera (Green gazpacho for spring) 14

Salmorejo cordobés (Chilled Cordoba tomato cream) 14

Gazpachuelo (Warm potato soup with eggs and vinegar) 16

Conejo en ajillo pastor (Rabbit with aromatics and saffron) 16

Puchero de hinojos (Fennel stew with beans and pork) 17

Remojón (Salt cod and orange salad) 19

Ensalada de alcauciles y pimientos rojos (Artichoke and red pepper salad) 20

Fritura malagueña (Malaga mixed fried fish) 21

Salmonetes en escabeche (Red mullet salad) 22

Urta a la rotena (Fish with onions and brandy) 22

Soplillos de Granada (Granada almond meringues) 25

Pestinos (Fritters in honey syrup) 25

Extremadura

Sopa de tomate con higos (Tomato soup with fresh figs) 29

El matambre (Crispy bread balls in tomato sauce) 29

Escarapuche (Cold trout in vinegar with chopped salad) 30

Caldereta extremeña (Stewed lamb from Extremadura) 30

Prueba de cerdo (Fried pork with paprika and vinegar) 33

Costillas con niscalos (Pork ribs with wild mushrooms) 33

Liebre guisado (Hare in red wine, Spanish style) 36

Pato con aceitunas a la antigua (Duck with olives the old-fashioned way) 37

New Castile and La Mancha

Crema de Aranjuez (Aranjuez cream-of-asparagus soup) 40

Perdices estofados (Partridges in wine and vinegar) 41

Queso frito (Fried cheese) 41

Alajú (Arab honey and nut sweetmeat) 41

Sopa de la abuela castellana (Granny's garlic and bread soup) 42

Pisto Semana Santa (Peppers, tomatoes and onions with canned tuna) 42–3

Torrijas (Sugared wine toasts) 43

Tortilla de patatas con azafrán (Potato cake with eggs and saffron) 45

Pollo con salsa de ajos (Chicken with saffron and garlic sauce) 45

Madrid

Chuletas de cordero con pimientos asados (Lamb cutlets with soft red peppers) 52

Mama's merluza (Mama's hake with two mayonnaises and a soup course) 52

Torta de gambas (Prawn-glazed salad loaf) 53

Pastel de higadillos de ave, María Palau (Maria's hot poultry liver pâté) 54–5

Huevos Generalissimo Franco (Potato nests with eggs and mushrooms) 55

Redondo de ternera mechada (Pot-roast beef larded with ham) 56–7

Surtido de verduras rellenas (Stuffed vegetable selection) 58

Aceitunas a la importancia (Party olives with anchovies and peppers) 60

Tigres (Stuffed crumbed mussels) 62

Besugo al horno (Baked whole fish with lemon and potatoes) 62–3

Figuritas de marzapan (Marzipan pieces) 63

Intxausalsa (Christmas Eve walnut cream) 63

Old Castile and Rioja

Menestra con pollo (Cauliflower, artichoke and chicken hotpot) 67

Judías del Barco de Avila (White bean pot) 67–8

Menestra de ternera (Veal with new vegetables) 69

Carne con chocolate (Beef stewed with chocolate) 69–70

Tostón (Roast sucking pig) 71–2

Pimientos rellonos de merluza (Red peppers stuffed with hake or cod) 73

Calderillo bejarano (Potato, green pepper and rib stew) 74

Revuelto de ajetes o puerros (Cold scrambled egg with leeks and mayonnaise) 76

Jamon asado con pasas (Roast pork with red wine and raisin sauce) 76–7

Galicia

Gallina a la gallega (Buttered Galician chicken with noodles) 81–2

Sardinas rellenas asadas (Baked sardines with oregano stuffing) 82

Callos con garbanzos y costillas (Tripe with chick peas and pork ribs) 82–3

Zamburiñas rebozadas, cuatro en uno (Fried baby scallops, four to the shell) 84

Tarta de Santiago (St James's moist almond tart) 84

Empanada de berberechos (Cockle [or clam] pie) 86

Lomo de cerdo con castañas (Roast pork with chestnuts and cognac) 87

Castañas con berza (Chestnut, cabbage and sausage pie) 88

Castañas en almíbar (Chestnuts in vanilla syrup) 88

Vinagreta de mejillones (Mussel and potato salad with paprika dressing) 91

Tortilla de mejillones de La Coruña (Corunna mussel omelette) 91

Asturias and Cantabria

Croquettas de huevo (Egg croquettes) 95

Chirlas o almejas con arroz verde (Clam and green-rice soup) 95

Perdices con verduras (Partridges in wine with cabbage) 96

Casadielles (Walnut puff pastries) 96

Pote asturiano (Asturian bean and sausage soup) 98

Fabes con carabineros (Beans with big prawns) 98–9

Caldereta asturiana (Mixed fish and shellfish stew) 100

Salmón a la ribereña (Riverbank salmon in cider) 100

Arroz con leche requemado (Rice pudding with caramel topping) 102

Tarta de manzanas (Apple batter cake) 102

Basque Country

Endivias al Roquefort (Chicory with Roquefort cream) 106

Arroz a la vasca (Rice with everything from a chicken) 108

Helado Nelusko (Chocolate and almond ice cream) 108

Zurruputuna (Salt cod soup with garlic and peppers) 111

Bacalao al ajoarriero (Salt cod the mule-drivers' way, with garlic) 111

Revuelta de delicías (Spinach and sea treasures with scrambled egg) 113

Merluza a la koxkera (Hake or cod with clams) 114

Gastaíka (Ray or skate with chilli oil) 114

Budin de merluza (Pink souffléd pudding) 116

Solomillo con salsa de berros (Steak with watercress sauce) 116

Reinettas en salsa de limón (Baked apples with lemon sauce) 117

Aragon and Navarre
Lentejas de urdesa (Lentils with leeks and mushrooms) 121
Chilindrón de cordero (Lamb stewed with peppers) 122
Pichones con pasas y piñones (Pigeons with raisins and pine nuts) 122
Pâté del Alto Aragón (Pork pâté from the mountains, with apples and nuts) 124
Truchas con serrano y hierbabuena (Trout with raw ham and mint) 125
Conejo con patatas (Rabbit stewed with potatoes) 125
Espárragos con huevos (Asparagus with poached eggs) 127
Cogollos de Tudela (Lettuce heart and anchovy salad) 127
Cordero a la pastora (Lamb with new vegetables and milk) 128
Guirlache (Almond and aniseed candy) 129

Catalonia
Rap amb all cremat (Monkfish with caramelized garlic) 133
Pechugas de pollo Villeroy (Chicken breasts in cream-and-crumbs) 134
Crema fría de melón con virutas de Jabugo (Iced melon soup with raw ham shreds) 135
Lechugas a la catalana (Braised stuffed lettuce) 136
Pésols a la catalana (Peas with fresh herbs and pork) 136
Allioli (Garlic and oil sauce for fish) 137
Musclos gratinats (Grilled mussels with spinach and allioli) 138
Romesco de peix (Shellfish soup with hazelnut and chilli sauce) 138
Escalivada amb anxoves (Barbecued vegetable salad with anchovies) 140
Pollastre amb escamarlans o gambes (Chicken with scampi or prawns) 142
Sopa de setas (Wild mushroom soup) 145

Levante
Ajotomate (Tomato salad with tomato dressing) 148
Esgarrat (Red pepper and cured fish salad) 149
Bajoques farcides (Cold stuffed peppers with rice and tuna) 149
Mújol a la sal (Whole fish baked in salt) 150

Arròs amb forn (Oven rice with pork and tomato) 154
Arroz en caldero (Rice with peppers and allioli followed by fish) 154–5
Pollo all y pebre (Peppered chicken) 155
Lola's caracoles (Snails with piquant sauce) 156–7
Bunyols de vent (Hot orange puffs a wind could lift) 158
Tocino de cielo (Sweet temptation) 158
Paparajotes (Fritters with lemon or bay leaves) 161
Refrescos (Refreshing drinks) 161
Granizado (Iced lemonade) 161
El pixer (Iced coffee liqueur and lemon punch) 161
Carajillo (Brandied coffee) 161

Balearic Islands
Calamares rellenos a la menorquina (Squid stuffed with pine nuts, mint and raisins) 165
Oliagua amb escarrats (Tomato and garlic soup with asparagus) 165
Motllo d'alberginies de Mallorca (Aubergine timbale from Majorca) 166–7
Mahonesa (Mayonnaise) 168
Cocorrois (Chard or spinach pasties with raisins and pine nuts) 170
Escaldums d'indiot ode pollastre (Turkey, or chicken, fricassee) 171
Ponx d'ous (Rum and milk punch) 171
Ponche de sanguineas (Iced white rum with blood oranges) 171

Index